W9-BIW-356

JOINERY
SHAPING
& MILLING

JOINERY

SHAPING & MILLING

Techniques and strategies for making furniture parts from *Fine Woodworking*

The Taunton Press

Front cover photo: Sandor Nagyszalanczy
Back cover photos: Anatole Burkin (top left), Alec Waters (top right)
Charley Robinson (bottom)

for fellow enthusiasts

Printed in the United States of America
10 9 8 7 6 5 4 3 2 1

The Taunton Press, Inc., 63 South Main Street, PO Box 5506,
Newtown, CT 06470-5506
e-mail: tp@taunton.com

Distributed by Publishers Group West

Library of Congress Cataloging-in-Publication Data

Joinery: shaping & milling : techniques and strategies for making
furniture parts from Fine woodworking.
p. cm. — (The Woodworker's Library)
ISBN 1-56158-304-9
1. Furniture making. 2. Joinery. 3. Timber joints. I. Series.
TT194.J648 2000
684.1'04—dc21 99-05321

About Your Safety

Working with wood is inherently dangerous. Using hand or power tools improperly or ignoring standard safety practices can lead to permanent injury or even death. Don't try to perform operations you learn about here (or elsewhere) unless you're certain they are safe for you. If something about an operation doesn't feel right, don't do it. Look for another way. We want you to enjoy the craft, so please keep safety foremost in your mind whenever you're working with wood.

"He builded better than he knew."

—RALPH WALDO EMERSON

CONTENTS

INTRODUCTION

Jointing a smooth face on a rough-sawn board is a particular woodshop joy. It offers the first sight you get of the true run of the grain and color. With a small dab of mineral spirits, the board will reveal itself completely. Sometimes you uncover treasures, such as unexpected curly figure. But whether you find unexpected beauty or not, the smooth face is a window on the final piece of furniture. And that's fun to see.

Unfortunately, there isn't much more good to be said about milling rough lumber. It's tough, repetitive work, even with a well-tuned jointer and planer. By hand, milling can be described charitably as a healthy workout and drudgery after you've flattened a stack of boards. The far more enjoyable work comes next in shaping parts and cutting the joinery. Consequently, buying lumber premilled can seem a wise course to save yourself a lot of work and to make time for the fun parts.

Still, milling lumber to dimension has an important place in the woodshop. It is the first of five essential steps in building furniture, and it's the basic foundation on which everything else rests. The other four steps are shaping dimensioned stock into parts, cutting joinery, assembly, and, finally, finishing. This book covers the first three steps in building furniture: milling, shaping, and joinery. These are the cutting stages; beyond them, you put down your chisels and saws and pick up clamps, glues, and finishes.

You should be able to come away from this book with a solid foundation of techniques and options for making a wide range of furniture parts. However, remember that the articles collected here from *Fine Woodworking* magazine don't try to have the final word, or even list all the possible techniques. You might find some favorite technique missing; then again you might find something neat that you didn't expect.

ONE

Straight, Flat, and Square

Straight, flat, and square are ideals toward which woodworkers strive, but obtain only in relative degrees. Wood is very cooperative under the influence of sharp tools. If you know what you're doing, you can plane wood within a thousandth of a gnat's eyelash; but wood is constantly expanding, contracting, warping, cupping, and twisting due to the changes in relative humidity and internal stresses. Gnat's eyelashes become irrelevant every time the weather changes.

This is why it's good to remember that woodworking is part science and part art. While every woodworker should own a dial caliper, none should be a slave to it. Fussing over different thicknesses only a dial caliper can recognize is futile. The best judge of equal thicknesses, for example, is your thumb. Only if you can feel the difference should you worry about it. After all, thumbs will be the gauges by which everyone else will measure your work. Woodworkers who pull out a dial caliper and climb under the furniture in other people's homes should be considered rude.

The art of milling lumber straight, flat, and square is to know when to stop. It's preparatory work, and though essential to get right, "right" is a relative term. The articles in this section help you tune up your tools to cut "straight," give you advice on how to plane "flat," and even teach you a dance step that will make a tablesaw cut "smoothly." But how smooth is smooth enough? Of course the answer is that it depends. Flat and smooth can feel relatively rough and be perfectly acceptable for a glue joint as long as it isn't uneven. If you're milling a tabletop that will eventually have a mirror-like gloss finish, then "smooth" takes on a new dimension. It's at this stage that you'll want to eliminate all imperfections and leave a very smooth surface that will be easy to scrape and sand to perfection.

SMOOTHING ROUGH LUMBER

By Gary Rogowski

I have paid lumberyards good money for some nasty-looking hardwood. Sometimes you just have to take what you can find, even if the stock has defects. But I do have some faith in the power of machines. Planks that look like they were pried off the hull of a beached boat can be made silky smooth and straight as an arrow with the push of a button.

Warped view of lumber

As wood dries and ages, strange things can happen to it, even under the best of conditions. Identifying the problem is the first step in milling the stock efficiently.

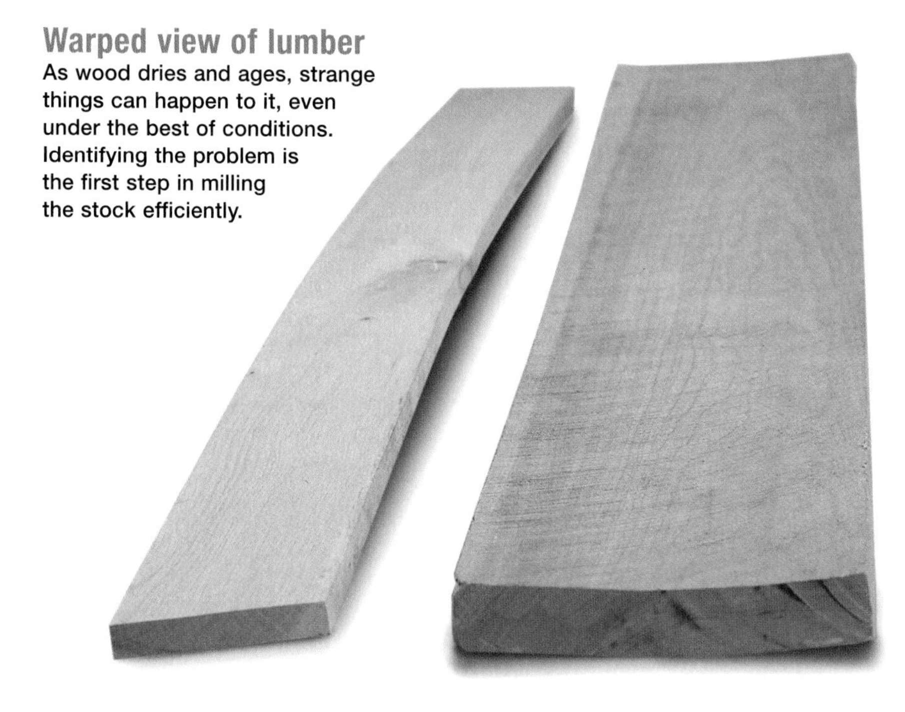

Bow

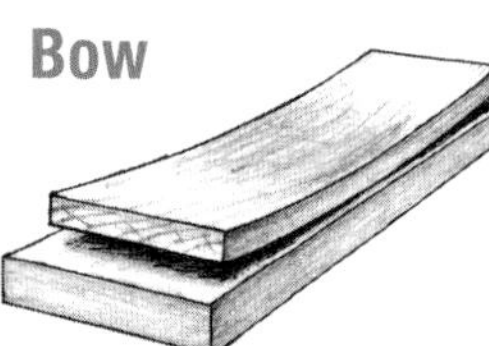

Bow occurs along the length of a board along the face side. If the bow is severe, it is best to cut the board into smaller sections before machining.

Cup

Cup occurs across the face of a board. If lumber is badly cupped, rip it into narrower sections; you'll end up with thicker stock after face-jointing and planing.

Twist

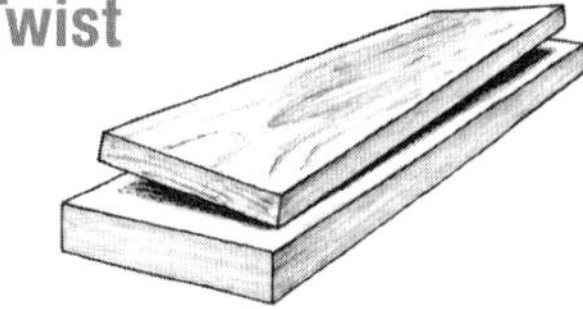

Lumber with a slight twist will give you fits if not removed prior to cutting joints or gluing panels together. If it's severely twisted, cut the lumber into shorter sections for better yield.

Well, almost. You can't blindly shove stock into the maw of a groaning machine and extract perfect boards. If you repeatedly pass the face of a twisted board across a jointer and don't apply proper pressure to the opposing corners, you'll end up with one big shingle—skinny on one edge and fat on the other.

The first step in milling is looking, not machining. Examine your stock, and identify problems such as bow, check, cup and twist. Different defects call for specific milling strategies. But even when you're careful to identify problems, surprises sometimes arise. Recently, while planing a plank of what looked like clear sycamore, I noticed a sudden color change in the machined face. I took a closer look. Smack in the middle of the discoloration was a chunk of buckshot. Fortunately, the soft lead didn't damage the planer's knives.

Although it may seem like more work, I prepare stock in two steps: rough milling and finish milling. First I pick through the stock and decide what boards to use for which parts of a project. Next I crosscut the pieces 1 in. oversize in length, rip them on the bandsaw, leaving them 1/8 in. over in width. Then I joint and plane the stock, leaving everything 1/8 in. over in thickness. When rough milling, I concentrate on the serious defects and don't worry too much about getting perfectly square edges yet. Then I sticker the stock for a few days to allow any hidden stresses in the wood to reveal themselves. Wood that's been sitting in a rack may hold hidden surprises that

Checks may occur throughout lumber, but they are most commonly found at the ends of a board (right), the result of too rapid drying.

Checks can be found anywhere. Though they are most common at the ends of boards, checks may also occur in the middle of a board (top inset). In the case of internal checks, the problem may not be obvious until a board is crosscut (left).

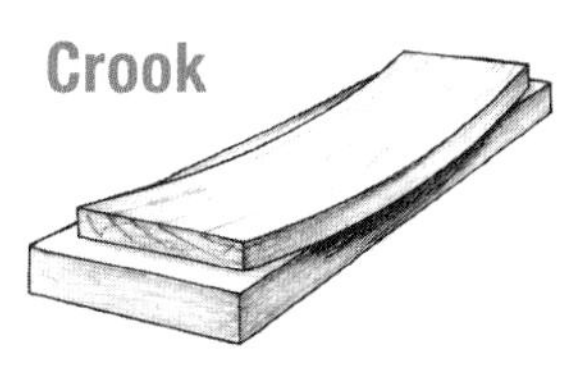

Crook is a bow along the edge. You'll end up with waste along both edges when ripping it straight and parallel.

Bowed lumber

To determine whether a board is bowed, sight down one edge (left). Bowed boards are best used for shorter pieces of a project. Mark sections using a pencil while eyeballing the amount of bow (right). Next crosscut the board into shorter sections; then join them flat, placing the stock bow side down on the joiner table (below).

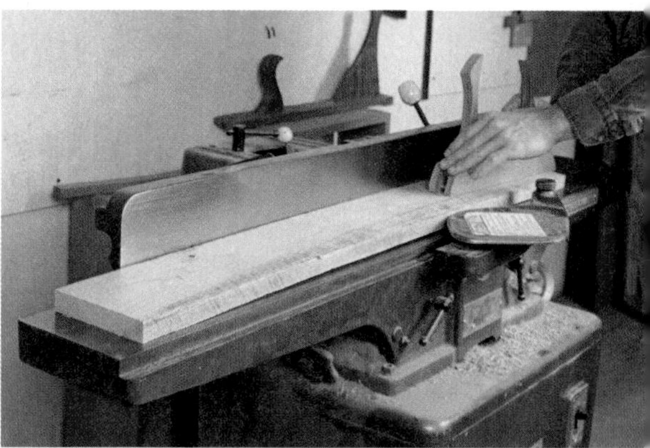

Set the machine to take shallow cuts, about 1/32 in., for all face-jointing. The jointer will remove material at the ends first (above). Be careful not to exert too much pressure on the board, or you may temporarily press the bow out, resulting in a board that planes unevenly and isn't flat.

Cupped lumber

A straightedge placed across the face of a board shows cup. Remove it by jointing the cupped side (top left). The machine will take off material at the outside edges first (bottom left). To avoid stock that's too thin, bandsaw into narrower pieces before face-jointing.

show up after milling. After letting the stock settle down, I'll do the final milling—getting stock square and cutting it to the final dimensions. By then, the stock is usually pretty stable and less likely to play tricks on me.

The defects found in lumber are often a result of what happened to the wood before you bought it. As wood dries, even under ideal conditions, it suffers some degradation. Improper drying—too fast, too slow, improper stickering and other mistakes—can play havoc with wood. Here are some of the more common problems and how to solve them.

Use bowed stock for short pieces

Bowing describes a board bent along its length on the face side. Bowing isn't too great a problem if you need short pieces. You can dress the face of a short bowed plank until flat. But for long tabletops, where you need the thickness, bowing can cause problems. One end or both will wind up too thin after repeated passes over a jointer. When a project calls for long pieces, and the lumber is bowed, select stock thicker than needed to allow for waste.

Face-joint bowed stock concave side down across the jointer. Severely bowed stock may catch on the outfeed table as soon as it passes over the cutterhead. If it does,

Twisted lumber

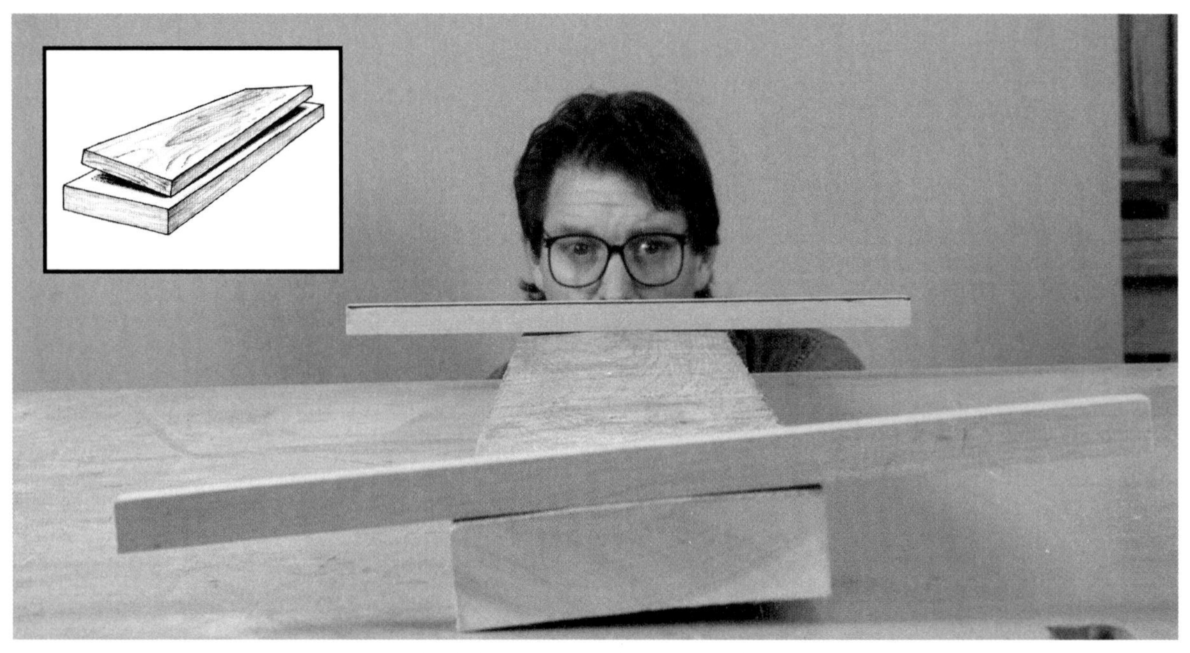

Use winding sticks to check lumber for twist. Lay the sticks across the board at opposite ends, and sight down the board. If the sticks aren't parallel, the lumber suffers from twist.

Removing twist on the jointer. This is accomplished by taking a diagonal cut across the face of a board. Begin by pressing the lead high corner flat to the table. Gradually transfer pressure to the trailing high corner as the board passes across the cutterhead. Don't let the board rock onto the low corners, or you will remove material where you don't want to.

Winding sticks help identify twist

Winding sticks are simple but accurate tools that help you spot twist in lumber. They're handy for truing up other surfaces as well, such as your bench or jointer tables. Mill up two sticks about 1 in. by 2 in. by 24 in. Make sure that the wood is dry, knot-free and straight and that the two pieces come out the same size. Mark along the edge of one stick using a dark marking pen, or for fancier sticks, make an inlay of darker wood.

To use the sticks, place one on each end of a board. Move away, and then hunker down and sight from the top edge of the near stick to the top edge of the far stick. If the two sticks are parallel to one another, the board is flat. If the sticks are tilted with respect to one another, the board is twisted. To remove twist, the board is face-jointed, and the high corners are removed first.

lift the board onto the outfeed table. Then push the stock through. Repeat until the board no longer hangs up. Alternatively, you can joint enough of a flat onto the rear of the board until the front end no longer catches. Don't exert too much pressure, or you may temporarily press the bow out. I set my jointer to take very light passes—about $1/32$ in.—for all operations, even on rough stock. It's easier on the machine and easier on you. A bigger bite means more vibration, which will reduce your ability to feed stock smoothly. I also use a push stick on the back edge of a board.

Jointing a high spot

A board with a hump on one edge requires a balancing act to get a true edge. Place the board on the infeed table of the jointer, and put your weight onto the trailing end of the board. This will lift the lead end of the board as it passes over the cutterhead. Slide the board along until it just starts to cut the hump. Then transfer all your pressure to the outfeed section of the board, which will lift the rear portion off the infeed table. Repeat until the stock doesn't rock and material has been removed across the entire face.

If your lumber has wild or swirling grain, often found near small knots, use a damp rag to lightly moisten the wood fibers before cutting. Take shallow passes when jointing or planing, removing less than $1/32$ in. at a time. This will help avoid tearout. The same method works well for lumber with wild grain, such as curly maple.

Taking the cup out of a board

A moisture imbalance between two faces will cause a board to pull itself into a cupped shape. The side with more moisture will expand at a greater rate and become convex;

Crooked lumber

Crooked boards can be safely straightened on a bandsaw. Use a batten or any straightedge the length of the stock, and mark the area to be removed with a pencil. The author prefers using a bandsaw for all rough-ripping because there's no chance of kickback.

the drier side will shrink and become concave. You can spot cupping by sighting across a board or by holding a straightedge across its face.

To flatten a cupped board, place the concave side face down on the jointer. Take light passes until the entire face has been touched by the cutter. Flatten the convex side by running the board through the planer, humped side facing the cutterhead, after face-jointing. When setting the depth of cut on your planer, reference it off the highest part of the cup.

Most rough lumber has checks in the end grain

End-checking or cracking is common in all lumber. As wood dries, moisture escapes faster from end grain than from the face or edge. That's why it's important to paint the ends of green lumber before drying it, which will help equalize the rate of shrinkage throughout the boards. Nevertheless, end-checking occurs frequently. When buying stock, factor in the loss of a few inches of length.

Although less common, lumber may also check along its surface, far away from the ends. This occurs more frequently in certain species such as oak. These checks tend to be narrow—1/8 in. or less. Lumber that has been dried too quickly may develop severe internal splits. These splits may be in the form of interlinked cracks called honeycombs or one large massive crack running the entire length of a board. You can sometimes spot a honeycombed section by looking for a bulge on the face of a board.

There are various methods for dealing with checked lumber. For a simple solution, cut off the afflicted sections, and use them for firewood. Some woodworkers celebrate these natural flaws by filling them with colored epoxy resin or cutting a butterfly key to stabilize the crack.

Gone with the wind

A twisted board is the most sinister of defects. Slight twist—also commonly referred to as wind—may go unnoticed until you begin face-jointing a board and realize too late that you've created a taper. When you try to correct it by more face-jointing, you may end up with stock that's too thin at one end.

Check for twist by sighting down one end of a board to the other. If one corner appears higher than another, the board is in a twist. Tools called winding sticks are a foolproof way to help you spot twist (see p. 10). A flat surface such as a workbench also can be used as a tool to look for wind. Place the lumber face down, and push on the adjoining corners. If the board rocks, it's twisted.

If lumber has other faults besides twist, such as bow or cup, deal with the twist first. Place the board on the infeed table of the jointer, and press down on the low corners. Exert greater pressure at the front of the board at the beginning of the cut; then transfer pressure to the rear as it approaches the cutterhead. The board will be cut across a diagonal line from one high corner to another. Repeat until the board is flat.

Remove crook with a saw

Think of crook as a bow along the edge of a board. The same problems encountered when jointing bowed lumber may occur with crooked boards. First crosscut the stock into approximate lengths needed for a project, then rip the boards slightly oversize using a bandsaw. This will make it easier to joint an edge straight without wasting a lot of wood.

As with bowed wood, if you're having a problem with the stock catching on the edge of the outfeed table, place the leading edge of the board on the outfeed table, just past the cutterhead, then push it through. Continue until the board no longer catches, jointing it in the usual way.

AN EDGE-JOINTING PRIMER

by Gary Rogowski

By hand or by machine—Edges may be jointed successfully with either handplane or machine. The basic approach is virtually the same: Read the grain of the wood correctly, and use sharp, well-tuned tools.

There was a time when I was convinced my jointer was possessed. It would thwart my every effort to make a crooked edge straight. Sort-of-straight edges became more humped, and wide boards became ever narrower at one end. Like many woodworkers, I found myself talking to my jointer, pleading for cooperation. My early efforts at handplaning edge-joints didn't go much better. When I would get an edge close to straight, it might not be square.

I have since happily discovered that edge-jointing problems, though common, are almost always correctable. A well-tuned jointer or handplane is essential, and some basic techniques will solve most problems. But the most overlooked detail when edge-jointing lumber is what the board looks like to start with.

To get a straight, square edge, you first need a flat reference face. If your boards are cupped or twisted, choose one face to be the reference face, and joint it or plane it dead flat. If you plane the other face parallel to the first, you can use either side against the jointer's fence to joint the edge.

Read grain to prevent tearout

The edge of a board is where the work will actually take place. Whether you're handplaning or using a jointer, your success depends on knowing where to start cutting and in which direction. The object is to take down the high spots without touching the low areas and to plane with the grain to avoid tearout.

Wood fibers generally rise up in one direction to meet an edge, although they sometimes rise in opposing directions along

the same edge or swirl in the board like eddies in a pool. When you try to plane or joint an edge against the grain, you're likely to get tearout. So how do you tell which way the grain is running?

The best analogy that I have for grain is fur. If you pet a cat from its head to its tail, the fur lies down smoothly. You're moving your hand with the grain. But if you pet the cat from its tail to its head, the fur will resist your hand and stand on end. You're going against the grain, and the cat may take offense at your insensitivity. With the cat, you risk a scratch; with a board, you risk tearout.

The first step is to read the grain direction on the face of a board to see how it rises up to meet the edge (see the drawing on p. 17). Check both sides of the board if you're uncertain. Look closely enough to see the grain lines, not just the more prominent growth rings. These often will line up with the grain direction, but not always.

Reading the wood—Sighting down the edge of a board quickly reveals humps and hollows and tells the author where to start the straightening process.

Check for high and low spots

If all edges were straight to begin with, we wouldn't need to joint them flat. But in the real world, most boards have high spots (humps) or low spots (hollows) along their edges. A humped board can pivot on its high spot when run across a jointer. Similarly, a handplane often will follow a hump, rather than flatten it. A hollow in a board can cause it to catch on the lip of the outfeed bed when pushed across the jointer.

To check the edge of a board, hold it face up, one end at eye level and the other end on your bench or shop floor. Now, sight down along the edge of the board where it meets the face (see the photo at left). If the board is grossly humped or hollowed, you'll be able to see it right away (I'll tell you more about dealing with that in a minute). If the board is nearly straight, showing only minor dips and humps, it can be taken right to a jointer. If you're handplaning the edge, however, you'll need to check it with a straightedge. Get a reliable metal straightedge (or a long board you've jointed flat and true), and set it on the edge of the board. If the board has a single high spot, the straightedge will spin freely as it pivots at the hump. If the edge is hollow, the straightedge will make contact with the board at two points, and light will be visible between the straightedge and the edge of the board. In either case, mark the high spots where the straightedge makes contact. Now you can begin straightening an edge, concentrating on these spots before working on the full length of the board.

Technique is key to hand jointing

Working an edge by hand is best done with the longest handplane you have. Although you can do the job with a smooth plane, a jointer plane's longer sole is better designed to ride over a series of high spots or traverse a hollow. Work the plane at a slight angle to the edge of the board so the iron slices through the wood (see the top left photo on p. 18). Skewing the plane like this will give you a cleaner cut, and it puts just a bit more plane body in contact with the wood, lengthening your reference surface.

Start the cut with all your hand pressure on the plane's leading edge (see the top right photo on p. 18). As you move through the cut, transfer pressure to both hands, and finish with all the weight on the trailing hand. This way, you won't taper a board at its ends.

This technique works fine if your board is pretty flat to start with. If it has a serious hump in it, though, you need to deal with that first. Start by checking the edge of the board with a good straightedge and marking the hump with a pencil. After taking several passes across the hump, check the edge again. The high spot should be longer and flatter. Keep marking the ends of this plateau. Remove material until you can take one full pass along the edge.

To straighten a board with a hollow along its edge, the process is similar. You need to plane down the high spots to either side of the hollow until they're at the level of the hollow. Usually this means just planing at the two ends of the board at first and then gradually lengthening the areas you are planing until they meet in the middle of the board.

If you've gotten this far and the edge is flat, congratulate yourself. But there's more to consider. How square is the edge to the face? Check with a small square, and mark the high side at several points along the edge. Hold the plane square to the face when cutting. This can be tricky because it means the plane will not be fully supported on the edge at all times. Over time, you'll develop a feel for it.

Another tactic for planing an edge square by hand is to use a shooting board (see the top photo on p. 20). My shooting board is a simple bench hook with a stop at the end and a fence on the inside. The edge I'm shooting extends beyond the shooting board so the handplane, held on its side, trims just the edge. The plane blade must be at precisely 90° to the shooting board.

Boards planed at complementary angles mate flat

The simplest method for getting two handplaned edges to mate perfectly is to plane boards as a pair. Clamp the two boards together in a vise, line up their edges and plane them flat, end to end (see the bottom photo on p. 20). When the boards are removed from the vise and held together edge to edge, whatever angle one board has been cut at will be mirrored by the other. These angles are always complementary. Just the same, try to keep your plane as flat as possible from side to side, because a steeply angled joint will be more apt to slip when you're clamping it.

Planing direction

To avoid tearout with either a handplane or jointer, check grain lines, and establish the best direction of cut (below).

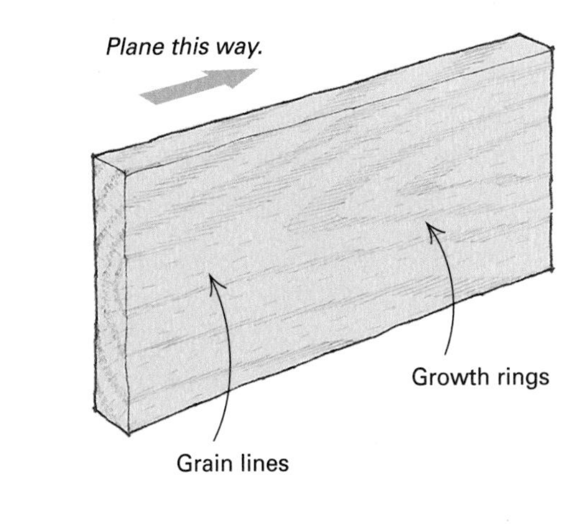

Jointer must be well-tuned for straight edges

To accomplish a task as precise as providing a straight, square edge over a long board, your jointer must be in tip-top shape. If its tables are twisted out of alignment or droop at either end, no amount of finesse is going to give you straight edges. You can check for twist with winding sticks, and a straightedge will tell you whether infeed or outfeed tables are drooping.

Assuming there's nothing seriously wrong with your jointer, the first thing to consider is the sharpness of your knives. If the knives are dull or pitted, take them out and have them sharpened. Sharp knives are essential to good edge joints.

The relationship of the knives to the outfeed table is also critical. If you're getting snipe at the end of your boards, your outfeed table is set too low relative to the knives (see the top drawing on p. 21). When the board clears the infeed table, it's dropping into the cutterhead and taking a deeper cut. This is easily corrected by raising the outfeed table so it's precisely parallel with the top of the knives' cutting arc. Make sure the table is locked down securely.

Jointing an edge with a handplane

To avoid planing ramps at the leading or trailing end of a board, transfer pressure on the plane from front to back as you move along the edge. Skewing the plane slightly will help give you a cleaner cut.

1. At the beginning of the stroke, all downward pressure should be on the leading hand, which is around the knob. The rear hand just pushes the plane forward and guides it.

2. Once the plane is completely on the board, apply pressure evenly at both ends of the plane.

3. As the leading edge of the plane moves beyond the end of the board, gradually transfer pressure to the hand on the tote, or rear handle.

When the outfeed table is too high, the result is taper (see the bottom drawing on p. 21). The board will seem as though it's cutting fine for most of its length. Then, toward the end of the cut, you'll notice that the knives are no longer cutting. As with snipe, this is easily corrected. You just need to bring the outfeed table down a bit, so it lines up with the knives.

The jointer fence also needs to be set square to the tables. Use a square you can trust, and check the fence just past the knives on the outfeed table. By looking at the square with a light source behind it, you'll be able to see even the slightest deviation from square. Loosen the fence-lock lever, adjust as necessary and lock the fence without moving it.

Jointer technique is important

If one of my students is having problems with tearout and the board is being fed through the jointer in the proper direction, the first thing I check is depth of cut. For hardwoods, I keep it around 1/32 in.

Feed rate needs to be constant throughout the pass. An excessively fast feed rate will cause noticeable scallops along the edge of the board left by the arc the cutterhead passes through as it cuts. Moving stock over the jointer too quickly also can cause tearout. Too slow a feed rate, or pausing in the middle of a pass, can cause burning. Neither surface is optimal for gluing.

Pay attention to grain direction when feeding boards over the jointer. Because you're moving the board past the cutterhead, the grain should be trailing down and away from the knives. But if the board tears out anyway, turn it around, and try it in the other direction.

Reading the grain will almost always tell you the best feed direction, but on occasion, boards do tearout in both directions. Choose the feed direction that tears out the least, and take a light, slow cut. If your jointer permits, skew the fence to help give you a cleaner cut.

Your stance is also important. Keep your feet spread comfortably apart, and maintain your balance. That may sound like advice from a coach, but keeping the edge of a 7-ft.-long, 10-in.-wide piece of hard maple flat on the jointer can be something of an athletic event.

Be especially careful at the beginning of the cut. If you apply too much pressure on the leading edge of the board, it could kick back. If it does, there's nothing between your hands and the cutterhead. Just keep your downward pressure back from the leading edge until the board is safely on the outfeed table.

Once the board is on the outfeed table, keep one hand just past the knives, and apply pressure with this hand, down and in, toward the intersection of the jointer table and fence. This will keep the cut square.

The length of a board will determine how you handle it. If it's short enough, place one hand near its leading end and your other hand at its rear. The forward hand will hold the board tight against the fence and table, and the rear hand will feed the board.

Longer boards will cantilever past the rear end of the infeed table, so you'll need to put pressure near the front of the board to keep it flat on the table. Start with both hands near the leading edge, and then use a hand-over-hand method to move the board along for a cut (see the photos on p. 22).

It's also essential to hold the board's jointed face tightly against the fence. If the edge of a board is angled so that it tips away from the fence when held on edge, it's easy to see. If the board tilts into the fence, though, it may appear to be tight against the fence when it's not. To be sure, look at the leading edge of the board before beginning the pass.

Problem boards

If you're jointing a short board with a hollow along its edge, it's fairly easy going. The board will ride on its two ends, and if the jointer bed is long enough, it will only allow a cut at these two spots. After a few passes, you'll be jointing the board's full length, well on your way to a straight edge.

If the hollow is really long, though, the front end of the board may dive into the leading edge of the outfeed table and get stuck there. Lift the board carefully off the knives, and place it on the outfeed table to continue your pass. After a few passes, the ends will have flattened out enough so you

Shooting board simplifies getting a square edge. Once the plane blade is set correctly—at 90° to the bench—a square edge is almost automatic. The side of the plane uses the bench as a reference surface.

Fold boards together, and plane as one. When their edges are brought together, the two boards will be perfectly flat. Variation from 90° in one board is exactly offset by the other.

can take a full-length pass. You could also take several passes just at the leading end right away, removing enough wood for the board to feed properly.

A hump along an edge is a bit more difficult to plane out. Guide the board at its leading edge, but exert all your hand pressure on the trailing end. This will lift its leading edge off the jointer table so that no wood will be removed until the high spot on the board gets to the cutterhead.

As soon as this happens, transfer all your pressure to the outfeed side, so the board essentially pivots on that high spot. This way, the trailing edge doesn't get cut either. All that gets cut is the top of the high spot. The high spot will gradually become a plateau, giving you enough of a flat surface that you can feed the board normally. If you don't use this technique, you'll end up jointing just the front end of the board, and it will taper. You could lose most of a board's width before getting a straight edge.

If you're having a hard time getting a square edge, you can joint complementary angles on mating boards just as you can with a handplane. On the jointer, though, joint just one board at a time, choosing the board with the most prominent grain direction. For the mating board, run its opposite face against the fence. If you're going against the grain, slow down your feed rate to avoid tearout.

Spring joint keeps glued edges together

After all this talk about getting a straight edge, now I'm going to tell you that you don't want one. When I edge-glue two boards together, I intentionally put a slight hollow along their edges. This is called a spring joint.

Because most of a board's moisture exchange occurs at the end grain, building in a little compression at the ends helps ensure the joint will stay closed. I keep the space between the boards to 1/32 in. or less, looking for just a little light between the two edges when the two boards are held together. Even without looking, you can tell if an edge-joint fits correctly. If there's friction at the ends of the boards when you try to spin them, then they are either straight or slightly hollow. If the boards spin freely, then there's a hump along one or both of the edges. Holding an edge against the jointer's fence or table will tell you which board is humped.

You can create a spring joint in several ways. One method is to handplane it after the boards have been jointed flat. This lets you control the amount of spring you want along the joint.

Another approach is simply to press down harder at the center of the board as you're feeding it over the jointer. It seems impossible, but there is usually enough flex in a board to provide just a little spring joint along its edge.

Start with a board that's already jointed straight. At the beginning of the cut, apply just enough pressure to keep the board flush against the jointer table. When you're about a third of the way along the edge, start to push down harder. Push down hardest in the middle, and then start letting up two-thirds of the way along. Finish up with normal pressure.

You can also get a head start on a spring joint by taking a board you have already jointed straight, lowering the board down gently and starting a pass from its end about one-third of the way along its edge.

Take a normal cut until you reach approximately two-thirds of the way along, and then lift the board carefully off the cutterhead. Finish up by taking one full cleanup pass, pushing down a little in the center of the board.

Diagnosing jointer outfeed table problems

A misaligned outfeed table leads to two of the most common problems with edge-jointing lumber: snipe and tapered cuts. Both problems are easily corrected by adjusting the height of the outfeed table.

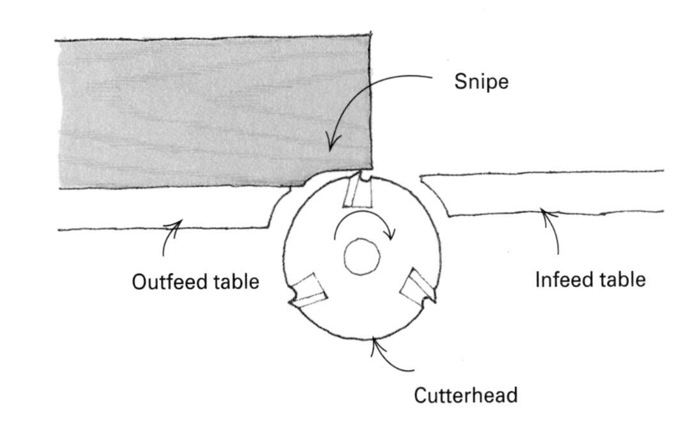

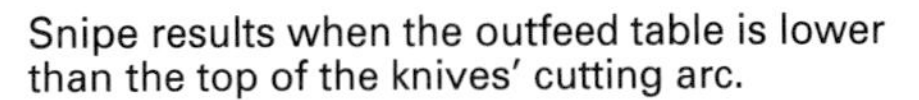
Snipe results when the outfeed table is lower than the top of the knives' cutting arc.

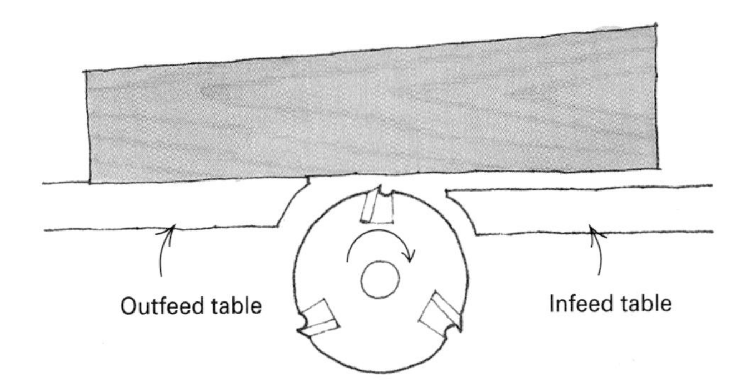

Taper occurs when the outfeed table is higher than the arc of the knives. As the board becomes established on the outfeed table, it begins to lift off the infeed table.The board tapers until it's no longer in contact with the cutterhead.

Jointing a long board

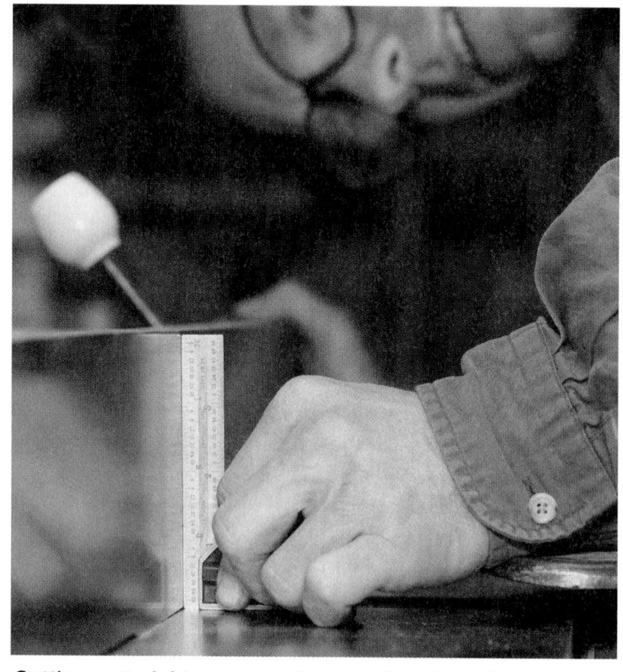

Getting a straight, square edge on a long board means paying careful attention to how pressure is applied as the board moves over the cutterhead. But before you start, make sure the fence is square to the bed.

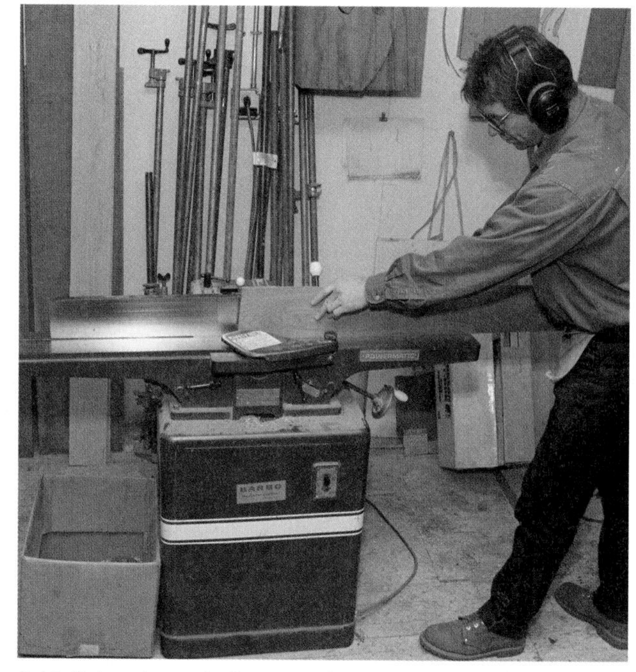

1. Both hands push down on the board at the beginning of the cut, so the board stays flush against the jointer's infeed table. The leading hand keeps the board tight against the fence while the rear hand pushes the board forward.

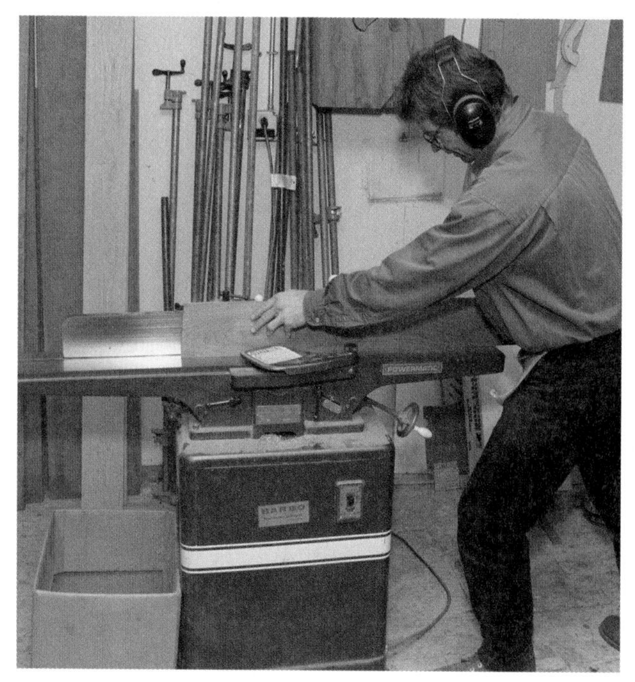

2. As less of the board hangs off the infeed table and the leading edge moves onto the outfeed table, push the board forward by switching lead hands. Keep one hand just past the cutterhead, and hold the board down on the table and tight against the fence.

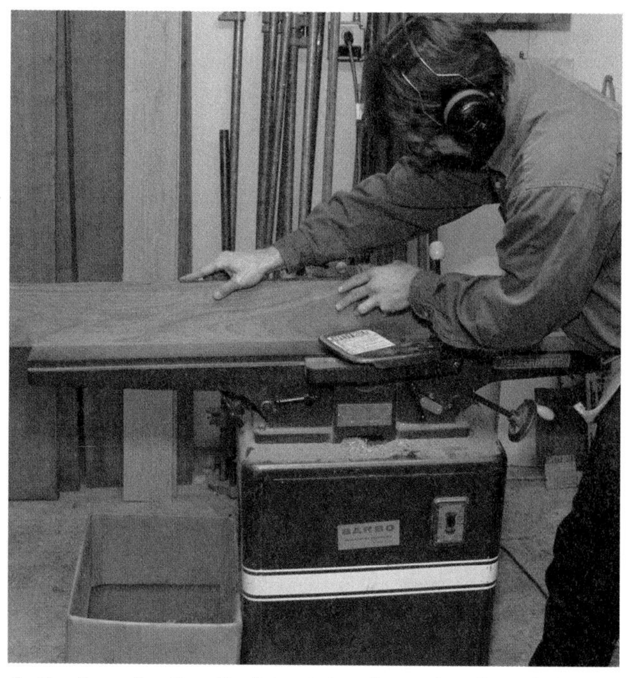

3. Continue feeding the board, hand over hand, until the weight of it requires two hands to hold it down on the outfeed table.

FLATTENING WIDE PANELS BY HAND

by William Tandy Young

Sooner or later, most woodworkers will have to flatten and thickness a plank of solid wood wider than their jointers or planers can handle. When I have a lot of wide panels to flatten, I take them to a local millwork shop. The big jointer and planer can do the job in minutes, and the wide-belt sander can thickness heavily figured wood without tearout. Typically, I can have all the major parts for a large, solid case-work piece sanded to 120-grit on both sides in about 30 minutes. Sanding usually costs about $30—money well-spent.

When I have only a few panels to flatten, however, I stay in my shop and do the job with hand tools. The work is satisfying, and it goes quickly. It took less than an hour to flatten one side of a 16-in.-wide cherry board. With a jointed straightedge and just a few commonly available hand tools (a No. 7 jointer plane and a No. 80 cabinet scraper), I can flatten just about any panel, even one many times wider than my planer.

Many woodworkers I know own 12-in. or 15-in. planers, but few have jointers with a capacity of more than 8 in. And there's the rub. By learning how to flatten one side of a wide board with hand tools, you can still take advantage of your planer for thicknessing. You won't have to rip boards down to size, joint them and then glue them back together. You'll save time and have fewer gluelines.

Using hand tools to flatten a panel that's too large for your jointer or planer is also more efficient and less annoying than other low-tech methods. I've surfaced solid panels with a belt sander, but I sure don't relish all the noise, dust and vibration. I've also seen panel-surfacing jigs that consist of a router in a large plywood base riding on top of wooden rails at either side of a workpiece.

Plane across the grain. Start at one end of the board, and work to the other, planing straight across. Skewing the plane at 45° or so may help it cut better. The jointer plane's length makes it a good reference surface, and its wide iron (2⅝ in.) allows you to make fewer passes. If the board starts to rock, tap wedges under the high corners.

Well-tuned hand tools make the work fast and fun

Set the chipbreaker $\frac{1}{16}$ in. or less from the end of the plane iron. This will help keep the throat clear of chips. Grind off the corners of the iron on a bench grinder so that they won't gouge the wood.

Wax the plane's sole to keep it gliding smoothly. Either beeswax or paraffin is a good choice.

Planes or scrapers that clog, leave chatter marks or produce only dust take the pleasure out of working wood. Experiences like these may send you scurrying for your belt sander. But it's not all that difficult to get these old-fashioned "cordless" tools to sing. Before you put a 60-grit belt on your sander, try tuning up your hand tools.

Tuning a jointer plane for flattening

Besides the basics of plane tune-up (a flat sole and a well-honed iron with a flat back), there are other steps that will improve the performance of a jointer plane used for flattening. The first thing I do is ease the corners of the plane iron on the grinder. As long as you adjust the iron so it projects through the mouth evenly across the opening, it won't gouge the wood. Sometimes I switch to an extra iron I keep on hand that's been ground to a slightly convex profile. I wouldn't use this iron to joint the edge of a board, but it's perfect for flattening.

I also set the chipbreaker close to the end of the iron (see the top photo at left). This will help keep the throat clear of chips. And sometimes I'll open up the mouth by moving the frog back slightly.

Finally, I keep the sole well-waxed (see the bottom photo at left). As soon as I feel the plane start to drag, I rub on a little more wax. It won't affect the finish because I'll smooth the surface later. A well-waxed sole makes a world of difference in how easily the work goes.

Tuning a cabinet scraper

The first thing I did to my cabinet scraper when I got it was flatten its sole with some fine-grit sandpaper on a flat surface (I used a glass plate). I ground a 45° bevel on the blade, honed it and flattened the back, and then turned a slight burr with a burnisher. This worked well enough, but sometimes I would get chatter when I scraped.

I determined that the blade wasn't seating well, so I trued the scraper body with a mill file to improve the bedding of the blade and the fit of the blade retainer bar. I also bent the retainer bar inward so that it contacts the center of the blade first as the thumbscrews are tightened. The result is a cut that's almost always chatter-free (see the left photo below). But you'll need to set the blade for the right depth of cut. I use a piece of paper to set the amount the blade protrudes through the sole (see the right photo below).

Once I have the proper depth of cut, I tighten the front thumbscrew just until it's snug against the blade. You shouldn't have to crank down on the thumbscrew. The more you do, the rougher the scraped surface you'll leave and the sooner you'll have to re-hone and burnish the burr.

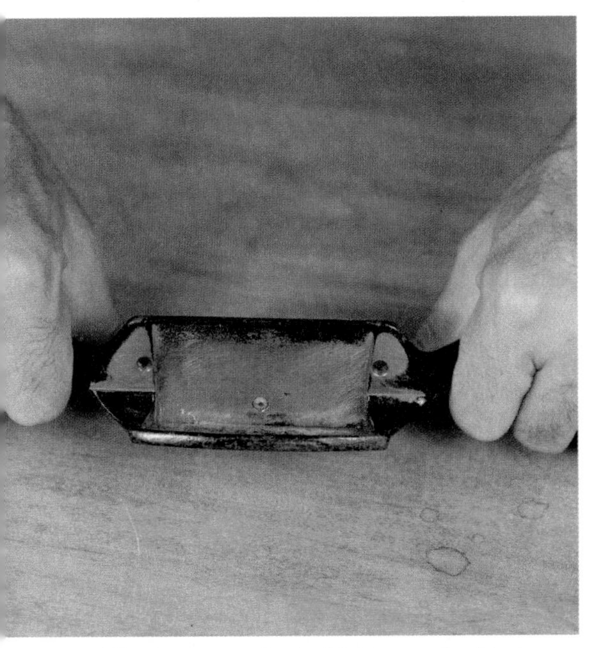

File the scraper body. Make sure the blade bed is filed flat, and file the scraper body so the retainer bar seats properly when tightened. This will help eliminate chatter and produce a better curl.

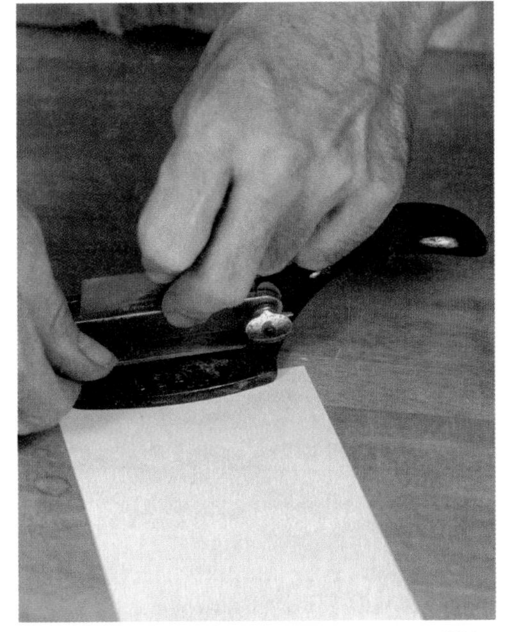

Use a piece of paper to set blade height. With a slip of paper under either the front or rear edge of the scraper sole, lower the blade until it rests on the bench. Then tighten the thumbscrews to exert pressure on the blade.

Plane off any high spots, continuing to plane across the grain.

Use a jointed straightedge to determine flatness. Check the board once the sawmarks are eliminated and the board is close to flat from edge to edge. Position the straightedge diagonally across the board to make sure it's not twisted.

Scrape with the grain across the width of the panel from either end until you've eliminated all cross-grain planing marks.

My reaction has always been, "All that jig-building and routing just to end up with a surface that still needs a lot of cleanup? No thanks, I'll stick with my jointer plane and cabinet scraper."

Plane across, and then scrape with the grain

The beauty of this technique is that I can flatten a board quickly while avoiding tearout altogether. I plane straight across the grain, eliminating the possibility of the plane blade catching the grain and lifting and breaking wood fibers. After using the jointer plane, I scrape with the grain. Because of the angle at which the cabinet scraper holds the blade, there's no chance of tearout. This lets me arrange boards for glued-up panels so they look their best, regardless of which way the grain goes. It also allows me to flatten even heavily figured wood.

After one side is flattened, you can feed the panel through your planer to take it to thickness. If the panel is too large for the planer (a tabletop, for example), take a marking gauge and scribe a line around the tabletop's edge, holding the fence of the gauge against the flat side of the tabletop. Then repeat the procedure. The gauged line tells you when to stop planing and scraping.

Once your panel is the right thickness, smooth the surface. If you're confident in your planing skills, smooth the surface with a finely tuned smoothing plane; otherwise, scrape and sand.

You should use flattened panels as soon as you can because they can warp or cup with changes in temperature or humidity. Then you'd have to flatten them all over again. If you can't use them right away, either stand the panels upright so they get plenty of air circulation on both sides or sticker them on your workbench and weight down the top.

RESAWING ON THE BANDSAW

by Ronald Volbrecht

I buy quilted maple for the backs and the sides of the guitars I make from a friend who is a lumber grader. Each year he inspects more than a million board feet of lumber, and if I'm lucky, he will find three good 2½-in.-thick planks. Some of the hardwoods and old-growth spruce I use are no less rare.

When it comes time to resaw these irreplaceable planks, I don't want anything to go wrong. Over the years, I've learned to adjust my bandsaw for consistent resawing with very little waste. I can get finished, 3/32-in.-thick guitar backs from resawn boards that are only 1/8 in. thick.

I do all my resawing on a 21-year-old Delta 14-in. bandsaw. It has a 6-in. column extension, which allows me to resaw planks that are up to 12¼ in. wide. The boards I resaw are usually 8 in. to 10 in. wide. I use a ½-in. blade with 3 teeth per inch (tpi).

Other than replacing the motor, I have not made any modifications to the saw, and I have no magic tricks. But there is more to getting good results than just running a board through the saw.

I tune my blade, set the guides close to the blade and then make sure that the blade is good and tight (for more on this, see the story on p. 35). I use wrenches to lock down all the adjustment points on the saw so that they can't vibrate loose. Then I feed the plank slowly against a high fence (see the photo on p. 28), judging the feed rate by the sound of the blade.

Blade-tension scales aren't exact. The author tensions the blade by ear, not by the calibrations on the saw.

Press the plank against the fence while pushing it through the blade. The right hand pushes the board while the left hand is positioned down low to press the workpiece against the fence. Use a push stick at the end of the cut.

A heavy-duty motor and new pulleys

When I bought the saw, it had a 1/2-hp, 1,750-rpm motor, but I soon replaced it with a 3/4-hp, 3,450-rpm motor. Because the bigger motor turned faster, I had to change the pulleys to keep the blade running near the factory speed of 3,000 feet per minute (fpm).

I used the formula given in the box above to determine the right combination of pulleys. I kept the 2-in. pulley that came with the motor. That pulley and an 8 1/2-in. pulley on the saw would have given me the right blade speed, but the big pulley wasn't in stock locally. I tried a 12-in. pulley, but the blade ran too slowly (about 2,100 fpm). Each time the weld went through the guides, the saw lurched. I ended up with an 11-in. pulley, which turns the blade at about 2,300 fpm. That's just about right for the work I do.

Choose a good blade, and keep it tight

I use the same type of blade for every cut I make on the bandsaw. It's a 1/2-in. skip-tooth blade with 3 tpi and a thickness of 0.025 in. I don't think the brand of the blade matters, but the quality of the welds does. I look for blades with good alignment at the weld and no blobs of metal. I check the back of the blade at the weld to make sure there is no offset. Problem welds cause the bandsaw to vibrate, and that makes the results inconsistent. I can tolerate a little offset or lumpiness because I carefully grind these defects smooth with a Dremel Moto-Tool and then dress the blade with a diamond stone.

I determine the correct tension by removing the blade guard on the left-hand column and plucking the blade as if it were a giant guitar string (see the photo above). The sound will go from a sloppy vibration to a smooth, low tone. At that point, you've reached the proper tension (see the photo on p. 27). For guitar players, the tone roughly corresponds to an E note on a bass guitar. When the blade sounds right, I replace the guard.

Pluck the blade to check the tension. Listen for a clear note, roughly an E on a bass guitar. The author replaces the blade guard after tensioning the blade.

A formula for blade speed

When I switched my motor for one with more horsepower and higher rpms, I had to change the pulleys to reduce the blade speed. Factory blade speed is 3,000 feet per minute (fpm), and I wanted my blade to turn slightly slower than that.

Here's a formula to determine blade speed of any combination of motor and pulleys:

Motor speed x (motor-pulley diameter ÷ saw-pulley diameter) x p x wheel diameter (in feet)

For example, this is the formula for blade speed on my 14-in. bandsaw with its new motor:

3,450 rpm x (2 in. ÷ 11 in.) x 3.1415 x 1.167 ft. = 2,299.7 fpm

Raise the guide bar, and adjust the blocks and thrust bearing. Set the gap between guide blocks and blade to 0.002 in., and bring the thrust bearing in light contact with the back of the blade.

I've never bothered to release the blade tension when the saw's not running. In theory, constant tension will shorten the life of the saw's bearings, but I'm still using the originals. I'd rather keep my saw ready to roll than fiddle with blade tension every time I want to use it.

After the blade is tight, I turn the upper wheel by hand to check the blade tracking. I spin the wheel and adjust the thumbscrew near the blade tensioner until the blade runs in the middle of the tires. When the blade tracks true, I tighten the thumbscrew and its locknut with Vise-Grips.

Next I set the table perpendicular to the blade. I raise the guides full height and use a long combination square. I put a light behind the square so I can detect and correct even small discrepancies (see the photo on the facing page). I tighten the knobs that lock the table in place with a wrench, so they don't loosen while I'm resawing. Before the next step, I check the squareness again.

Use a wrench to tighten the adjusting screws

Before I set the blade-guide adjustments, I raise the guide bar so the upper guides are about 9 1/2 in. off the table—high enough to clear my resaw fence. I tighten the thumbscrews that hold the guide bar in place as tightly as I can. For leverage, I use a pair of Vise-Grips. With this kind of pressure, the end of the thumbscrew becomes slightly mushroom-shaped over time. This can cause the guide bar to rotate slightly each time the thumbscrew is tightened, and the motion can twist the blade. To prevent this, I periodically remove the thumbscrews and file the ends square. With the guide bar set, I turn my attention to the guide blocks and thrust bearings. I usually adjust the lower guides first and then the uppers.

Some woodworkers prefer aftermarket guide blocks made of phenolic resin, but I've kept the original steel guide blocks that came with the saw. I prefer that the blade bear against a hard, flat surface, so I grind the guide blocks square and set them close to the blade to minimize its side-to-side motion. Because I clean up the welds on the blades, I can position the guide blocks only 0.002 in. from the blade. I use a feeler gauge to set the gap, and I tighten the setscrews carefully against the guide blocks so they don't shift. After they're locked in place, I double-check the gap. I locate the blocks just behind the blade gullet (see the photo on p. 32).

Make the table perpendicular to the blade. The author uses a light behind the square to highlight small misalignments. An out-of-square adjustment can ruin stock.

A wide board needs a high fence. A length of angle iron bolted to the top of the bandsaw's original fence supports a facing of ¼-in. Plexiglas. Wedges help square Plexiglas to table.

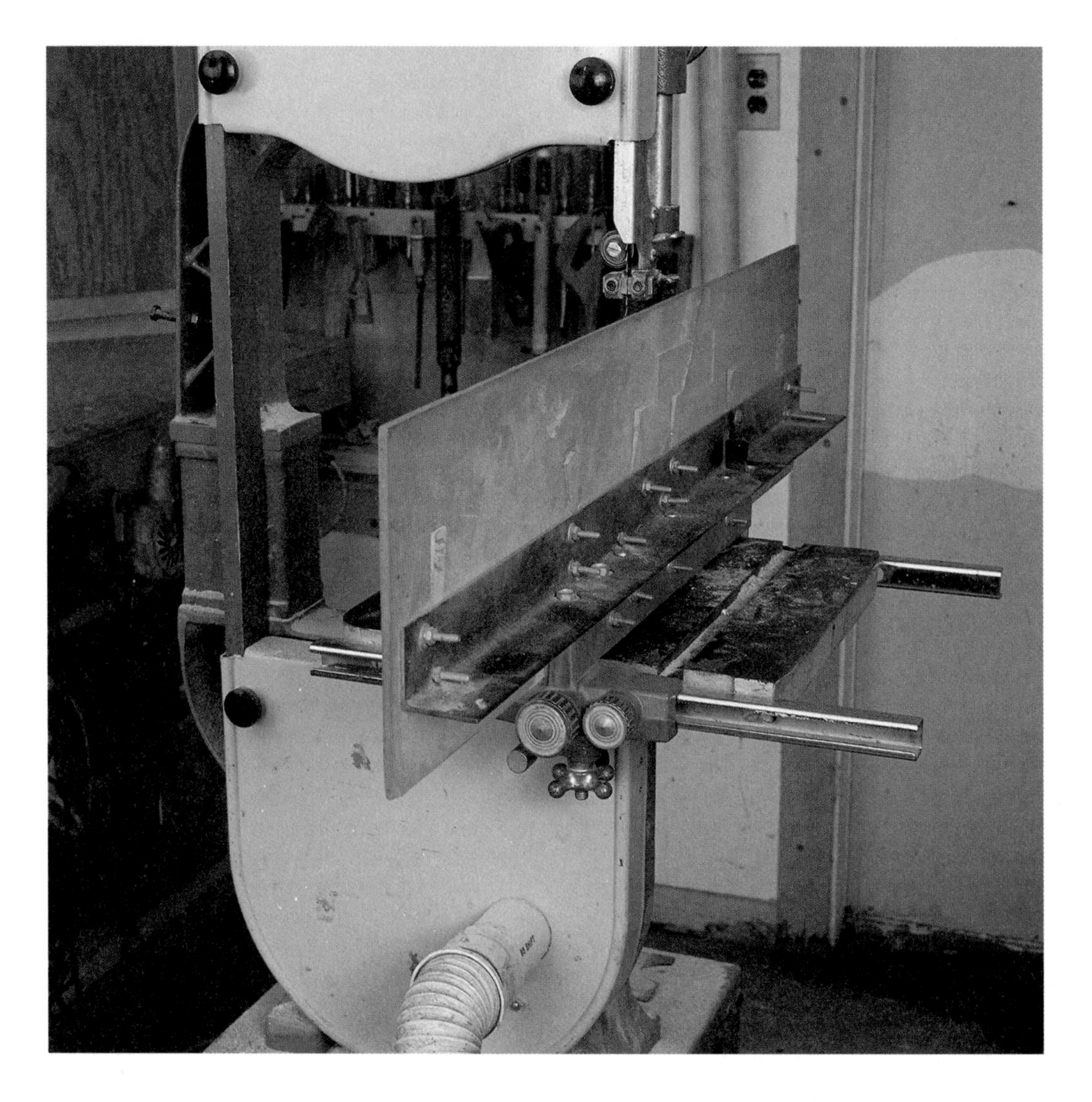

Before moving the bearing, I spin it to make sure it turns freely. If necessary, I give it a little oil. If one side of the bearing shows wear on the outer rim, I turn the bearing around. Then I move the bearing up to the back of the blade. It should just touch the blade but not spin until the saw is cutting wood.

When I first started resawing, I ruined a few boards because my carefully set adjustments vibrated loose. I tightened the adjustments as much as I could by hand, but that wasn't enough. I finally added locknuts to the lower guide adjusting screws. The nuts won't vibrate loose even after hours of resawing. I make them wrench-tight, which would be 20 to 25 ft. lbs. on a torque wrench. On the upper guide adjustments, I use Vise-Grips locked onto the thumbscrews to torque them tightly enough to be vibration-proof. These adjustments make my cuts very precise, but the tolerances are so close they have to be reset each time the guide-bar height is altered.

A high fence supports the plank

The resaw fence needs to be almost as high as the piece being sawn. If the fence is too low, when feeding a plank through the saw, the bottom of the board will tend to move away from the fence. The face of the fence must be 90° to the table. Even if the fence is out of square by only ½°, finished boards resawn from wide planks will have a pronounced wedge shape.

I built my resaw fence by adding a 9-in.-high piece of ¼-in. Plexiglas to the face of the rip fence that came with the saw. I used Plexiglas simply because it was handy. Plywood, Lexan (similar to Plexiglas but stronger) or aluminum might be better. Even a crack in the resaw fence hasn't affected its performance. To better support the Plexiglas, I bolted a length of 3-in. by 3-in. angle iron to the top of the fence (see the photo on the facing page).

When I first set up my resaw fence, the original rip fence wasn't square to the table. As a result, the top edge of the resaw fence was out of square. I fixed it by inserting wooden wedges between the Plexiglas and the angle iron (see the photo on the facing page). The wedges are about 1½ in. long and taper from $^3/_{16}$ in. to $^1/_{16}$ in. along their length. Each time I set up the fence, I make sure the Plexiglas is square to the table and adjust the wedges as necessary.

You may have to adjust your bandsaw fence for lead or drift. That's when the blade won't make a cut parallel to the edge of the table. To adjust the fence to account for it, I draw a line parallel to the edge of a jointed board and make a freehand cut along the line for about half the length of the board. Then I stop sawing, clamp the board to the table and set up the fence along the jointed edge of the board. Now the fence is parallel to the cut, and the blade will have no drift. I periodically check for drift, but I've never found any on my saw. I hear the same from other woodworkers who use the same saw.

When I'm ready to resaw, I install the fence $^1/_8$ in. to the right of the blade and lock it to the table at both ends with the clamps on the original fence. Then I prepare the plank by jointing both edges and one face. I run the jointed face against the fence. When using rare woods, it's important to waste very little. So I run the plank through a thicknessing sander to resurface it after each cut. The sander takes off less wood than a planer and without tearout.

Feed slowly, and support the piece

When resawing, I keep both hands on the piece, as shown in the photo on p. 28. My right hand is on the end grain, pushing the board through the saw (use a push stick for the last few inches of the cut). I keep my left hand low, and I spread out my fingers to press the planks against the fence across a wide area. Slow, constant feed pressure is the key to success. If you stop sawing for a moment, the blade will bite a little deeper.

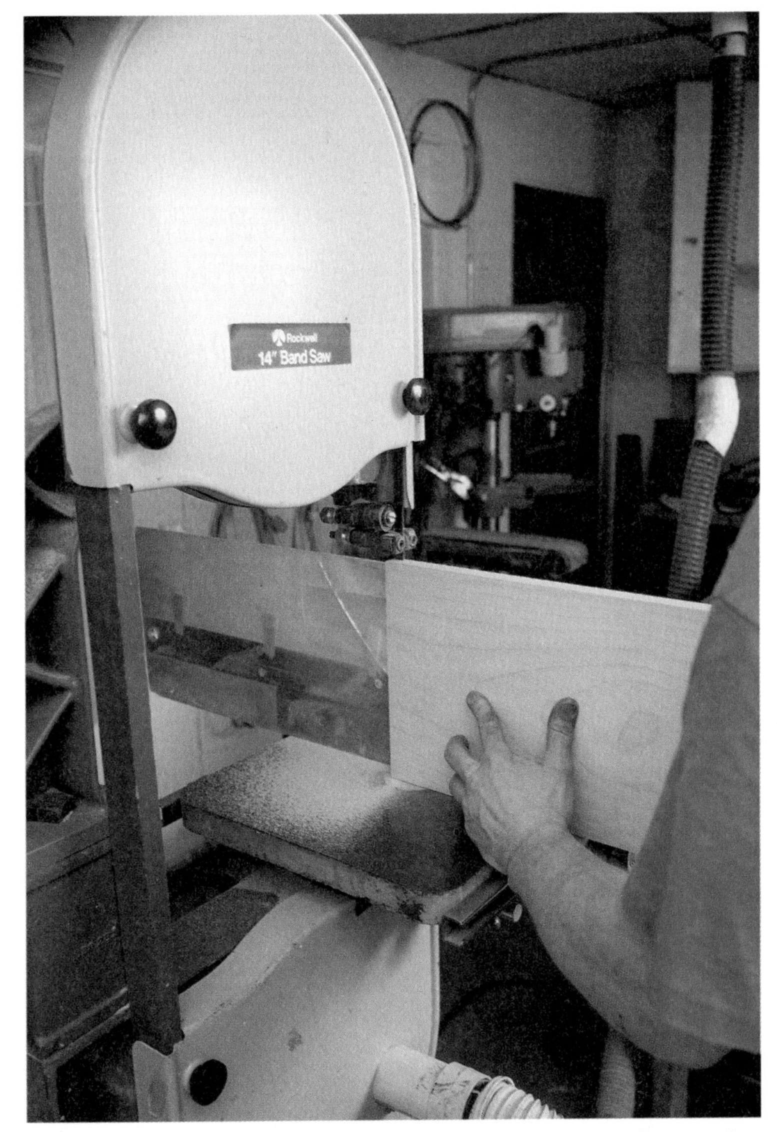

Slow, steady pressure—The author maintains a steady feed rate as he moves the workpiece through the saw. Stopping even briefly will produce a thin spot in the board.

I start out sawing slowly, listening to the sound of the blade. It should make a smooth, steady rasp with a light blip as the weld goes through the guides. I gradually increase the rate of feed, still listening. I feed steadily and strive to keep the sound of the blade steady as well. If I feed too fast, the sound switches to an uneven scraping as the saw vibrates more rapidly. If I push faster still, the vibration will smooth out, but the blade will wander, making an uneven kerf. I just keep the feed rate slow. It takes me about six minutes to resaw a quilted maple plank 8 in. wide by 3 ft. long.

The proof is in the pudding. By adjusting his bandsaw carefully and feeding the workpiece through the cut steadily, the author gets consistent results like this.

Keep your bandsaw singing, not whining

by Anatole Burkin

Like a stringed instrument, a bandsaw likes being under tension to perform well. But too much tension can de-tune your machine. We asked two tool manufacturing representatives to comment on what happens to a bandsaw when too much tension is applied. And we asked how to keep a bandsaw running smoothly.

Louis Brickner, vice president of engineering and product development for Delta International Machinery, says one way to spot overtensioning is to slide the guide bar up and down after tensioning the blade and setting the guide blocks. "If you have to readjust the blocks, it's a clue that you're bending or flexing the machine beyond its design capability," says Brickner.

Most woodworkers adjust blades by using the markers on the machine's tensioning adjustment screw and/or listening for a low tone by plucking the blade as it's tightened. Either method should get the blade in the 7,000 to 15,000 psi tension range (the low figure is bare minimum, and the high number is optimum). These numbers apply to carbon steel blades and bimetal blades, which make up the bulk of what's sold for small- to medium-sized bandsaws. If you have an industrial-grade saw, higher tensions may be possible.

The only way to measure the precise tension of your blade is with a tension gauge. You can order one through Starrett, but it will set you back $294.

Brickner also advises against keeping a guide bar raised too far above the work. The upper guide should just clear the surface of what's being cut. That greatly reduces the risk of injury.

A common problem customer's have is tires flying off the bandsaw because the motor they installed runs too fast, says Brickner. To upgrade the motor, pick one that runs at the same speed as the original (1,750 rpm), or change the pulleys after installing a faster motor (see the box on p. 29).

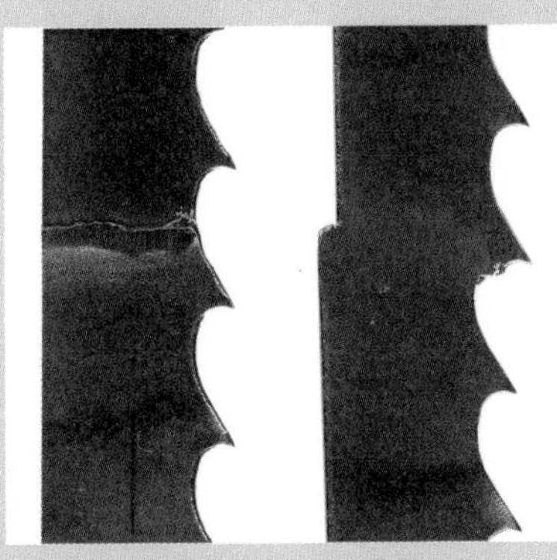

Get rid of the bumps. Ronald Volbrecht uses a diamond stone to smooth out a rough weld (left) or a Dremel Moto-Tool to feather out a misaligned blade (right).

Another problem is using a blade too wide for a 14-in. bandsaw. Machines of this size are not meant for 1-in. or wider blades. Tensioning them can bend or twist the machine. Best results are obtained with blades ½ in. wide or less.

As with all machines, proper maintenance can prevent problems and injuries. Brickner says it's important to inspect for wheel-bearing wear regularly. Unplug the machine, take off the blade and pulley belt, and spin the wheels. A clicking noise in the shaft spells bearing trouble.

Ray McPherson, product safety manager at Powermatic, says it's important to inspect the spring in the blade-tensioning screw occasionally. A broken spring can make it easier to overtension a blade.

Some woodworkers touch up bandsaw blade welds with a file or grinder. McPherson cautions against taking off too much metal. "A welded joint is stronger than the rest of the blade simply because there's more metal there. Just don't overdo it (grinding). Make sure the weld is complete and there's metal-to-metal contact," says McPherson.

For a comprehensive book on using and tuning bandsaws, a good source is *The Bandsaw Book* by Lonnie Bird (The Taunton Press, 1999).

JOINT-QUALITY EDGES CUT ON A TABLESAW

by Lon Schleining

Dance Steps for a Smooth Ripping Technique

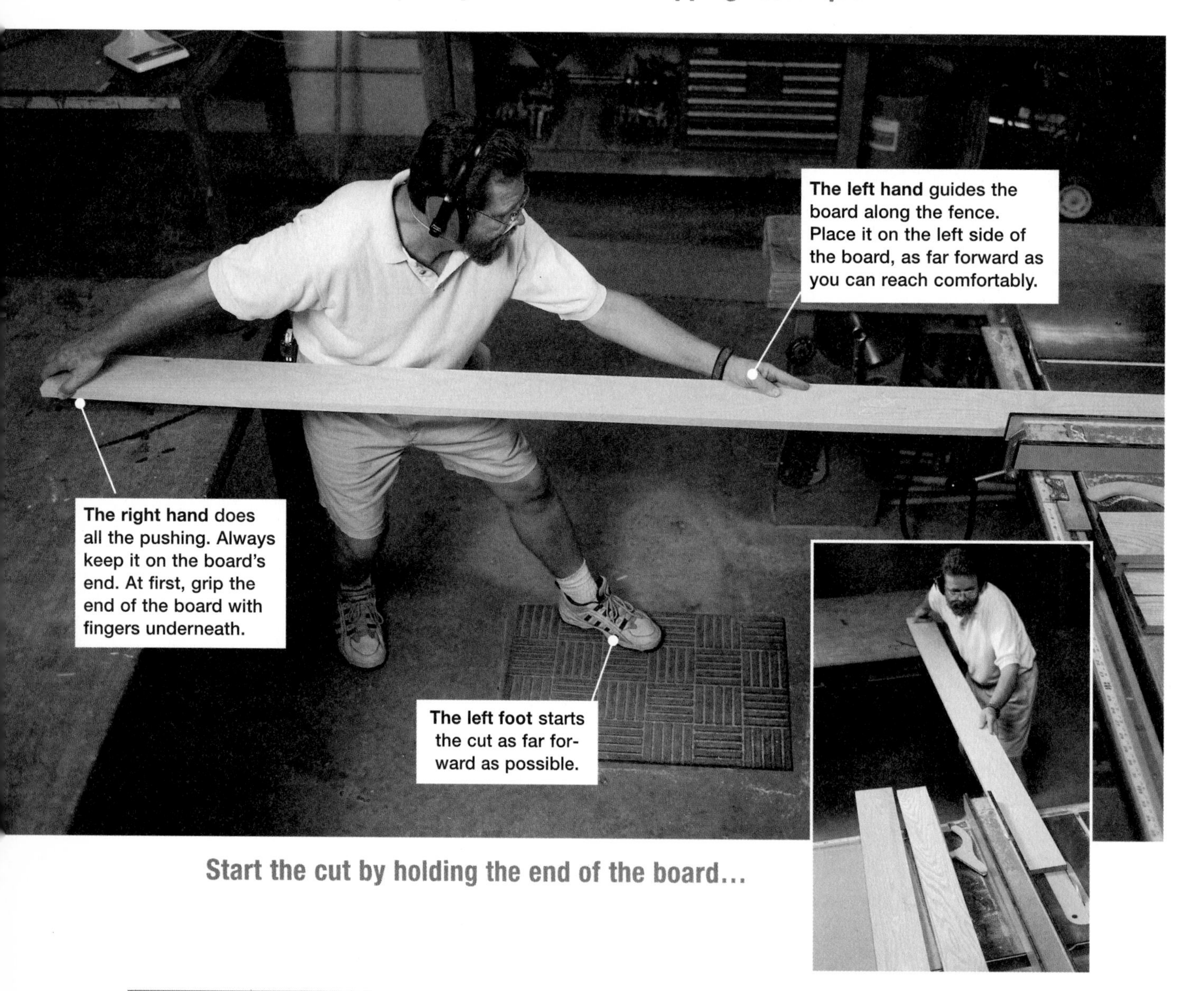

The left hand guides the board along the fence. Place it on the left side of the board, as far forward as you can reach comfortably.
The right hand does all the pushing. Always keep it on the board's end. At first, grip the end of the board with fingers underneath.
The left foot starts the cut as far forward as possible.

Start the cut by holding the end of the board...

When I tell my students that a lot of professional woodworkers use a tablesaw to get glue-ready edges, I sometimes hear gasps of disbelief. Most woodworkers think the tablesaw cuts crude, uneven edges, which must be cleaned up on a jointer. The assumption is that the smoother surface a jointer gives is better for glue, but this isn't always true. Glue must penetrate below the surface of the wood to do its job, so it needs open pores to seep in and grab hold. Jointer knives can compress the wood as they cut, glazing the surface and preventing maximum glue penetration—especially if the knives are dull or if the board is run over the jointer too slowly. However, running an edge over a jointer too fast cuts a pronounced wave pattern. If severe enough, only the tips will touch when two boards are put together, creating a wider glueline than is desirable.

The right technique on a tablesaw creates a straight, square and slightly abraded surface, which is ideal for glue joints. And a properly sawn edge, if it's to be left exposed, needs only light sanding to be finished. The trick is mostly in the way in which you feed

The left hand stops at the table edge, holds the board down and pushes it against the rip fence. Use the heel to help keep your balance.
The left foot starts to support most of the body's weight.

lean into the cut, shifting your weight forward...

the board through the cut. It has to move through the blade at a constant speed without wavering. All you need is a tablesaw with a powerful motor (3 hp or more), a good quality triple-chip blade and an outfeed table. The rewards are great—less milling time for stronger glue joints and finished edges.

Two-step at the tablesaw

To cut a clean edge on a tablesaw, you'll need to rethink how you move the board over the saw, as well as how you move. The commonly accepted technique of standing next to the saw and feeding boards hand over hand ensures an uneven edge and, frankly, is a dangerous habit. There is a total reliance on friction between the hands and the top face of the board to feed it forward, hold it down on the table and press it against the rip fence. The body is out of balance, and the hands (especially the left) move very close to the blade. One slip and the unthinkable might happen.

The following technique is a lot safer, but somewhat more complicated. It's very much like a bowling step. You need to coordinate your feet, hands and body into one fluid movement to ensure that the board goes over the saw steadily. I'll walk you through the technique presuming that you have one edge of the board straight already. As you

Rotate your right hand so that your fingers are on top of the board and your thumb on the end. The tricky part is to keep the forward motion constant.

The right foot comes forward and bears weight after the left hand touches the table.

turn your right hand over when the board's end comes alongside you...

might have guessed, I straighten the first edge on the tablesaw instead of the jointer (see the box on p. 40), but use whatever method suits you.

The main focus of the technique is to keep the board moving safely and at a constant speed during the cut. This requires that you start and end the cut with your right hand pushing from the end of the board. Guide the board with your left hand, placing it as far forward on the board as you can comfortably.

Depending on how long the board is, you may need to start the cut standing a certain distance back from the saw, and take a step or two toward the saw during the cut. This is when keeping the cut steady becomes more difficult, though by no means impossible. The key is to start with your left foot as far ahead of you as possible so that you need only take one smooth step with your right foot to reach the saw and finish the cut (the photos show how to complete this movement).

A triple-chip blade on a powerful saw

The right blade with this job, as for many things in life, is a compromise. In my experience, combination teeth can't remove material rapidly and produce a smooth edge. But pure rip grinds are often a bit too

The right hand pushes the board all the way through the cut. To keep the board tight against the fence, use your thumb to exert a twisting action to the right on the end of the board.

and finish the cut with your right hand only.

Getting the first edge straight on a tablesaw

The jointer is unmatched at making a warped board straight and flat on its face. It's what they were designed to do. However, they aren't the only machine that can get a first edge straight on an uneven board. For edge-jointing the S2S lumber I buy, I choose my tablesaw every time. I find it works faster. Where it might take 10 passes over a jointer to get a straight edge, I can do it on the first pass over my tablesaw with a minimum of setup.

Unlike the jointer, the tablesaw needs a guide to do this. A piece of ¾-in.-thick plywood for a template, slightly wider than the board to be cut, and a few brads are all you need. Make sure that the edges of the plywood are straight and parallel.

I align one edge of the plywood along the board exactly where I want the cut to take place so that the waste edge of the board is peeking out from under the plywood. I then nail the plywood to the top of the board with small brads. You usually only need one nail at each end, and by using a longer-than-needed board, you can cut off each end where the nails left holes.

I set the fence to the width of the plywood and guide the assembly through the saw as I would if it were a single board (see the photo on the facing page). I keep the edge of the plywood against the rip fence, and just like magic, the edge of the board below is cut straight as a string pulled tight.

This technique can be used to straighten rough edges, crooked edges or to cut tapers.

A clean joint line fresh from the tablesaw. Sawn edges without further preparation can make perfectly good glue joints.

aggressive to cut cleanly. They remove material much faster than a combination grind but leave an edge that is too rough for gluing. Triple-chip grinds are less aggressive but remove material rapidly enough to provide the cleanest overall ripcut. However, beware of cheap triple-chip blades: I've found a range of quality among them that substantially affects performance.

Tablesaw setup is just as important as blade choice. The blade must run parallel to the fence. If it doesn't, you'll get a condition known as heel and toe, which can produce deep swirl cuts down the edge of the board. For ripping long boards, the hands of a well-intentioned helper are no substitute for a solid outfeed table. The smallest amount of lateral wandering from the line of cut will give you a less than perfect edge.

There is no substitute for power to get the best edges. It's possible to do it with less than 3 hp, but lower horsepower machines have smaller sweet spots—the range of feed rates that a motor can handle without burning the edge or bogging down. The technique isn't impossible on a contractor's saw with a 1½-hp motor (I used one for years), but it's a lot harder.

Edge-jointing without a jointer. Template registers against rip fence and guides uneven boards through a straight cut.

If you push a board through any saw too fast, the motor will bog down and the blade will wobble, producing an uneven cut. But if you slow down too much, accumulated friction will burn the board. Both problems will leave you with a flawed edge. Higher horsepower motors can handle a wider range of feed rates—between burning at slow feed rates and bogging down at high feed rates. This makes it much easier to get a clean edge because you're not walking a tightrope between too slow and too fast.

Practice makes perfect

If this all sounds complicated, it is—at first. My suggestion for learning this technique is to practice. I recommend using an 8-ft. length of 3/4-in. particleboard about 10 in. wide. Its weight and cutting resistance are similar to hardwood. Using particleboard keeps you from turning a lovely piece of cherry into kindling. The idea is to practice the hand and foot movements until the motion is entirely fluid.

Make several cuts in succession, taking off about 1/4 in. with each cut, but never less than 3/16 in. or just enough so the blade is fully engaged with the board. If the blade runs free, it will oscillate slightly. As it engages the wood, the kerf made in the wood dampens this oscillation. The design of a good blade takes this into account. If it is cutting only on one side—not fully engaged in the wood—a tablesaw blade will continue to oscillate and produce a gouged edge.

For the learning session, use your utility tablesaw blade because particleboard is quite abrasive and will quickly dull a triple-chip blade. After a dozen or so cuts, the process should start to feel familiar and will become as natural a movement as any.

TWO

Making Curved Pieces

Working with curves strikes about as much fear into the heart of woodworkers as finishing does. Not quite as much fear, you understand, but nearly the same. While finishing is a totally alien art of plastics, bug excretions, alcohol, and other chemicals, making curves is at least grounded in something familiar—wood. But the art of making curves asks wood to do things that seem fundamentally unnatural. For example, when steam is applied to normally rigid boards that could support your weight, they wrap readily around curved forms, shrinking substantially on the inside surface, then become rigid again when cool.

Curves in wood play with our understanding of the material. The apparent structural qualities of wood are strength, rigidity, and maybe a little springiness when cut thin. Wood has beauty and grace, but that comes from its grain and color. When wood is bent or cut in a curve, it abandons the appearance of strength in its structure but gains beauty and grace. And curves cut from straight stock are indeed weak where the grain runs short. Looking at a Morris chair, with all its straight parts, sturdiness comes to mind. But look at a bent wood chair, such as a Thonet design, and grace and beauty come to mind first, and maybe strength doesn't at all.

This is why learning to make curves in wood is such a valuable ability for every woodworker. You're no longer limited to statements of 90° and strength; you can add flowing beauty and grace. The problem, as every woodworker knows, is that curves are difficult to make. Straight tape measures don't go around bends easily, and working with π to figure dimensions is a headache. When you're joining two curved members, you may have no point of reference whatsoever and need to fly blind to get anything done. But woodworkers are an ingenious lot and have found solutions to all of these problems. Read on and find out about them.

STEAM-BENDING BASICS

by Andrew K. Weegar

Steam-bending is fairly simple: Choose the right wood, pay attention to the grain and give it plenty of steam. A plumber's propane torch boils water in a 5-gal. can, and a section of auto radiator hose conducts the steam to the simple wooden steambox. A bending jig that uses dowels or wedges to secure the bent stock will save a lot of time, effort and clamps.

Several times a year, I give boatbuilding demonstrations at county fairs and woodworking shows. Nothing attracts more consistent interest than steam-bending. When-ever I fire up the steambox and start to bend wood, a crowd gathers; it seems the idea of bending wood makes even the most experienced woodworker nervous. But with relatively few tools and a few simple procedures, most woods can be bent to surprising curves.

The process

When we steam wood, the steam doesn't actually penetrate the wood but brings any moisture already present in the wood to a boil, softening or "plasticizing" the wood fibers. The high humidity of the steambox keeps the wood from drying out. With sufficient exposure to the steam, you have anywhere from a few seconds to several minutes to coax it into a new shape. Boiling works as well as steaming, and if your workpieces are small—thin strips for Shaker boxes for instance—then boiling them in a shallow tray may be easier than fussing with a steaming apparatus.

The setup

The makeup of your system has a lot to do with how much bending you anticipate doing. Most makeshift rigs work in a pinch. When I was a graduate student living in Boston, I hoisted a 17-ft. boat through a third-story porch door with a block and tackle, so I could use the kitchen stove, my girlfriend's tea kettle and a length of stovepipe to bend new gunwales.

Whatever you use, it must be capable of providing large quantities of wet, hot steam. Although many people use portable camping stoves, I've never had much luck getting them to provide enough heat to really build up steam. An outside fire fueled by scrapwood works well but requires constant tending: Too little fire and the water won't boil, too much and your tank will boil dry, baking your stock. Many snowshoe makers and Windsor chair bodgers use simple rigs that fit over the top of a wood stove.

A portable propane torch, the kind plumbers used for melting lead, works well for me (see the photo on the facing page). I had legs added so that the torch would be freestanding and used an adapter that allowed it to run off a hose from a larger propane tank. I use a 5-gal. kerosene can to hold the water. Initially, I directed the steam into the steambox with a short length of radiator hose, as shown in the photo at left. To increase the volume of steam, I later cut a 4-in. circular hole in the top of the can and directed the steam through a length of 4-in.-dia. stovepipe.

The steambox

The steambox is just that: a box to hold steam. A number of things will work. For long awkward pieces, such as snowshoe frames, wooden skis, sleigh runners or the 20-ft. gunwales on a canoe, schedule 40 PVC pipe works well, but it tends to sag in the middle. Support it on wooden boards as long as the pipe. Clean metal stovepipe can be used as well, though it tends to bake the

A steambox can be made of almost anything. The author connects sections of PVC drain pipe for long pieces and uses a couple of cobbled-up wooden boxes for shorter pieces. For best results, especially on thicker pieces, the box should be as small as possible.

pieces near the sides. For most stock, a simple wooden box works best, providing insulation and holding the steam. I use several steamboxes, as shown in the photo above: PVC pipe for bending long stock, a 6-ft. wooden box 16 in. sq. that can hold more than 50 boat ribs at once, and a smaller 5-in.-sq. wooden box just over 4 ft. long for bending hardwood stem stock, chair parts or barrel staves.

In choosing a steambox, especially when bending hardwood over an inch in thickness, always use the smallest box that will hold the stock. In any steam chamber, some kind of internal rack is needed to keep the stock separated and off the floor, so the steam can circulate freely around it. Copper wire will work, as will clothes-hanger wire, though the iron will stain the wood. Most of my steamboxes use dowels. The end of the box should be loose-fitting to provide a relief; pressurized steam is unnecessary and dangerous. A hinged lid can provide easy access to the box, but a blanket or rag stuffed in the end works just as well.

You can't bend that wood—Common opinion is that kiln-dried wood, particularly pine, can't be bent. Carpenter Greg Marston of S. Bridgton, Maine, who built the kiln-dried, white pine hand rail on this banister, didn't know that.

The stock

No point in the steaming operation is as important as carefully selecting your stock. No matter how elaborate your steaming setup, poor-quality wood simply will not bend. The grain should travel in a straight line through the stock that will be bent and not wander off the sides. Any part of the stock that will be bent must be absolutely free of knots, wavy or irregular grain, surface checking or any imperfections. Avoid wood with insect damage or fungal stains, which weaken the wood. Some sources claim that wood bends better with the flat of the grain parallel to the face of the bending form, while others prefer the grain perpendicular to the face of the form. (For reference in this article, we'll call the former flatsawn, the latter quartersawn, regardless of how the stock was milled.) After bending thousands of ribs for the canoes that I've built, I've found that, for the most part, it makes no difference. I often bend quartersawn white oak to show off the medullary ray patterns and haven't noticed any increase in failure. In fact, on the especially tight bends required at the ends of a canoe, I select quartersawn northern white cedar, which I find less likely to tear out along the grain than flatsawn stock.

Riven vs. sawn stock, green vs. dry stock

If you own or have access to a woodlot, you may want to cut your own trees and try riving your stock. This has several advantages. You can select the best trees, and you can split green wood, which follows the grain, whereas a sawblade follows an indifferent path. Wood you've split yourself can be bent immediately while the wood is still green. Steaming drives the sap out of the wood, which dries it. After the wood has cured on the form, it will be ready to use.

Perfectly good stock also can be had from lumber piles at a local sawmill. I have found most sawyers will go out of their way to help a customer with an unusual request, if you let them know what you're doing and tell them what you need. And partly dried wood may have some advantages. It is easier and faster to obtain for most people, and some sources (including the British Ministry of Technology) indicate the cells of green wood may actually be more likely to rupture during the bending process, leading to failures. In addition, air-dried stock needs less time to dry and set on the form and is less likely to distort or split during bending.

If you use stock that has air-dried, it can be soaked to regain some of its moisture content. In this way, I've steam-bent cherry that had been drying in a barn loft for 30 years. Boards can be sunk in a pond or stream, or they can be wrapped in wet cloth and sealed in plastic. Woods can be stored indefinitely like this; I have some white oak boards that have been sunk in my duck pond for more than two years, but a few days of this treatment is usually enough. Some woods, such as white ash and white oak, tend to discolor near the surface when soaked for too long, but this can be planed off or removed with oxalic acid.

The one type of wood that should always be avoided is kiln-dried, which has baked-in defects such as casehardening (tiny cracks in the surface of the wood) that can lead to failures. The first rule in bending wood, however, is that there are no hard and fast rules. Not long ago, I saw a house carpenter bend a piece of kiln-dried white pine, a poor species for bending to begin with, to a fairly impressive curve on a staircase banister (see the photo on the facing page). Against all expectations, it worked "slicker than a smelt," as they say here in Maine.

Stock preparation

Bending wood places it under a great deal of stress, and therefore, the stock to be bent should be carefully prepared. Because the ends of a curve often distort (see "Making a bending form" on p. 49), I cut pieces several inches longer than I will need. I leave stock that will take a sharp bend slightly oversized in thickness as well, usually about 1/16 in., which allows me to plane off any slivers that pop up when the wood is bent.

To prepare the stock, first plane off any sawmarks, and then handplane off any snipes left by the thickness planer. Chamfering the edges that will be in tension with a block plane or sandpaper will keep loose fibers from plucking up. Clearly mark stock that has to be bent with a certain face down, and be sure to use a pencil or indelible ink, or the steam will erase your mark.

Experience also has taught me that some stock is better shaped after it is bent. I follow this simple rule: Pieces that have to take an acute bend and are likely to experience a higher failure rate are finish-shaped after steaming.

A trick used by snowshoe makers is to relieve or cut away some of the wood where it takes the sharpest bend. This can be determined and marked off by eye and accomplished with a simple jig for a handplane or thickness planer. While this may slightly reduce the strength of the finished piece, it will greatly improve the ratio of success in bending. Finally, it's always good practice to prepare and to steam several extra pieces in case one breaks.

Two kinds of bending failures— Compression failure (inside curve of the bottom piece) is often due to oversteaming. Tension failure (outside curve of all pieces) can be reduced by using straight-grained stock and a backing strip.

Getting ready

Some of the other important factors in bending success are also the most basic. Preparedness is certainly one. At all costs, avoid the urge to fire up the boiler and to figure out the rest while the wood is steaming. I know the results: more fuel for the fire. Have everything ready, laid out and clearly marked before starting. This can be

Woods that bend

A number of sources offer confusing, often contradictory, information about which species of wood are appropriate for bending. One source that I read listed ash, probably everyone's favorite, as a poor choice, and others offered general advice such as "softwoods do not bend well," which would no doubt come as a surprise to boatbuilders who rely on white cedar and tamarack for steam-bent ribs.

In my applications, I use mostly cedar, white oak and white ash, which all bend well. Oak, ash and beech are probably the woods chosen most often for bending and with good reason. They are readily available in the quality needed for bending and bend easily. Often I'll bend several dozen pieces without breaking one. Oak and ash are almost always seen on bent chair arms (see the photo below), sleigh runners and toboggans. In other applications, I've found American elm, the birches, maples, walnut and hop hornbeam all bent well. (Many older snowshoe frames were yellow birch.) Other species, such as cherry, bend with difficulty, but I have bent inch-thick cherry to a tight radius by choosing the stock carefully and leaving it in the box a long time.

Mahogany, pine and spruce need great care, good luck and druidic supplications to bend at all, but again, determination and preparation can often overcome the reluctance of even these species to take a bend. Over the last century, canoemakers in Maine routinely used spruce and mahogany for gunwale stock, and bent pine is seen on many an old staircase banister.

Boatbuilders are good sources of information on bending wood because they do it regularly. Luthiers are another. Many books also offer good advice. Read as many sources as you can rather than making up your mind on the basis of one author's advice—unless it's mine.

Above all, experiment. I wanted to use black locust for the stems of a canoe I was building but wasn't sure it would bend well, and I got as many different answers as people I asked. I begged a board from a local sawmill, telling them I'd buy more if it bent well. It did and I did. Whenever I think of it, I set aside scraps of species I haven't tried. Then, when I'm firing up the steambox, I throw them in.

Woods that bend— Although oak and ash may be the most popular woods for bent chair parts (like the arms and backs of these chairs built by Greg Marston, S. Bridgton, Maine), maple, birch, beech, American elm and walnut will also work well.

Making a bending form

The shape of the curve you're bending will be only as good as the form you bend it on. Boatbuilders and others who work in curves speak of a curve being fair, which holds the same meaning here that it did in chivalry: pleasing to the eye with no distracting bumps or dips.

To develop a fair bending form, you can trace a curve you want to duplicate, or eyeball a curve, full-sized, directly onto your stock. A word about the jig stock: It need not be fancy. My jigs are built from waste pieces of plywood and dimension lumber, and I am shameless about finding it wherever I can: construction sites, demolition sites and even the dump. All of it works about the same. Stack the pieces to give you the necessary thickness.

Two things will ensure your finished form will give the wood you bend over it the shape you're after. First, because the ends of bent wood often distort, continue the curve for several inches at either end of your form. Second, because wood tends to spring back, make the last quarter of the curve from 1/4 in. to 3/8 in. tighter than the actual desired shape.

Once you've established a line, flex a clear, flawless 1-in. by 1/4-in. pine or spruce batten to follow it. Nail on opposite sides of the batten along its length; then sight along it. Any humps or hollows where the nails force the curve should jump out at you. Remove and retack the nails until you're satisfied with the finished curve, and mark it with a sharp pencil. Saw wide of the line, and use a spokeshave, block plane and rasp to smooth to the line. Carefully running the curve past a sanding disc mounted on a tablesaw saves time on wider forms.

One last piece of advice: It's a good idea to make the form thick enough to bend several pieces at once. It always pays to steam an extra piece in case one breaks. And design it so dowels or wedges can be used to secure your bent stock (see the photo on p. 62). Otherwise, you'll tie up a lot of clamps in a hurry.

particularly important when making repairs, as shown in the photo on p. 51. Make sure that you have enough clamps handy, and always remember that you're dealing with live steam. The steam can cause serious burns to the face and hands if not handled properly.

Nonwork-related factors can lead to other failures. Here are some things to remember: Make sure your shoelaces are tied; clean up clutter, and check that an extra long piece won't take out the overhead lights when you bend it around.

Steaming

Start timing how long the wood has been steaming from the moment you see steam coming out of your box. Opinions vary as to how long the wood should spend in the steambox. Most sources recommend one hour for each inch of thickness, but those on the more conservative side recommend an hour for each 1/4 in. of thickness. Much of the discrepancy can be related to the species used, whether it is green or dry, and the tightness of the curve the wood is being bent to. Because it is possible to oversteam wood, making it more brittle, the best solution may be a compromise. For stock under 3/4 in., I use the inch-an-hour schedule. But, I'll leave a 1-in. piece in the steam for two hours or more. With experience, you'll be able to feel when the wood is ready: Properly steamed wood will feel floppy when you wiggle it from one end and will take a slight test-bend around your knee with no resistance.

Bending

As wood is bent, the fibers on the outside of the curve are stretched into tension, while the inside fibers are pushed into compression. This can lead to two kinds of failure, as shown in the photo on p. 47. The first, compression failure, occurs when the wood crumples and folds during bending. This is

Heating-pad bending eliminates the steam

by Bruce Gray

I like steam-bending wood. It's fun to see wood do something it's not supposed to do. But I admit, I hate scorching my hand on a hot pipe heated by a butane torch, ammonia gas stinging my nose or steam billowing up into my shop rafters where I store kiln-dried wood. When I was faced with removing a back slat from a Shaker-style chair I had made, I knew standard methods wouldn't work. My solution was the heating-pad approach. Let me explain how it works (see the drawing at right).

Heating-pad bending

A drug store heating pad and a wet towel supply enough damp heat to soften wood for bending.

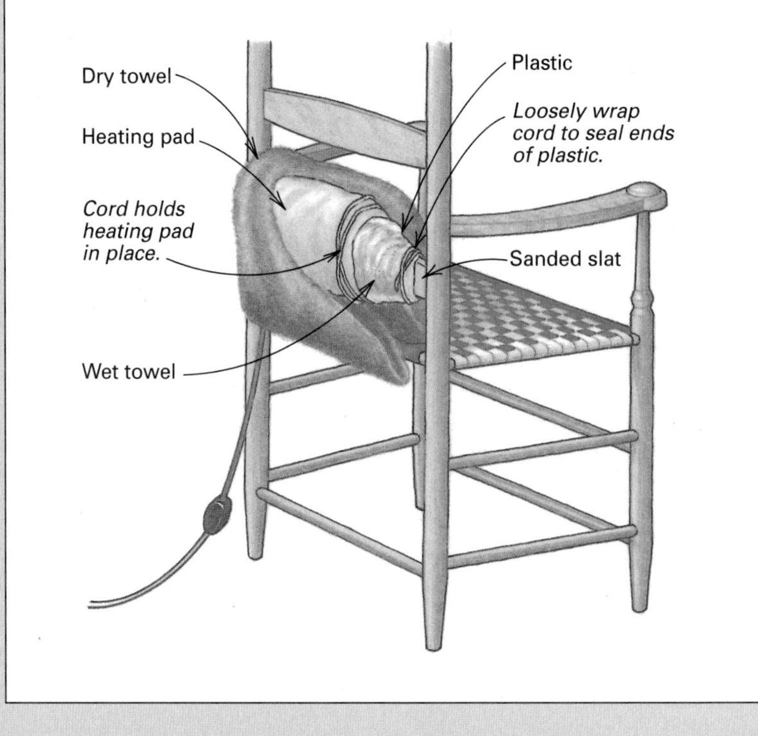

After sanding the slat to remove any existing finish, soak a bath towel in hot water. The towel should be quite wet but not dripping. Fold the towel around the back slat; then wrap the towel with thick plastic sheet (I use 6-mil plastic) to keep the moisture in. Loosely tie the plastic in place with a cord, pulling only the ends tight. Don't use knots, just a few overlapping wraps to keep the cord from slipping, because the cord needs to be removed quickly. Now that you've built a wet-towel and plastic-sheet steambox, you'll need some heat. The heating pad I use is the drug store variety used to soothe sore joints. Mine is rated at 120 watts, 125v and measures 12 in. by 14 in. Fold the pad over the plastic, and secure with a cord as before. Cover the pad with a folded, dry towel for insulation. Turn the heater on to high and presto: one efficient steambox without steam!

Heating time varies with wood species, thickness and initial moisture content. About 1½ to 2 hours turned the ¼-in.-thick, kiln-dried, bird's-eye maple slat to putty and the same for a 1-in.-dia., air-dried ash back post. Like traditional steaming, the method is quick. Like soaking, steam time is flexible, and the wood has a relatively long working time. Because there is little need to monitor the process, you can focus your attention on other work while you are steaming.

It's easy to see if the wood is ready to bend, just test-bend the wrapped assembly with your hands. A slow yield to your force indicates the wood is ready. Leather work gloves will protect your hands from the hot wood.

If you have just a few small pieces to bend, you can't beat the heating-pad approach for low cost, ease and speed.

Be prepared—When making repairs such as replacing the rib in this canoe, it's important to have everything ready, pieces marked for proper orientation and clamps at hand because of the limited working time of steamed stock.

often a sign of overexposure to steam. The second, more common failure is tension failure. It occurs when long slivers of wood break off and peel away on the outside of the bend. Minor slivers can be glued down or sanded or planed away, but severe slivers will continue through the work, sometimes breaking the piece in half.

Several factors will reduce tension failure: proper selection of stock and supporting the outside edge with some kind of strap, a thin, wooden batten or an elaborate spring-steel strap with adjustable end stops. I usually opt for the wooden batten. Waxed paper between the stock and a steel strap will prevent staining.

For any piece that takes an acute bend, lay a tension strap over the stock as soon as it comes out of the box, and fasten the wood to the jig either at one end or in the middle. Bend the wood slowly and deliberately, pausing occasionally for a few seconds to allow the fibers to stretch. You can help "stretch" the wood by bending the stock with your hands.

Once the wood is bent, it should be left on the form for at least 24 hours to avoid springback, which is relaxing of the fibers that occurs when the wood is unclamped too soon. There are several other ways to reduce springback. One is to work quickly: the sooner the wood is bent after it's removed from the box, the less it will spring back later. You can also compensate for springback by making the curve of the bending form slightly tighter than the curve of the finished piece.

Repeated bending failure can be attributed to several factors.

1) The wood itself: Trying to bend the wrong species, poor stock of the right species or kiln-dried wood of any species can lead to failures (see "Woods that bend" on p. 48). 2) Problems with the steam: You need a lot of consistent, hot steam to limber the wood. 3) Not using bending straps.

Finally, there's one trick that might work when all others fail: Sing to your wood as it's steaming. The English playwright William Congreve noted in 1697 that "music hath charms to bend the knotted oak"—something even steam can't do.

BENT LAMINATION

by John Michael Pierson

The completed music stand, with its curved legs and pedestal, looked great in the San Diego State University shop where I made it as a student. The stand seemed like a perfect gift for my father, a concert violinist in Corpus Christi, Texas. This was my first bent-lamination project, and I was very pleased with the results and anxious to send it on its way. Little did I know that soon the stand would be back for repairs because I had made the mistake of using yellow glue for the laminations. Even after the glue was fully cured, it continued to creep with changes in the temperature and humidity; the glue even began squeezing out from between the laminations. The smooth, curved surfaces gave way to a rough, bumpy texture. I ended up refinishing that stand

three times before the problem was brought under control.

That was 20 years ago, and despite my rough start, I'm sold on the possibilities of bent lamination. Curved shapes add movement and life to my furniture designs. But many of the species that I want to use don't steam-bend well, and bandsawing curves from solid stock can result in weak furniture parts.

Bent lamination, which is simply gluing a series of thin plies together over a form, provides strength and allows a greater freedom of wood choice. Many people hesitate to try bent lamination because they think that it's too difficult. Nonsense! Making bent shapes is relatively easy.

Parts can be built up with uniformly thick plies. Or for a more dramatic effect, you can taper the plies to develop finished parts of varying thicknesses (see the story on p. 59), as I did on the tea cart in the photo above right. The procedure I'll describe works equally well on tapered plies or plies of uniform thickness.

Coaxing plies into shape requires a strong form and heavy-duty clamps (facing page). Bent laminations make furniture, such as this tea cart, graceful, light and strong.

Choosing wood and ply thickness

Ash, oak and other tough, long-grained woods bend more easily than brittle, short-grained woods like mahogany and purpleheart. But any wood can be bent if you use the proper ply thickness for the desired bend radius. This relationship is about 50:1. So, for example, a 5-in.-radius bend would use plies 1/10 in. thick.

Also, keep in mind the more plies the less springback after the laminate is removed from the form. Success depends on the quality of the individual boards. Knots, erratic grain and uneven thickness will give poor results. Stock must be made from clear, straight-grained lumber that's surfaced flat with at least one jointed edge.

Accurate form, accurate bend

The bending form can be a shaped piece of stock to which the plies are clamped, but I generally prefer a mating, two-piece form. It's harder to make, but it captures the laminates and distributes pressure evenly with fewer clamps. This makes glue-up faster and gluelines nearly invisible.

The form must be strong and accurate because thin plies will conform to any bump or irregularity. I build up the forms with layers of medium-density fiberboard (MDF) or particleboard to match the width of bending plies (plus an extra 1/32 in. of clearance between the edge of the laminates and the edge of the form). If needed, I'll use a thin plywood shim between layers of MDF to make a final adjustment in the form thickness.

The best way to get identical form pieces is by pattern routing. Bandsaw and carefully shape a full-sized pattern from 1/4-in. MDF. It's much easier to shape a single 1/4-in.-thick pattern accurately than it is to shape a number of 3/4-in. or thicker pieces of form stock. Screw this pattern to a piece of MDF or particleboard, and bandsaw the rough shape, staying about 1/16 in. to 1/8 in. away from the pattern. Then, using either a hand-

Making a pattern saves time. Identical layers of form stock are made by pattern routing with a flush-trimming bit.

held router or a router mounted in a table, trim the excess stock to match the pattern with a flush-trimming bit (see the photo above). Pattern rout as many layers of form material as necessary to build up the needed thickness, and then glue, align and clamp the layers together.

Upright forms let glue cure faster

Feet glued and screwed to the bottom of the form hold it upright and provide clearance for the jaws of the clamps. This upright arrangement promotes air circulation and faster glue curing. Also, it's easier to see what you're doing when you're tightening the clamps.

I also add alignment keys to my forms. They are just pieces of hardwood, 1/2 in. by 1/2 in. by 8 in., screwed and glued to the sides of the form. The keys (see the top photo on the facing page) speed glue-up dramatically by ensuring the exact location of the mating halves and preventing plies from slipping off the form's side. I line the matching edges of the keys with two layers of masking tape when attaching them to the form. When I remove the tape, there's a slight clearance between keys so they won't bind. A generous chamfer on the inside faces and matching edges of keys allows smooth engagement of the keys when the form halves are brought together.

I finish the forms with two coats of Varathane Diamond finish, a fast-drying, water-based topcoat. Then I apply paste wax (see the bottom photo on the facing page) to all the parts that will come in contact with glue and buff out the wax thoroughly.

Consistent plies give best results

When the form is completed, rip the plies with a tablesaw. Start by drawing reference lines on the stock (see the photo at left on p. 56) so that the plies can be reassembled in the original order for grain continuity. Set the fence-to-blade distance at 1/8 in. This should put you in the ballpark on thickness, but you should cut a test ply to see if it's flexible enough. Bend a test ply by hand (no clamps) in your form to test for flexibility (see the photo at right on p. 56). It should bend easily. If you hear the sound of cracking or see visual fractures, the ply is too thick. Bump the fence over 1/32 in., and try again.

Once you're satisfied with the bendability of the test ply, rip the rest of the plies and stack them in their original order. I rip plies less than 2 1/2 in. wide on the tablesaw; for wider plies, I use a bandsaw. Try to keep the board moving without pause, from the beginning to the end of the cut. This minimizes sawmarks on the ply faces. As you feed the board, be sure that the edge stays against the fence. When some discrepancy develops after cutting a number of plies, simply re-joint the edge, and go back to ripping. Assuming your finished lamination will be of uniform thickness, your goal is to produce consistent ply thickness. Sawmarks do not interfere with a good glue-up nearly as much as erratic thicknesses in plies.

Use a throat plate and splitter

Ripping thin stock on the tablesaw is intense business, but there are ways to make it safer. It's absolutely necessary to make a special throat plate that has a slot only as wide as the blade (see the drawing on p. 56). This throat plate prevents a thin ply from being sucked down the wide slot of a standard throat plate, possibly resulting in an accident. A wooden splitter mounted on the outfeed side of the plate adds another level of safety and prevents the flexible ply from bouncing against the blade. The height of the splitter should be slightly less than the stock thickness so that it won't interfere with the push stick.

Use a substantial push stick like the one shown in the photo at left on p. 56. It is important to keep the stock flat on the table. Don't allow the front end to rise up at the beginning of the cut, as is its tendency.

Alignment keys keep the two halves of the form meshed correctly and prevent plies from side slipping.

Wax forms thoroughly, especially around the keys, so they don't stick together. Forms should get two coats of finish first.

Use a hefty push stick for ripping. Reference marks (in white) help you reassemble the plies in their original order.

Throat plate and splitter for ripping thin plies

A dedicated throat plate for ripping plies minimizes the risk of kickback and ensures good results. Cut the slot with the blade used for ripping the plies. The splitter height should be slightly lower than the thickness of the stock being ripped. Locate the splitter close to the back of the blade.

Slot width same as tablesaw blade

Hardwood splitter glued to throat plate

Grain is vertical.

Make plywood throat plate to fit the tablesaw.

Test a ply by bending it over the form. If the ply bends easily, the thickness is correct.

A stippled roller helps spread the glue with speed and consistency. Apply glue to all but the two faces that will contact the form.

Start clamping in the center, and work out to prevent bubbles between plies.

Use plenty of clamps, and space them so the plies are compressed against the form. To avoid springback, keep the clamps on the form until the glue has completely cured.

Separate the form. Sometimes a rap with a well-placed chisel and mallet is needed to free the cured part.

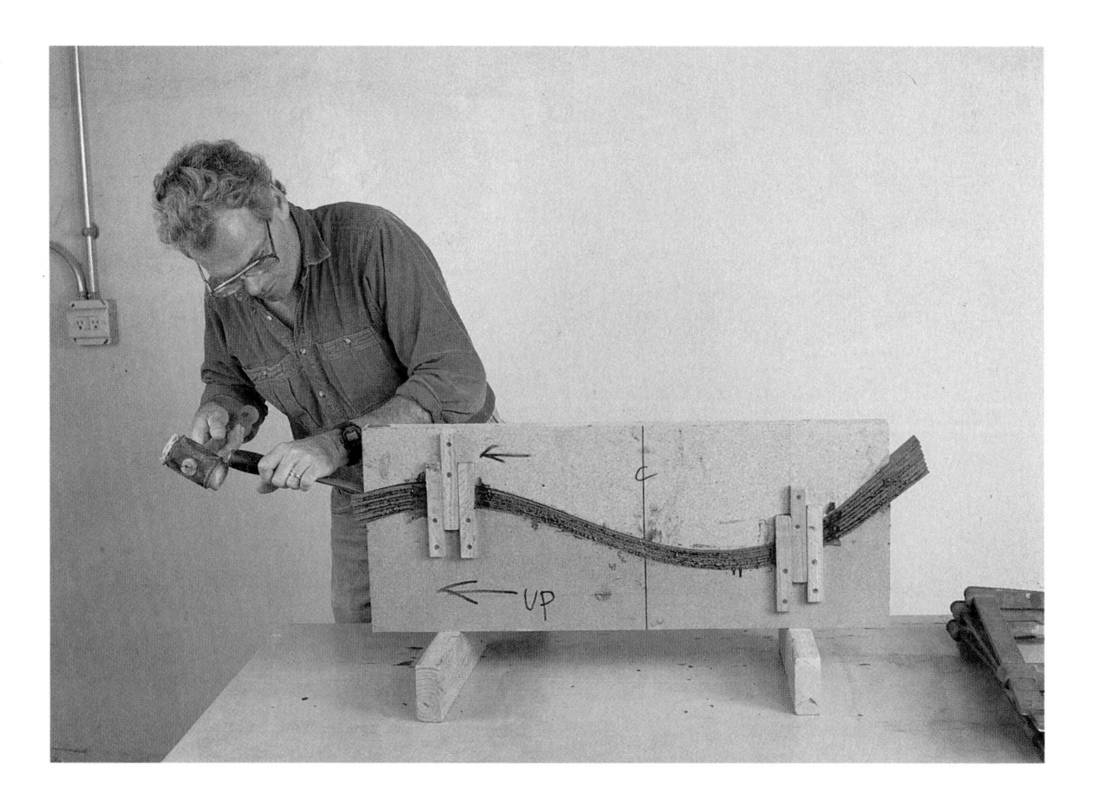

Grind off glue. A coarse-grit sanding disc and mini-grinder quickly remove squeeze-out once the glue has dried.

Wrap your thumb and index finger around the handle of the push stick, and hook your third and fourth fingers over the top of the tablesaw fence. If the push stick kicks out from underneath your hand, the position of these fingers over the fence may prevent your hand from falling onto the blade. Be certain to continue pushing the stock completely past the back of the blade before lifting off the push stick. The push stick will pass directly over the blade during the completion of the cut. Do not readjust the position of the push stick during this stage.

Place the push stick against the tablesaw fence, and press down firmly on the stock as the end of the board approaches the blade. Keep it in this position until it clears the back side of the blade. When the stock has been cut down to 2 1/2 in. wide, you can change to a narrower push stick to maintain a good purchase, or you can cut the plies on the waste side of the blade. Sanding the plies after ripping isn't necessary.

A tapering jig for contoured parts

Tapered bent laminations add another dimension to my furniture designs. To get this effect without bandsawing through plies and disrupting the grain continuity in the finished piece, I taper the ply thickness first. I make a jig similar to a standard tapering jig, except I create a slight crown along the length of the jig equal to the amount of stock that I want to remove (see the drawing at right).

In use, I simply attach the plies, one at a time, to the jig with three patches of double-faced tape and re-rip all the plies for a thinner center section.

Other contoured forms are possible with this approach. For example, with a convex curve, the jig will produce plies with a thicker center section, and a straight taper jig will give uniformly tapered plies.

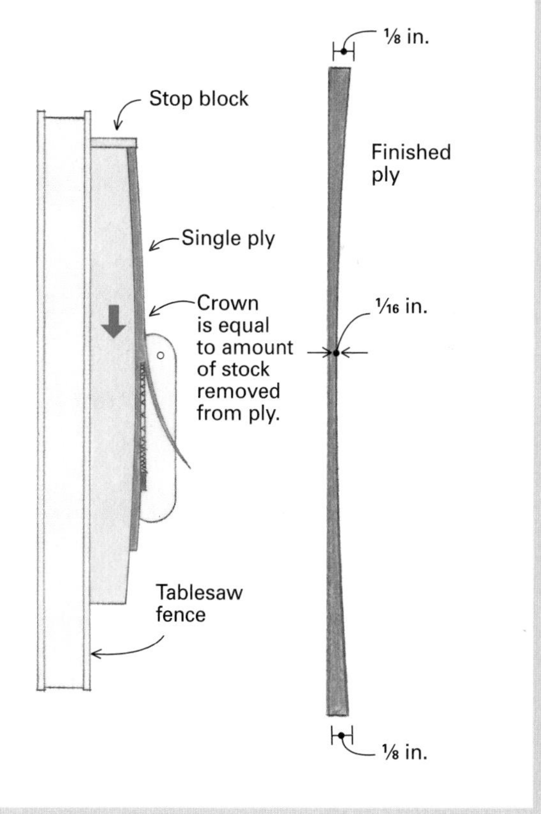

Slow-setting glues work best

I usually use Urac 185 urea formaldehyde glue for the plies (Cytec Industries Inc., P.O. Box 32787, Charlotte, NC 28232; 800-243-6874). It has a long pot life (it doesn't harden too quickly after you've mixed it), dries hard, doesn't creep and won't clog sanding discs when you grind it. Plastic resin glue, another form of urea formaldehyde, also will work and is more readily available in small quantities.

Yellow and white woodworking glues don't work as well for laminating. They remain somewhat plastic, even when cured, allowing glueline creep and springback. They also set too quickly, which can be anxiety-producing when clamping takes longer than expected. If the glue skins over before clamp-up, there is a chance of delamination (possibly after the piece is completed and delivered).

Epoxy works best for oily woods like teak. The glue must be fully cured before unclamping to control springback and to prevent delamination.

How to glue up

Before applying any glue, place the dry lamination stack against the form face, adjust the plies so that the middle of the stack is aligned with the middle of the form, and draw a reference line across plies and onto the form. This reference line will help you see excessive slippage during glue-up, which would reduce the usable length of your finished piece.

Using a stippled roller (sold at larger paint stores and used for applying contact cement), apply a thin layer of glue to each face of the plies except the two surfaces that will contact the form (see the top photo on p. 57). Then set the stack against one face of the form. Be careful to align the reference mark on the stack with the matching mark on the form. Clamp across the center. I prefer to use heavy-duty bar clamps to reach the center of the form. Pipe clamps are less satisfactory because their shallow jaws tend to pull the form to one side.

Position and tighten the center clamp first, and then work toward each end. This will prevent trapping a wrinkle in the lamination. There's no magic to spacing the clamps; just use enough to compress the stack uniformly along the entire bend (see the photo on p. 52).

Plies probably will slip and slide around as excess glue is squeezed out. If necessary, release the clamp pressure, readjust the plies and clamp again. Allow the glue to cure thoroughly—this is very important. Prematurely releasing the part from the form will result in springback.

Knock the cured piece free

After the glue is cured, remove the clamps, and tap the bent piece with a mallet to pop it off the form (see the top photo on p. 58). Especially stubborn pieces may require a sharp tap with a chisel between the lamination and the form.

Once free of the form, I clean off the hardened glue with a 24-grit sanding disc in a mini-grinder (see the bottom photo on p. 58). If you are gluing up duplicate parts, carefully clean off any dried glue residue on the form, reapply paste wax and buff it out. You're now ready for another glue-up.

FORMING CURVES FROM LAYERS OF BLOCKS

by Kirt Kirkpatrick

Building furniture is a pretty linear process, as long as the parts are straight, the joinery is simple and the framework is rectangular. But many pieces aren't straight at all (see the photo at right). Tables can have curved aprons and edges. Mirror frames are often oval or circular in shape. Drawer fronts can be serpentine. So what do you do when a piece of furniture throws you a curve?

Bricklaid curves are built in layers. To build curved furniture parts, glue up blocks of wood in rings or arcs, and then layer them. The technique is strong and versatile, as shown in the circular apron in the glass-topped imbuia table

Tempered hardboard is ideal for templates. Use a trammel, a straightedge and a knife to scribe a template for a segment of a circular frame. Then trace the template onto stock.

To get tight butt joints, trim the ends carefully. After bandsawing the segments, the author disc sands their ends just to the knife line (darkened with pencil). He'll sand inner and outer curves later.

Gluing up the segments. To form rings, apply glue to the ends of the segments; then rub the ends together to force out any air from the joints. A polished stone slab, as flat as a patternmaker's surface plate, makes an easy-to-clean assembly table.

I've found that segments of wood, glued together like a mortared wall, are just what the doctor ordered to make strong, stable curves. I first used this construction method, known as bricklaying, in 1975 while serving my patternmaker apprenticeship. I rarely make wooden patterns anymore, but I continue to use the bricklaying technique for curved furniture components. The bricklaid form can be a full circle, an arc or any curve. For strength, a curve needs at least two layers of glued-up segments, but three or more is best. A single layer isn't strong enough unless you use some additional joinery, like splines, biscuits or dowels to bridge the butt joints between individual segments.

Just as with ordinary laminations, I always make the bricklaid form oversize. That way, I can adjust the layout of the finished part onto the glued-up stock. Once the glue sets, I can cut joinery into the form and shape and sand it just like it is a solid piece of wood. In the case of a circular mirror frame (like the one that's described in the story on the facing page), the form is ring-shaped. Bricklaid curves can be more complex, but because the mirror frame is simple, it's a good example of how the technique works. First, though, it's helpful to see why bricklaid segments are so versatile and to understand the importance of making accurate templates.

Why patternmakers use bricklaid segments

Patternmakers glue wooden blocks together like layers of bricks to build the curved areas of wooden patterns, which are full-sized models used to form molds in sand. The sand molds are then used to cast metal (for more on this, see the story on pp. 66-67). The pattern can be reused to make many molds.

Patterns must be strong and stable. As long as the wood grain in the segments is about the same density and runs the same way (no short grain), movement of the form due to moisture exchanges should be uniform. In bricklaid circular and spherical

Making a circular frame

The teak mirror frame in the photo at right consists of two ring layers, each with six segments. To make the frame, determine its inner and outer diameter. Have the mirror glass in hand so you can make the inner diameter of the frame 1 in. smaller, allowing for a ½-in. rabbet in the back of the frame. Next make a segment template (see the main article).

If you select a big enough board, all the segments will have the same color and characteristics. If not, cut the wood for the most visible layers from the same board. Using the template, trace out 12 segments onto ¾-in. stock. Bandsaw and sand the segment ends. Next glue up half-rings of segments, flipping every other one. When dry, true up where the halves will be joined. Flip opposite halves, and glue them into full rings. After the glue has cured, scrape the joints, so you can stack and glue two rings together. Clamp the form, and let it dry.

Trim the frame, and rout the back rabbet for the mirror. Using a roundover, chamfering or molding bit, ease the inner edge of the frame, and add an outside profile. Final-sand, apply a finish and then inset the mirror in the frame.

It's hard to tell this mirror frame is made of segments. The reason is that all the joints between segments and between layers are tight.

structures, the grain configuration is especially important because the form must expand and contract concentrically without becoming oval-shaped. After a pattern has been used at the foundry, it is usually retired to a warehouse. It may sit there for years before it's needed again. This is another reason why patterns must be strong and hold their shape over time.

Segments are ideal for bowls and furniture

Bricklaid segments are common in woodturning. Stack-laminated segments can prevent bowls from warping. The grain of the segments can be arranged so that the bowl appears homogeneous. Or different woods can be used to make contrasting segments. Layers can be built a couple at a time and once the glue has set, turned to make large, deep bowls safely. That way, you don't have to reach way inside the bowl with your tools.

Aside from circular shapes, you can bricklay wood into partial curves, such as arched door and window frames; waves in sculpture; and aprons for oval and semielliptical tables. I used this technique to form the built-up table edge in a large conference table.

Complex furniture parts can be bricklaid, too. For example, to create flowing lines in a contemporary glass-top table (see the top photo on p. 61), I bricklaid segments of imbuia that were all cut from one board, and then I shaped them with a router jig and hand tools. The offset segments in the bottom layer provide sockets for the three

Bricklaying a six-segment ring

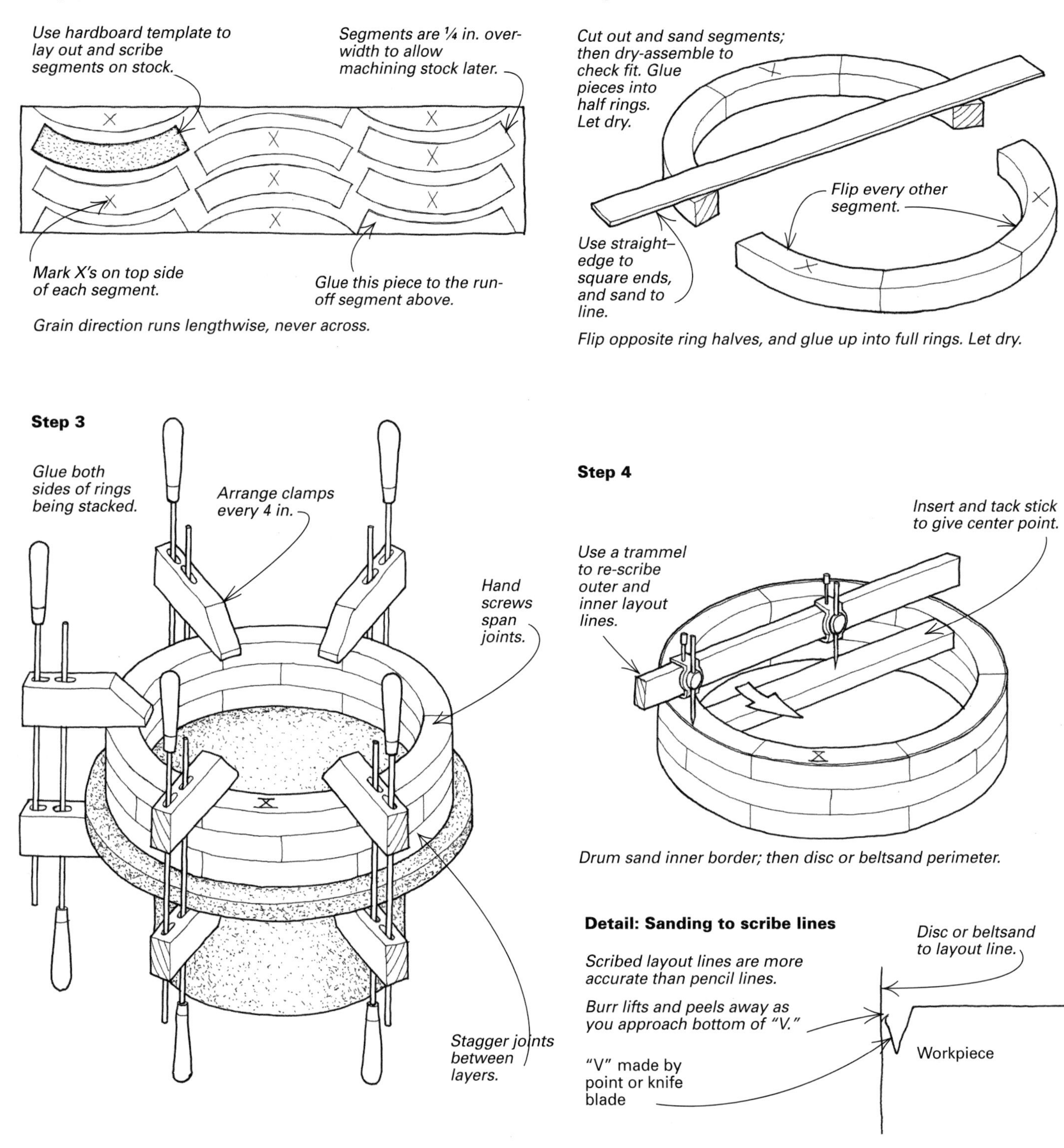
Step 1
Use hardboard template to lay out and scribe segments on stock.
Segments are ¼ in. over-width to allow machining stock later.
X
Mark X's on top side of each segment.
Glue this piece to the run-off segment above.
Grain direction runs lengthwise, never across.
Step 2
Cut out and sand segments; then dry-assemble to check fit. Glue pieces into half rings. Let dry.
Flip every other segment.
Use straight-edge to square ends, and sand to line.
Flip opposite ring halves, and glue up into full rings. Let dry.
Step 3
Glue both sides of rings being stacked.
Arrange clamps every 4 in.
Hand screws span joints.
Stagger joints between layers.
Step 4
Insert and tack stick to give center point.
Use a trammel to re-scribe outer and inner layout lines.
Drum sand inner border; then disc or beltsand perimeter.
Detail: Sanding to scribe lines
Scribed layout lines are more accurate than pencil lines.
Burr lifts and peels away as you approach bottom of "V."
"V" made by point or knife blade
Disc or beltsand to layout line.
Workpiece

tom layer provide sockets for the three legs—another advantage of the technique.

Strength comes from layers

Bricklaid forms derive their strength from bonded layers. The butt joints between segments are relatively weak because only end grain is being glued. To give those joints integrity, it's critical that the template used to lay out the segments be exact and that the segment ends be cut and sanded precisely to make the joints tight. By contrast, the bonds between adjoining layers of segments are strong because long grain is glued to long grain and because each segment bridges a joint. This is why the joints in adjacent layers must be staggered (see the drawing on the facing page).

Start by making a segment template

I start by making a template for the segments using 1/8-in. hardboard like Masonite. For bricklaid forms that are full circles, I use six segments. This process requires only simple tools and basic geometry, which makes layout a breeze. But if you need to make an arc shape or curve with an odd number of segments, you can look up the proper angles and chord lengths from charts often printed at the back of geometry and trigonometry textbooks. For tools, you'll need a scribing knife, a steel straightedge and a trammel, which is basically a large compass (see the top photo on p. 62). You can buy the trammel at most woodworking-supply stores.

To lay out the template for a six-segment circle, set the trammel 1/8 in. less than the finished inside radius you want, and scribe about a quarter circle onto your piece of hardboard. Next, using the same center, scribe a quarter circle 1/8 in. larger than the desired outside radius. Without changing the trammel setting, place one point on one end of the outside arc, and using the other point, drag a small hash mark across the outside arc. Now lay a straightedge from each point back to the center point, and scribe the ends of the segment (see the top photo on p. 62).

If you were to draw a full outside circle, you could use the same radius setting to step off points around the whole circle. You would get six equal divisions and end up at your starting point. Each of the six chords would be the same length as the radius. This is also an easy way to draw a hexagon or, by skipping every other mark, an equilateral triangle.

Bandsaw out the template, and drum sand the inside radius with a sanding drum mounted in a drill press or an oscillating spindle sander. Next take the template to the disc sander. If you don't own a disc sander, clamp your belt sander on its side. Make sure that the platen is perpendicular to your benchtop and that the belt can spin freely. As you sand the template, go easy, especially on the ends where the segments will contact one another.

The beauty of using scribed lines is that when you've sanded just up to the line (the bottom of the "V" made by the knife edge), a tiny burr will form and peel off the end (see the detail in step 4 on the facing page). So that you don't change the angle on the template ends, ease the piece into the disc (or belt) until you see an even burr lifting all along the top edge. Once you've sanded both ends, you'll wind up with a template for a six-segment, one-layer ring. The extra 1/8 in. on the inside and outside circumference will allow for machining to exact size.

Lay out and cut the segments from stock

Select your stock, and plane all the boards to the same thickness. Trace out all the segments, so the grain runs lengthwise. If your wood is especially precious and you can permit a glue joint in the segments, lay them out close to each other across the width of the board, so they look like stacks of arches. Let the last segment run off the stock. Then glue up the waste from the other side (under the bottom arch) with the incomplete segment to make a full one (see step 1 on the facing page).

Patternmakers: masters of wooden curves

by Alec Waters

I peeked into the cavernous warehouse and saw what looked like spare parts for the Tin Man. The character in The Wizard of Oz came to mind because I was surrounded by hundreds of silver-painted wooden patterns. I was visiting the pattern-making shops in Atchison, Kansas, where Kirt Kirkpatrick had learned his trade.

To see the fruits of a patternmaker's labor, look in your own shop. Your jointer tables and tablesaw trunnions probably are cast iron and each required a pattern at one time. The pattern was used to make an impression in sand—the mold for the casting. All the patterns I saw were unrecognizable, though. The more complicated ones looked like jigsaw puzzles.

When you're making impressions for a mold, the pattern has to be exact in size and shape. The casting will faithfully reproduce whatever is molded in the sand. In areas that won't be machined, the clearances can be critical, and the tolerances can be close. For example, the casting for an aircraft part often can't stray more than 0.010 in. to 0.015 in. from the dimensions shown on the blue print. To achieve this, the pattern must be oversized so that when the casting cools, it will be the intended size.

Guiding molten metal at the foundry—Wearing a fireproof suit, a worker at this Kansas foundry guides a ladle as it pours liquid-hot alloy. The flask (frame), containing compacted sand, has an upper (cope) mold and a lower (drag) mold that were formed with wooden patterns.

Kirkpatrick told me of one pattern that was a few thousands of an inch shy in places. It had to be sprayed with thin coats of lacquer to bring it up to specification.

When a pattern is laid out, the patternmaker has to allow for the contraction of the metal in the mold as it cools off. To compensate for the change in dimensions, shrink rules are used, which have built-in shrinkage factors based on the metal being poured (see the bottom left photo on the facing page).

Wood is the logical choice for patterns because it is relatively inexpensive, strong and tools easily. Patternmakers prefer woods that are dimensionally stable and shape consistently. The stock should have grain that is straight and tight. There should be no figure and no defects, such as knots or checks. For these reasons, clear mahogany and sugar pine are commonly used. If a pattern is too big to be made of solid wood, it can be made from bricklaid segments or from beveled, tapered pieces, like staves for a barrel. To sculpt the wood, patternmakers use bandsaws, routers, shapers, grinders and sanders (see the top photo on the facing page).

Most patterns are made in two parts: the pattern, which describes the outside of the casting, and the core box, which forms the interior (cavity) shape. Core boxes can be complex, so they're made in sections, which can be removed without disrupting the sand. Each side of the pattern is tapered, called draft, to allow the part to be withdrawn. Pieces often interlock or overlap (see the bottom right photo on the facing page) and frequently are painted to indicate the order of assembly or the relationship to other pieces. Parts often will have appendages for anchoring, gas venting, cooling and pouring.

As soon as the pattern is assembled, it's coated with a release agent, such as non-stick paint or powder. Then a frame that looks like a big sand box is prepared to hold the bed of sand. The sand is mixed with binder additive to make it compact better.

The last stop on my tour was watching a casting being made at one of the biggest foundries west of the Mississippi. As a pickup-truck-sized ladle of molten steel headed toward a sand mold (see the photo at left), I suddenly realized the significance of all the patternmaker's meticulous work. If there were any errors in the pattern that made the sand mold, lots of money, labor and time would be poured down the drain.

A disc sander is indispensable in a pattern shop. Using a 42-in. disc sander, Terry Scholz shapes a glued-up block, called a riser. The riser will be used to make a sand impression for a metal reservoir used in the casting process.

Tools only a patternmaker knows—Starrett squares and the Emmert vise are familiar to most woodworkers. But other items on this bench, like the ball-ended fillet irons and shrink rules (center), are best known by patternmakers.

A complex pattern from many pieces. To make a casting for a welding robot, Wilson Bros. Pattern Co. built this mahogany pattern. Each part is scribed on a painted hardboard layout board.

Bandsaw out all the segments, leaving a bit of your pencil line. Then go back to the disc sander, and just as with the template, carefully sand the segment ends (see the center photo on p. 62). Your disc sander's table angle could be slightly off, so mark all the segments with an X to identify the top side. You can cancel out any sander error by flipping every other segment when you glue up the ring (the Xs let you keep track). Before you glue up, though, check your joinery by dry-assembling the form.

Glue up segments, then layers

If everything checks out, glue up the first layer. It's easiest to form half circles—groups of three segments—and then join the halves. Glue on a dead-flat surface, such as the machined top of your tablesaw (protected by plastic). I use a big polished gravestone as a surface for gluing up. When joining two segments, apply glue to both ends being joined, and rub them together as they lay flat (see the bottom photo on p. 62). Rubbing the joint will press out any air, which would compromise the glue bond. Stop rubbing when the segments come into line. You shouldn't need to clamp the segments, but if a particular joint wants to open up, span it with a pinch dog, lightly driving the prongs into the adjoining segments. Only do this if the holes created by the prongs will be buried by another layer or will be in an unseen part of the project, such as the back of a mirror frame. Let things dry.

After you have all the half-circle groups glued together, take a straightedge and draw a line across the ends of the outside segments. This will create a straight surface (like a diameter) where the half circles will be connected (see step 2 on p. 64). Use the disc sander to sand to these lines. Be sure to mark each group with an X, as described previously, and flip one of the halves. Glue the half-circles into full rings.

Once the glue has cured, you can either run the rings through a wide-belt sander, or you can scrape and sand the joints until the tops and bottoms are flat. Then as you glue the rings together, be sure to stagger the segment joints from one layer to the next. Apply glue to both surfaces. Repeat stacking and gluing layers until you achieve the form thickness you need. If you are forming an arc, follow the same basic procedure. Finally, clamp the form generously around the circumference (see step 3 on p. 64).

Mark and trim the form to final size

You'll need to make a center point on the same plane as the top of your form, so you can re-scribe the outlines with the trammel. To do this, fit a stick of wood between the opposite inside edges of the laminated form. The stick should look like a diameter. You can secure it with hot glue, auto-body filler or tack it with tiny brads (you'll be trimming off any adhesive residue or nail holes later). Use the trammel to find the center point on the stick, allowing enough excess stock all around the form for clean up. Re-scribe the inner and outer circles with the trammel (see step 4 on p. 64). If the form is shallow (say, two or three layers deep), you probably won't need the stick. Just secure the ring over a piece of hardboard marked with a center point, and extend one of the trammel points to re-scribe the boundaries. These should pretty much match the pencil lines you drew when you were tracing the individual segments. Use a drum sander and a disc or belt sander to trim the form to the new lines. If you have a big lathe, you can mount the form to a faceplate, and turn it down to your scribe lines.

CURVED PANELS FROM A VACUUM VENEER PRESS

by Mason Rapaport

One of the most used tools in my shop is my vacuum veneer press. In fact, its use in creating veneered curved panels, which are the major components in all of my furniture, is absolutely fundamental. My first encounter with a vacuum press was as an apprentice to woodworker Roger Heitzman in Scotts Valley, California, in 1990. At the time, I had no idea how essential to my woodworking that tool would become.

Before the advent of vacuum presses, it was necessary, if you were laminating curved shapes, to build separate male and female forms that both mated very precisely with the layers to be laminated. The whole assembly had to come together as a perfect sandwich, with the forms as bread and the veneers and substrate layers making up the fixings.

But with the vacuum press, I need to build only one form. The vacuum bag and cauls (layers of flexible material that distribute clamping pressure) made from whatever material I'm using as the substrate, take care of the rest. The process can be divided into four main steps: making the form, preparing the substrate and veneer, gluing up and using the vacuum bag to clamp everything together.

Veneered curves are easier with a vacuum press. One form and a simple caul are all that are necessary to press a curved, veneered component in a vacuum press. This table, veneered in cherry and walnut, consists of two simple laminations spline-tenoned together.

Bending forms are easy to make. Using yellow glue and nails (or screws), you can assemble a form quickly from ribs of medium-density fiberboard (MDF). Use a combination square to make sure all the ribs are aligned.

Making the form

My bending forms are pretty simple. They consist of sections of particleboard or medium-density fiberboard (MDF) that are bandsawn and routed to the exact profile of the finished curve. These sections, or ribs, are then attached to one another with spacer blocks. The result, as shown in the photo at right, looks sort of like an upside down boat without its hull.

The form needs to be 2 in. or so longer than the final length of the finished lamination. This excess allows you to glue up an oversized piece that is trimmed to fit later. Don't forget to add the excess, or you'll be sorry.

Because all the ribs have to be uniform, the first step is making a master template to cut all the ribs. I start with a scale drawing of the curve I want, and then I enlarge it to full size on a sheet of 1/4-in. plywood to make the template. It's important that the template be cut and sanded to a fair curve. Any dips, chips or kinks in the edge of the template will show through on your finished piece.

Trace around your template onto the particleboard or the MDF, and then cut just shy of the line on a bandsaw. Next use a router with a flush-trimming bit, following your template, to get a clean, fair curve.

This process ensures that each rib will be identical.

Once the ribs are all cut, take the waste MDF and cut small pieces to use as spacers. Spacing keeps the weight of the form down but maintains sufficient rigidity so that the form will not deflect under pressure. To assemble the form, I use yellow glue, along with nails or screws, and a good combination square to make sure the form goes together square. The form should be as wide as the final piece, plus an inch or so on either side to allow for final, accurate trimming.

Preparing substrate

I use 1/8-in. Italian bending poplar or 1.5mm (about 1/16 in.) Finland birch for the substrate, depending on the radius of the curve I'm bending. The Italian poplar will bend to a radius of about 2 1/8 in.; the 1/16-in. birch will bend to about a 1-in. radius. When rough-cutting thin sheets, use an auxiliary fence or some other means to prevent the sheets from sliding under the tablesaw fence. Remember to cut the sheets of plywood slightly oversize; final trimming takes place after the piece comes out of the press. Bending plywoods are available in sizes down to 0.4 mm (about 1/64 in.) from specialty plywood dealers, such as Harbor Sales (1401 Russell St., Baltimore, MD 21230; 800-345-1712).

Preparing the veneer

If one sheet of face veneer will do the job, I just rough-cut it slightly oversize with a sharp razor knife or veneer saw. But if the face veneer has to consist of several pieces, things get a little more complicated. Their edges have to be precisely jointed. To joint two sheets of veneer, I just sandwich them between two boards; the edge of the bottom board must be jointed and stick out ever so slightly (say, 1/32 in.) beyond the top board. When clamped together with both pieces of veneer between and their edges sticking out past the bottom board, jointing is a simple matter of routing. With a bearing-guided, flush-trimming bit, make a pass down the board, and that's that (see the photo above).

Laminate trimmer and flush-trimming bit joint veneers. To joint veneers for wide panels, the author uses a laminate trimmer (a small router) and a bearing-guided flush-trimming bit.

Use veneer tape (a water-activated adhesive tape available from veneer suppliers) to tape these jointed veneers together. Tape them along the seam on the face side. Then use a hot iron on the veneer tape to dry the tape and to shrink it a bit, so the joint between the veneer sheets is very tight. The veneer will warp a bit from the iron's dry heat but not enough to matter when it goes into the vacuum press.

The last thing to do before glue-up is to mark each ply and sheet of veneer on one edge with a tick mark at the center to help align the layers on the form.

Glue-up

Next I glue up the stack of plies and veneer using a urea-formaldehyde or plastic-resin glue. I use these glues because of their longer open times compared to yellow glue and because they don't creep. The glue I use most often, Unibond 800 (available from Vacuum Pressing Systems, 553 River Rd., Brunswick, ME 04011; 207-725-0935), also is available in different colors and can be

Foam roller spreads urea formaldehyde or plastic-resin glues easily. These two types of glue have longer set times than white or yellow glues, so they're better for most veneer work. A thin, even layer of glue on one of the surfaces is sufficient.

dyed to make gluelines or squeeze-out less obvious. Unibond cleans up with warm water—not an easy thing to do with plastic-resin glues. And set-up time can be modified by the application of heat and by the ratio of resin to hardener you use.

Apply either of these types of glue with a thin, foam-covered roller (available at most hardware and paint stores). A thin, even coat on one of the two surfaces will create a strong glue bond (see the photo above). Finally, after you've glued and stacked all the layers, use the tick marks on the veneer and substrate to align the stock correctly. Use masking tape to hold the stack together at the center on both sides.

Into the vacuum bag

Inside the vacuum bag, I use a melamine platen (a large flat plate on which something is pressed). I cut 1/8-in.-wide, 1/8-in.-deep grooves with a tablesaw to make a grid of 6-in. squares on the platen, as recommended by the manufacturer. The platen is 2 in. to 4 in. larger than the base of the form, so there's plenty of bag to wrap around the form. The form goes in the bag and on the platen. I keep the form as close to the opening as possible to make it easier to put the lamination into the bag. I also roll up the unused end of the bag. That way, the vacuum pump doesn't have to work as hard at evacuating air from the bag initially, and the pump cycles-on less often while the glue sets.

Now I put the laminations into the bag with waxed or paper-wrapped cauls top and bottom to ensure even pressure over the entire lamination. The edges of the form and of the cauls are rounded over, so they don't puncture the bag. I usually duct-tape the whole lamination to the form at a center point I've marked on the form. The masking tape that I put on earlier over the center mark of the lamination locates its center. The duct tape keeps the lamination in place, but it still allows the plies to slide by each other as they get squished against the form.

Once I've closed the bag and started to pump out the air, I move quickly. It's important to make sure the bag isn't pinched between the form and platen, between lamination and form or between layers of the lamination itself. If you do pinch the bag, you'll end up with a void in the lamination and a bump on its surface.

It's also essential to check that the bag is bearing against the entire lamination, that it isn't hung up anywhere (preventing it from contacting the lamination) and that the bag

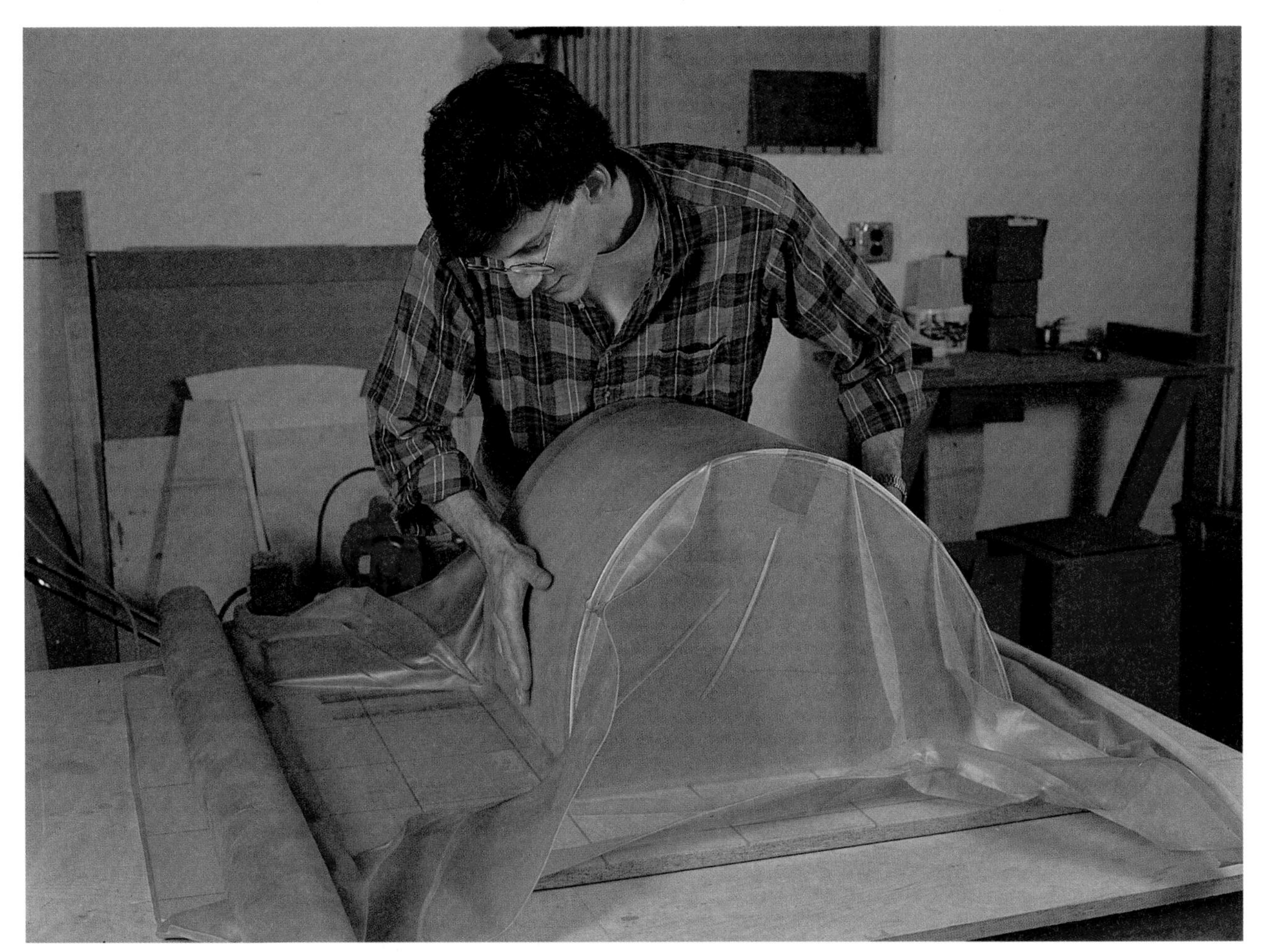

Make sure the bag isn't pinched. Check that the bag isn't caught between layers of the lamination, the form or the platen. There should be no air pockets between the bag and the lamination, which would mean a weak bond in that spot.

has been evacuated completely (see the photo above). Sometimes air pockets remain because the bag has closed off any exit channels, which can keep layers of the lamination from bonding. If I see any gaps between plies at the edges, I'll turn off the vacuum pump, open the bag, let some air in, close the bag and start evacuating it again, taking more care to see that the bag seats flush against the entire lamination.

Electric blanket speeds drying

To speed the glue-cure time once the lamination is under pressure, place an electric blanket, set on high, over the bag. This can reduce the cure time of the Unibond from about four hours to just over an hour. Electric blankets weren't designed to be folded over a plastic bag, though, so don't leave the blanket on unattended.

I leave my glue-mixing stick underneath the blanket on top of the vacuum bag, and I set an inexpensive plastic thermometer next to it. By knowing the temperature just outside the bag and comparing this information with that provided by the manufacturer of the adhesive, I can get a rough idea of how long before the glue will be cured; then I can turn off the blanket and the vacuum pump. The reason for keeping the glue-mixing stick there is just to play it safe. It will show me for certain when the glue has cured. When the thin film of adhesive that remains on the mixing stick has turned brittle and dry, then the lamination is ready.

COOPERING A DOOR

by Garrett Hack

Before I went to woodworking school, all of my work tended to be flat, straight and square. It wasn't intentional. Rectilinear work was all I had ever seen. When I arrived at school, everyone was designing and building curved forms, making tapered laminations—doing all kinds of curved work. It was a liberating experience to see beyond flat and square.

My first project with curves was a toolbox with a pair of coopered doors. I chose to cooper the doors—that is, to create the curves from a number of relatively narrow, bevel-edged pieces called staves—because I wanted the doors to be solid, not veneered. Coopering seemed like the simplest and best technique.

Coopering has been around since biblical days and has been most commonly used for making barrels and buckets. It appeals to me because it yields predictable results with a minimum of effort, and few tools or special fixtures are required. With careful layout and accurately cut bevels, I can make curved doors (or other furniture elements) of nearly any radius.

The only real alternative to coopering for making curved doors is laminating, either of solid layers or of veneer over plywood. Although laminating is somewhat stronger than coopering, it requires either carefully matched forms or a vacuum press, and results are less predictable. Laminated curves always have some degree of springback, and it's impossible to know just how much before they come out of the press. If you're willing to make a trial lamination or two to check springback and fine-tune the form, laminating will give you a very strong curved door. I've found, however, that it's not worth the effort for just a door or two.

Coopering is not without its disadvantages, but they're minor. If you want a smooth curve, rather than a faceted one, the whole door must be planed and scraped after assembly because the curve is fashioned from a number of flat pieces. The convex outer face is fairly easy to smooth. And I generally leave the inside faceted, intentionally revealing the method of construction. As for strength, as long as the glue joints are sound, a coopered door should last as long as any flat-panel construction. Also, a coopered door will shrink and swell as any solid timber will, but because of the angles at the joints, it can subtly change shape as it changes dimension. If you're concerned that a single wide door might move too much (its movement will be equal to a board as wide as the length of the curve), make two narrower doors instead.

Curve layout takes place on a pattern

The key to building any coopered door is an accurate pattern. It's on the pattern that I figure the number of staves, their width, thickness and the bevel angle at each joint. Just before assembling the case, I draw a curved pattern from the case top, bottom or even a shelf. Then I build the door to match

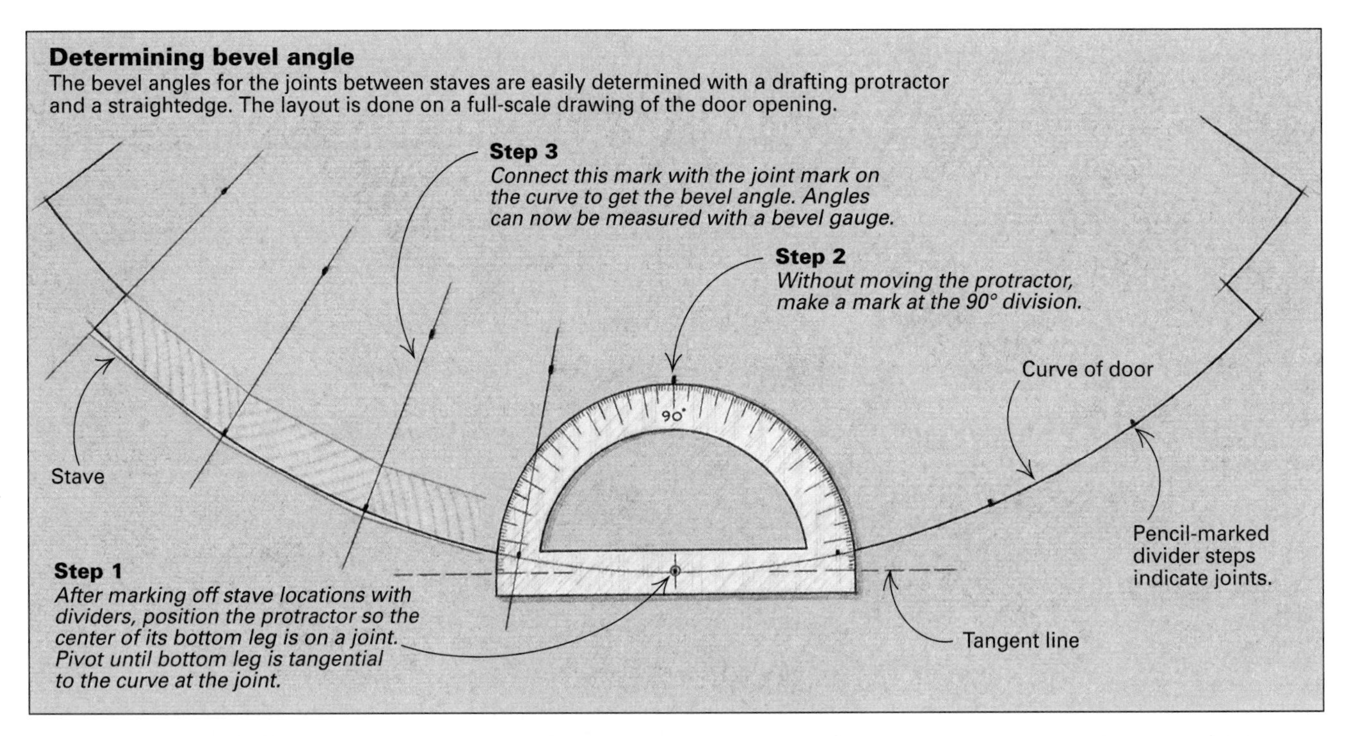

Determining bevel angle
The bevel angles for the joints between staves are easily determined with a drafting protractor and a straightedge. The layout is done on a full-scale drawing of the door opening.
Step 3
Connect this mark with the joint mark on the curve to get the bevel angle. Angles can now be measured with a bevel gauge.
Step 2
Without moving the protractor, make a mark at the 90° division.
90°
Curve of door
Stave
Pencil-marked divider steps indicate joints.
Step 1
After marking off stave locations with dividers, position the protractor so the center of its bottom leg is on a joint. Pivot until bottom leg is tangential to the curve at the joint.
Tangent line

Record each angle. Use a bevel gauge to measure the angles on the drawing. Then record them on scrap.

Transfer angles to the saw. The author uses the bevel gauge to set the tablesaw blade at the correct angle.

With the angle set, make the cut. Cut all the bevels of the same angle before changing the blade angle.

this curve. I include the case stiles (where the door hinges and latches) on the pattern to make fitting the finished door easier. When making the coopered door for the cabinet shown in the photo at left, I started with the curved, laminated drawer fronts. I used the shape of the drawers to determine the curve of the case and the pattern for the door.

To establish the number and width of each stave, I used a trial block cut to what I guessed the thickness and width of the completed staves would be. By laying this out around the curve on the pattern and tracing around the block each time, I got a good idea of what the profile of the finished door would look like. This approach allows me to change a trial layout by simply trying a different-sized block.

Keep checking the door against the drawing. To avoid having to remove a large amount of material after the door has been glued up, be sure the bevel angle between staves conforms exactly to the full-scale drawing.

The more staves you use, the smoother the curve, but for every stave you add, there's another joint to fit and glue. For doors with a nearly consistent curve such as this one (it's a section of an ellipse), I use staves that are all the same width. For asymmetrical curves, increasing the stave width where the curve is flatter simplifies construction. For a tighter curve, narrower staves work better.

If I am going to fair the curves (either just the outside face or both inside and outside), I allow extra thickness for each stave because some material will be planed away. The fewer the staves, the thicker they need to be because more material will have to be removed to create a smooth curve. Superimposing the trial block on the curve of the door drawn on the pattern gives me a good idea of how thick to make my staves.

I rough cut the staves about 1/4 in. wider than their final dimension and at least an inch longer. I start out with this much extra because after the bevels have been ripped, I still want to have roughly 1/16 in. per joint to allow for the fitting between each pair of staves and for the final fitting of the door in the case. Any extra material can be trimmed equally from the two outside staves when fitting the door. Once the staves have been milled, I lay them out to get the best color

Gluing the door

Gluing up an entire door at once would be nearly impossible, so the author starts with a pair of staves and then adds one stave at a time as the glue cures. When clamping the first pair (1), downward pressure helps close the joint on its outside face. Cauls that match the faceted inside curve of the door can make clamping the joints much easier as staves are added (2). On this door, the author glued up two halves separately; then he joined the two in a final glue-up (3).

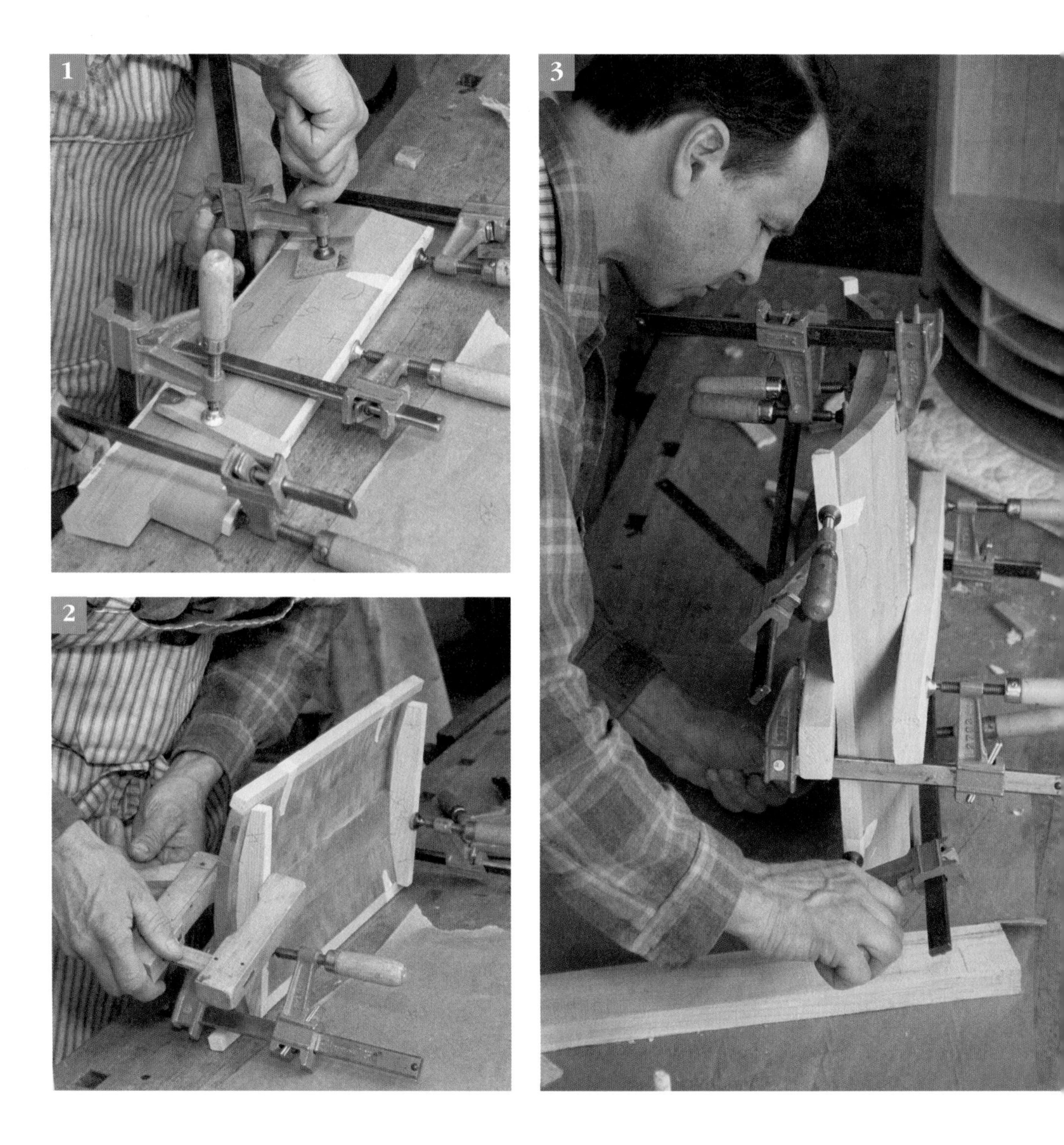

and grain match. I mark each joint so I know which side is the face and which end is up.

Although the trial block tells me how many staves I need, I still have to mark off the exact location of each joint on the drawing. I do this by walking a set of dividers around the curve, marking off equal segments (for a symmetrical curve) from one end of the curve to the other. As the drawing on p. 76 shows, a pair of staves will meet at each of the marks on the curve.

It's not absolutely essential that each pair of staves meet at the same bevel angle, but their surfaces will be flush inside and out if they do. This makes clamping and fairing the curves a bit easier. For a curve that is an arc of a circle, each bevel angle is the same. For any other curve, I determine the bevel angle at each joint by bisecting the angle formed by the two staves. The easiest way to do this is to draw a line perpendicular to the tangent of the curve at each joint (see the drawing on p. 76). Then I take a bevel gauge and transfer the angle from the drawing to a piece of scrap I call a bevel board (see the photo at left on p. 76). All the angles are now safely recorded.

Rip bevels on the tablesaw; joint with a handplane

I set the blade angle on the tablesaw by referring to my bevel board (see the center photo on p. 76). To bevel the first edge, I set the fence 1/8 in. or so wider than the stave's final width and passed the stave over the saw with a jointed edge against the fence (see the photo at right on p. 76). In general, if there are any other bevels that need to be sawn at the same angle, I'll rip them all before changing the blade angle. It's easy to get a stave oriented incorrectly, so I double-check every setup.

For the second edge on a stave, I set the fence so the stave was about 1/16 in. over its final width. Repeatedly resetting the tablesaw blade angle and fence for all the bevels results in slight differences in stave width, but it doesn't affect the result.

To get good glue joints, I jointed the tablesawn bevels with a No. 5 jack plane. (For a taller door, I would use a longer plane.) This also let me fine-tune the bevels. I started with the first stave in the curve and clamped it in a shoulder vise at a comfortable height. I took a very light cut, just enough to get a straight, polished edge. Then I did the same to the matching joint in the next stave. After shooting both bevels, I held the staves together on the pattern and checked for fit. (If need be, I can reshoot one of the bevels, taking a slightly heavier shaving toward one side of the edge or the other until the stave angles match the pattern exactly.) Before gluing them, I jointed the second bevel on the second stave. I wanted the back of this door faceted, so I also finish-planed the inside surfaces of both staves. If I had wanted the inside surface to be a smooth curve like the outside, I'd have skipped this step.

Glue and clamp just one joint at a time

Gluing the staves together is, without a doubt, the trickiest part of coopering, often demanding some creativity. The trick is to exert pressure evenly across the joint so that it doesn't open up either on the inside or outside. Many strategies will work: using shaped cauls, driving pinch dogs in the ends of the staves, gluing pine blocks to the faces of the staves temporarily to get a good clamping angle (with a sheet of paper in the joint so they can be broken off cleanly afterward), or just rubbing a joint together and holding it for a few minutes until the glue grabs. I always try to use the simplest clamping method that suits the scale and curvature of the door.

You can use a spline, a few biscuits or even brads (with their heads cut off) to help maintain alignment when gluing staves together. For a door this small, alignment was not very difficult. I just took the time to get it right when clamping each joint.

The bevel angles for this door were close enough to 90° that I was able to clamp them almost as I would two square-edged boards. You may find it helpful, as I did, to exert pressure both across and down onto the joint to close it up on the outside face. I used three clamps across the top side of the staves and then clamped right into the joint

Fitting the door

With the glue fully cured, the door can be cut to the right height on a tablesaw (1). The author strives for a snug fit. Pencil lines drawn on the top and bottom edges of the door (2) are reference marks that guide the final shaping of the door front (3). When the door has been planed and scraped to the lines, it will be flush with the rest of the case.

(using cauls to prevent marring) against the top of my bench (see the top left photo on p. 78).

For this door, I glued up two halves, one stave at a time, and then joined these two assemblies together. Because there were an odd number of staves, one-half had four staves, and one-half had only three. I glued up the first pair of staves for each half and let the glue cure before adding the next pieces. Building the doors a piece at a time makes the glue-up slower but much more manageable. Cauls can help. To glue the third stave to the first pair, I shaped two cauls with a bandsaw and block plane. I clamped the staves to these cauls and clamped across the joint with light bar clamps. Because the angle between staves can change as you work your way around the curve, the cauls may have to be reshaped (see the bottom left photo on p. 78).

When I spread glue on a joint, I kept it very thin toward the inside surface so that there would be little or no squeeze-out to clean up afterward. Nevertheless, I still used a rabbet plane and a small scraper that I ground to the angle between staves to get the inside joints sharp and distinct. I reshaped the scraper with a fine file to fit each successive joint.

Before gluing on each successive stave, I checked the joint against the pattern by holding the stave tight to the ones already glued together. I fine-tuned when necessary and finish-planed the inside surface. The final glue-up—connecting the two assemblies, one with the first four staves and the other with the last three staves—was the most complicated. It required another pair of shaped cauls and battens (see the right photo on p. 78). Even so, it wasn't that unwieldy because there was only one joint to worry about.

Fit the door to its opening

After the door was assembled, it was about an inch taller and just slightly wider than its opening. I crosscut the door on the tablesaw, leaving it slightly long to allow for a precise fitting after I'd cut it to width (see the top left photo on the facing page).

To fit to width, the hinging and closing edges need to be beveled to match their respective stiles. I could have cut these edges when I was beveling the staves initially, but I decided to keep them wide so no harm would be done by the inevitable clamping dings. Because I was very close to the width of the opening, I just took the bevel angles off the pattern and planed them by hand, checking as I went with a bevel gauge.

Once I had the door cut very nearly to width (the final fitting took place after it was hung), I planed its ends to length so that it would fit snugly, but all the way into its opening. Then, with the door in its opening, I traced a light pencil line of the curve around the top and bottom edges (see the bottom left photo on the facing page). This gave me reference lines to plane to when fairing the outside to a smooth curve. For designs where the door's final shape can't be traced so easily, another possibility is to cut out the paper pattern and transfer it to the ends of the door.

I shaped the outside with a block plane, working initially across the grain and at a diagonal, paying attention to the reference lines on the top and bottom edges (see the right photo on the facing page). Most of the wood to be removed is at the joints. This is also when I fine-tune the shape of the door by checking it in its opening often. Planing the door to match the case opening precisely may leave the door slightly thinner in places, but it's hardly ever noticeable. For the final smoothing, I use a scraper and fine sandpaper.

The inside is harder to plane to a smooth shape. Coopers use a stoup plane with a doubly compassed sole. When I want a smooth inside face, I use spokeshaves and shaped scrapers.

Once you understand the basic technique, it's not that great a leap to make a tapered door with tapered staves or even one curved in three dimensions. By tapering the staves, steam-bending them to shape and then shooting the joints between them, you can cooper some dramatic curves. But you don't need to go this far to add a pair of elegant doors to your next project.

THREE

Milling Complex Shapes

If you've ever stared at a piece of woodwork and wondered how on earth it could have been created, then this chapter is for you. Beyond straight cuts, and even beyond curves, are complex shapes that either don't seem possible or look awfully difficult to do. Among these are cove moldings, impossibly deep through mortises, and the dish-shaped seat of a Windsor chair. You'll find solutions to all of these and more in this short chapter. Even if you don't find a specific technique, there are still plenty of ideas to adapt.

What may surprise you are the types of tools used. There's no need for purpose-built industrial machines or fancy and expensive accessories: just a router, a tablesaw, and a few hand tools are all you need. Complex shapes are, after all, just a whole lot of simple shapes brought together. The trick in getting simple tools to make complex cuts is to use a little ingenuity and a lot of shop-made jigs.

The router is perhaps the most adaptable woodworking tool of all. Through shop-made templates and jigs it gains infinitely adaptable guidance systems. And so the nearly impossible becomes possible with the router, including milling multiple identical pieces and cutting very small pieces. The same goes for the tablesaw: It is not a tool that comes to mind for milling curves; however, by means of a simple jig or two, it becomes the very best tool for the job.

The exceptions to the jig rule are specialty hand tools. Adzes and inshaves, for example, have specially curved blades that are excellent for scooping out wood from a flat surface; otherwise, their use is limited. This specialization of certain types of hand tools has two advantages. First, the tool doesn't need a jig. Second, when you need a tool to make a slightly different cut, you have a very good reason to buy it for your collection.

TEMPLATE ROUTING BASICS

by Pat Warner

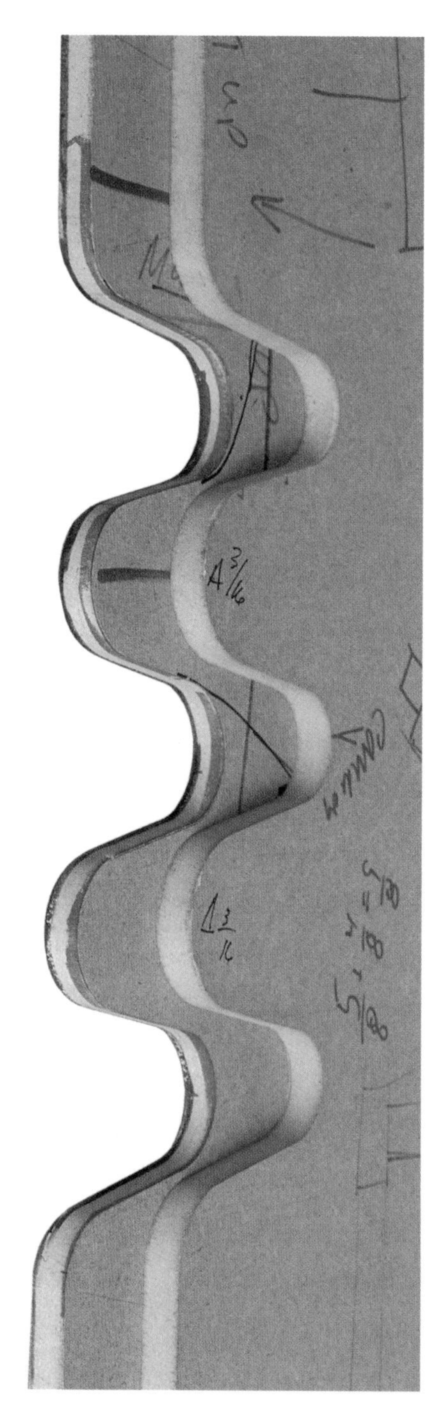

In 24 years of self-taught woodworking, I've made a lot of mistakes. Early in my career, though, I made a fortunate one. It started a learning process with the router that I'm still working on today.

I had discovered what looked like a devilishly simple technique for cutting dadoes. I used a board clamped across the workpiece to guide the router base. The first dado looked great, but the second wandered visibly off course. That day, I learned that a router base is never concentric with the bit. Turning the router as I cut the dado put a curve in it.

I began to look for better ways to guide routers. Some of the best, I have learned, are with templates. These are simply patterns of the shapes you want to cut. The router registers against a template, using it as a guide through the cut. The simplicity of templates, though, gives no hint of how powerful a tool they make the router.

The router's usefulness and versatility begin with the tremendous variety of bits that are available. With only a ball bearing on the end of the bit as a guide, you are really limited to detailing edges. When you use a template, however, you free the router from following the edge of the workpiece. The router becomes capable of two more fundamental woodworking tasks: milling repeatable patterns and all kinds of joinery.

You can easily make your own inexpensive, simple and accurate templates for a wide variety of joints and patterns. The initial investment of time to make a template for a precise task is well worth it. Your router will perform that task far faster and far more reliably than other tools can. And it's much harder to make mistakes when you are using templates.

Three bits for routing with templates

Straight bits and collar guides

Straight bits and collar guides are the most versatile: Collars are not as accurate as bearings, but they have the decided advantage of allowing you to cut at any depth in both side and bottom cuts. Fitted to the router's base and used with straight bits, they work much like pattern bits. Collar guides also act as a shield for the bit. You'll find that you will inflict a lot less injury to the template and the work by using them.

Collar guides do have disadvantages. Because the collar must be larger in diameter than the cutter, the line of cut is displaced from the template. This offset means the finished work will never be exactly the same shape as the template. And collar guides are never exactly concentric with the bit: 1/16 in. eccentricity is typical. A way to compensate for this is to keep the same part of the collar in contact with the template throughout the cut.

Pattern bits

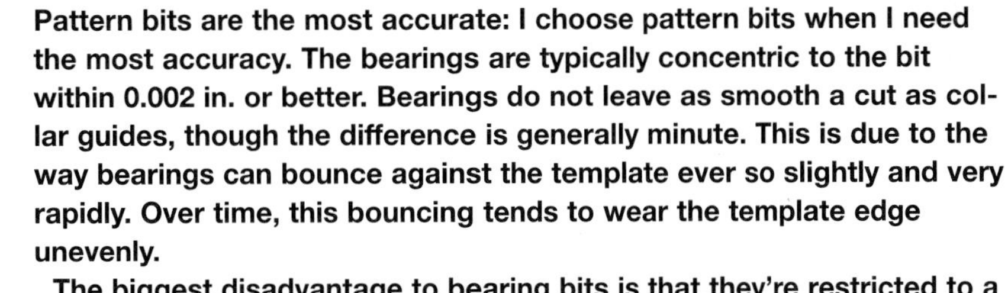

Pattern bits are the most accurate: I choose pattern bits when I need the most accuracy. The bearings are typically concentric to the bit within 0.002 in. or better. Bearings do not leave as smooth a cut as collar guides, though the difference is generally minute. This is due to the way bearings can bounce against the template ever so slightly and very rapidly. Over time, this bouncing tends to wear the template edge unevenly.

The biggest disadvantage to bearing bits is that they're restricted to a small range of depth settings. The bearing must always engage the edge of the template. I've also found that bits of this design often have diameters slightly larger than their bearings. If you run this kind of bit with some of the cutter in contact with the template, you'll rout away some of the template. Measure your bits with calipers or test them to make sure this doesn't happen.

Flush-trimming bits

Flush-trimming bits are the most common: The main advantage to using flush-trimming bits for template work is that they are easier to find and slightly cheaper than pattern bits. They also come in smaller diameters than pattern bits, allowing cuts into tighter inside curves.

Otherwise, they have many disadvantages. Bottom cuts such as mortises are impossible. In other applications, the workpiece can hide the template from view, and the router must ride on the work. If it's a small or thin piece, the router will not be stable.

Templates will allow you to repeat cuts and shapes perfectly, but only if you remember to use the same bit with the same collar at the same depth. The best place to record this information is on the template itself.

Make precise templates

The best way to learn the basics of template routing is to make and use some simple templates. But before looking at the practical applications for templates illustrated here, it's a good idea to start with some advice about how to make them, what materials to use and the best ways to use them.

The most difficult part of template routing is making the template itself. All the important information about the final shape you want to rout is encoded in the design of the template. The more accurately you make your templates, the more time you'll save in the long run. You'll do less sanding, fitting and fudging afterward.

Sawing, rasping and filing are time-consuming and tedious ways to make templates. It's also very hard to make a perfect curve with hand tools. I never make a template by hand unless there is no other way. I've found that accurate templates are most easily made with sanders and, yes, routers, templates and other guides.

Templates should be dimensionally stable, durable and capable of taking fine details. Solid wood is a poor choice because it's not dimensionally stable. Steel is stable and durable, but to a fault. If you accidentally touch a spinning bit to one, you'll probably wreck both the bit and the template. Acrylic and Lexan are transparent and allow you to see the work beneath. They also won't kill bits. But be aware that a slow bearing will generate enough heat from friction to melt them. Medium-density fiberboard (MDF) is the best all around choice. Mind you, it isn't perfect. It's toxic and unpleasant to work with.

Four everyday templates

You can use any one of the three kinds of router bits designed for template work. Each has its own strengths and weaknesses (for more, see the box on p. 85). Some bits are especially well-suited to certain kinds of templates, but all of them can bring speed and reliability to repetitive work.

Template for repeatable shapes

Using a scroll saw and an oscillating sander to make a single curved shape, like a decorative shelf support, might be just as fast as template routing it. But only the first time. If you make any more, template routing will be faster and easier. A router bit leaves a much smoother edge than a scroll saw, and the edge will need far less sanding. Make the template much the way you would make the support if you had no templates. Smooth, gradual curves on MDF are best obtained by sanding to layout lines on a stationary belt sander.

For this kind of work, it's easiest to use a straight bit with a collar guide because you can adjust the cutting depth to match the thickness of the shelf-support stock (see the photo and drawing at right). Collar guides, however, will displace the cut from the exact edge of the template. With straight lines, this merely entails positioning the template the offset distance from the layout line. The lines will be just as straight.

It's a different story with curves. A collar will make the bit cut slightly larger radii on outside curves and smaller radii on inside curves. The result will be a finished piece slightly different from the template. In complementary template work, this is a crucial consideration. But with something like the profile of a shelf support, the difference is not consequential. To tell where the bit will actually cut, run a pen in a loose bearing with the same offset as the collar along the template to draw the layout line.

Cutting shallow mortises

Cutting shallow mortises that are clean and evenly deep—like those that you would want for butt hinges—is a difficult task with traditional tools. Except for the very smallest hinges, a router guided by a template will give you more accurate cuts faster and with less variation between them. The photos and drawings on p. 88 show you how to make one.

Cutting multiples

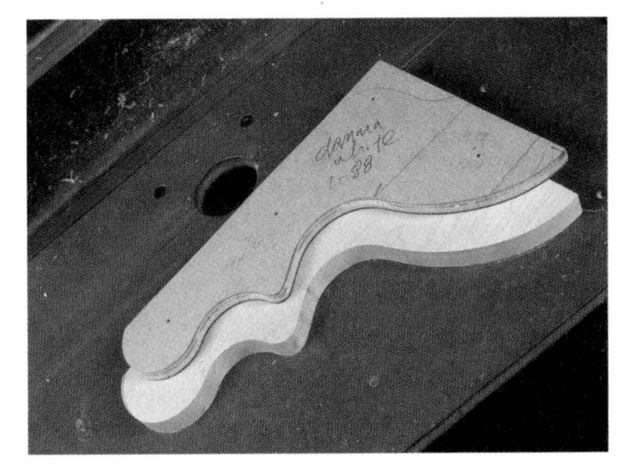

A straight bit and collar guide make a good combination for cutting a stack of profiled pieces, like decorative shelf supports. The bits can cut stock of any thickness and will produce a smoother edge than a bearing-guided bit. One thing to keep in mind: The template and the finished piece will not be identical because the collar guide keeps the bit away from the edge of the template.

Straight bit and collar guide with template over work

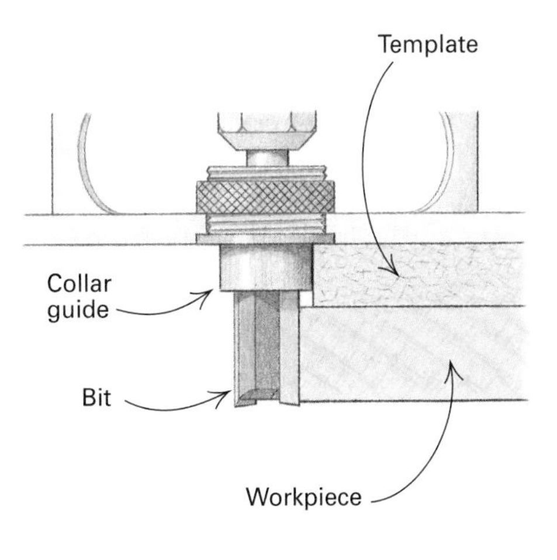

A template for butt hinge mortises

A pattern bit is a good choice for cutting shallow mortises precisely and quickly. To make the template, align the hinge on a piece of template stock, and then mark the outline with a pencil. Bandsaw out most of the waste, and reposition the hinge on the template stock. Clamp straight-edged scrap around the hinge to define the edges of the mortise (1). A paper shim will prevent the mortise from being too tight. Then remove the hinge, and rout to the line with the scrap as a guide (2). Remove the scrap, and you have a finished template that cuts an accurate mortise (3).

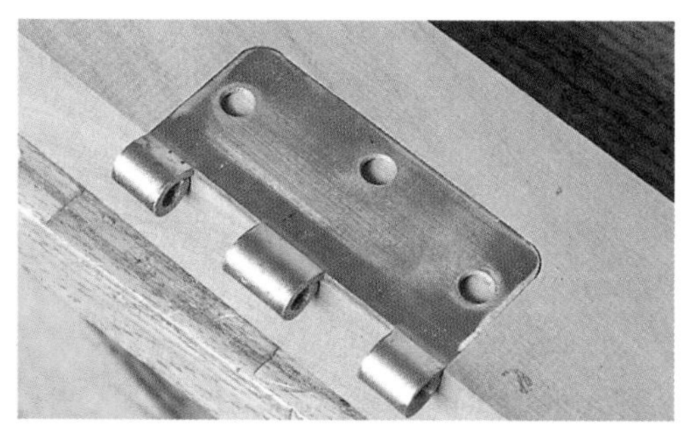

Making the template

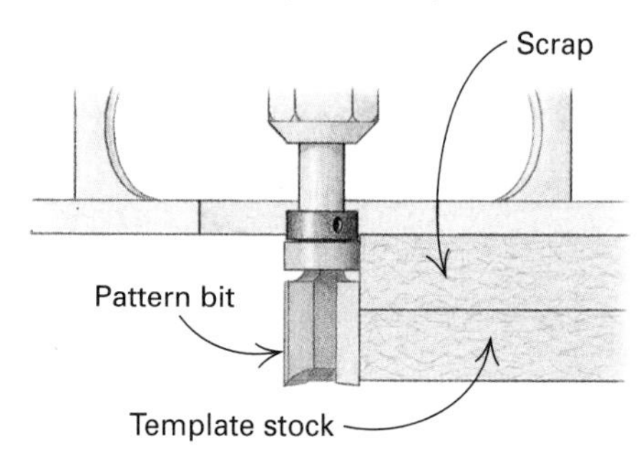

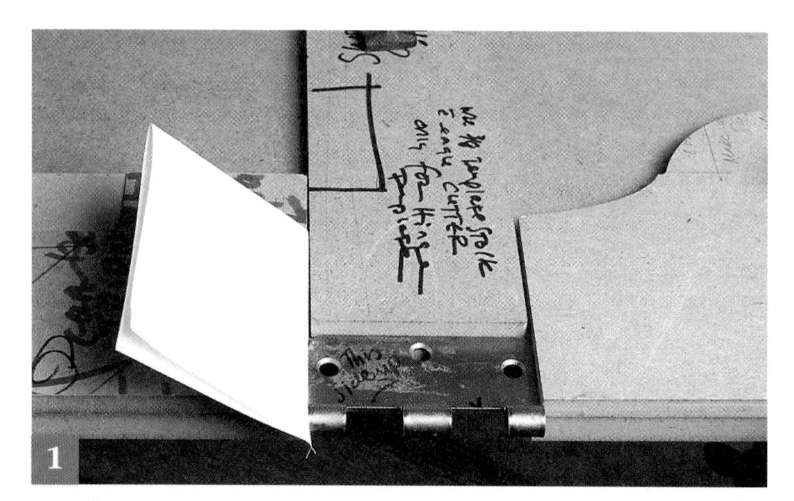

1

Cutting the mortise

Pattern bit

Template

Workpiece

2

3

Once you've made this template well, it's hard to go wrong using it as long as you are careful. Router stability on the template is essential to an accurate and safe cut. A 6-in. round base router with a 1/2-in.-dia. bit will have no more than 45% of its footprint on the template in an edge cut. If you make a turn around a 90° corner, that percentage is reduced to less than 20%. A router that wobbles with a lot of cutter engaged can break the cutter, tear the stock and template, or even cause a kickback that sends the router to the floor. The machine has to stay flat and stable at all times.

This butt hinge has rounded corners the same diameter as the bit. If it had square corners, you'd have to do some handwork to make the hinge fit. A bit with a larger diameter than the corners would also require handwork. Just never use a bit with a smaller diameter, or you'll have gaps to patch.

Cutting tapers on small pieces

Some workpieces are too small to rout safely if they are sandwiched between a workbench and template. To taper legs for a coffee table, for instance, I built a template that holds the workpiece in place with toggle clamps, as shown in the photos and drawing at right. Guide blocks position the side and end of the leg but leave enough room behind them to clamp the template upside down to a workbench edge. In use, neither the toggle clamps nor the clamps holding the template to the bench get in the way.

To get a good, smooth taper, you need to secure the guide blocks at the desired angle in relation to the edge of the template. As the router follows the edge, it cuts the taper angle of the blocks in the leg.

Template for through mortises

The plunge router is the best tool for inside template cuts, such as mortises, but it needs a lot of support to make it safe and accurate. Plunge routers are top heavy and have comparatively small bases. This make them good candidates for router teeter-totter problems. A template for mortising must be large enough so that the plunge router's base is completely supported by the template during the cut. The photos and drawings on p. 90 show a simple technique to make a through mortise deeper than any bit you own.

Template for routing small pieces

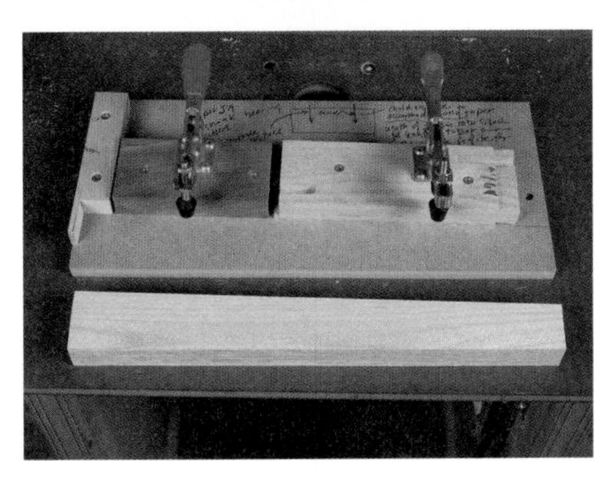

Use a pattern bit for tapered legs

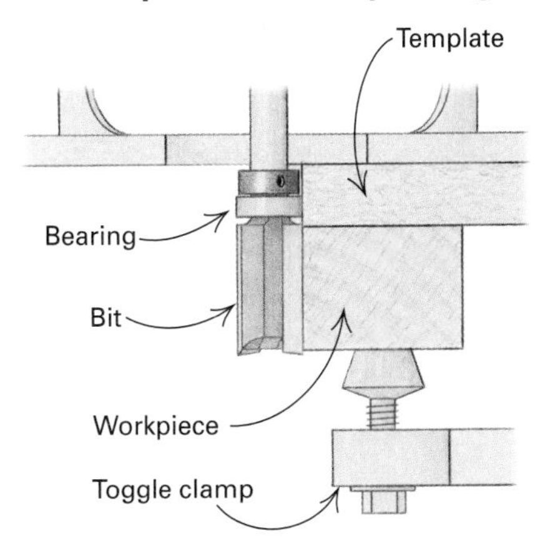

Templates can be made so they hold small pieces as well as guide the router. Coupled with a pattern bit, the template above makes short work of cutting tapered coffee table legs. The workpiece is held on the template with toggle clamps. To keep toggle clamps out of the way while routing, the author flips the template upside down on the workbench (above). Blocks between template and bench provide room for the toggle clamps.

Routing a through mortise

Deep mortises can be cut accurately by starting with a template and straight bit with a collar and finishing up with a flush-trimming bit. First rout the mortise as deeply as you can with the template as a guide (1). Then drill through to the other side. Remove as much waste as you can, and then flip the workpiece over (2). A flush-trimming bit that follows the upper part of the previously cut mortise will finish the job.

First pass with pattern bit

Collar guide
Template
Bit
Workpiece

Finish with flush-trimming bit

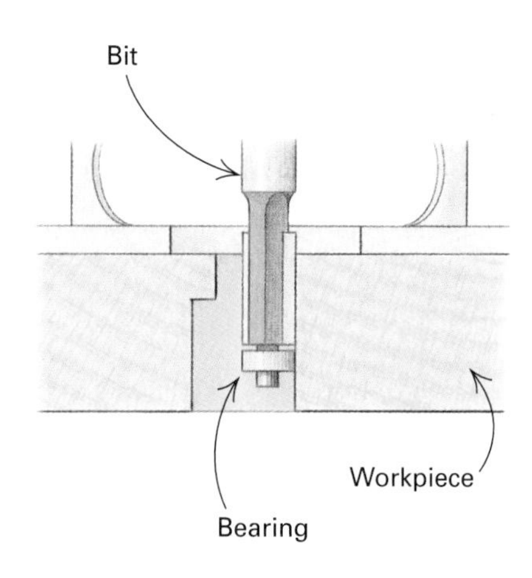

CUT COVE MOLDING ON THE TABLESAW

by Frank Klausz III

Moldings enhance the appearance of furniture and architectural millwork with their ability to catch light and make shadows. Most moldings are a combination of beads (convex curves) and coves (concave curves). Large coves are most often made with a shaper, but shaper blades are expensive, especially when they have to be custom ground—not to mention the cost of shapers themselves. So for short runs of molding or for shops that don't have shapers, tablesawn coves are a surprisingly versatile alternative. This article explains how to make a variety of coves using your tablesaw and examines ways of simplifying the usual trial-and-error set-up process. Safety issues raised by tablesaw coving are discussed in the box on p. 94.

There are two main types of coves: symmetrical and asymmetrical. Symmetrical coves, the more familiar kind, are cut by changing the angle of approach to the blade while leaving the blade perpendicular to the table. The stock rides along a skewed fence and passes over the top of the blade, removing an elliptical arc of wood, as shown in the bottom photo on p. 92.

Asymmetrical coves are cut by changing the angle of the blade's tilt as well as the angle of approach. This type of coving yields logarithmic, or accelerated, curves as shown in the drawing on p. 96. Partial coves can be cut using special fence setups, such as the one shown in the photo on p. 95.

Symmetrical coves

Symmetrical tablesawn coves are often used to approximate arcs of circles, but with one exception, they are actually sections of ellipses. As the drawing on p. 93 shows, skewing the fence slightly from the normal

Klausz finds the angle of approach for a symmetrical cove with a parallelogram set to the cove's width. With the blade raised to match the cove's highest point and the parallelogram just touching the blade at front and back, he marks the front fence location.

Symmetrical coves are cut with the blade vertical. Klausz shaves the last 1/16 in. from a piece of symmetrically coved cornice molding. The fence is set up to the infeed side of the blade, so the cutting action holds the stock against the fence.

ripping position produces a steep-sided elliptical cove; then, as the angle of approach is increased, the ellipse broadens and flattens out until, at 90° from the normal angle of approach, the cove is an arc of a true circle. Because there are only two factors to contend with, the height of the blade and the angle of approach, setting up for symmetrical coving is not too complicated.

Setting up

It's best to start by drawing the cove full size on the end of one of the pieces of stock you'll be cutting. Then you can make an accurate setup directly from the drawing of the cove. The height of the blade determines the depth of the cove, so butt the end of the piece up to the blade, and raise the blade to the highest point of the drawn cove.

Next you need to find the correct angle of approach, and clamp a fence to the saw table. An easy way to find the angle of approach is with an adjustable parallelogram like the shopmade one in the top photo above. Flat-head machine screws work well at the joints. Countersink the heads so that the parallelogram will lie flat on the tablesaw, and use wing nuts with them so that you can easily lock in particular settings.

Symmetrical coves

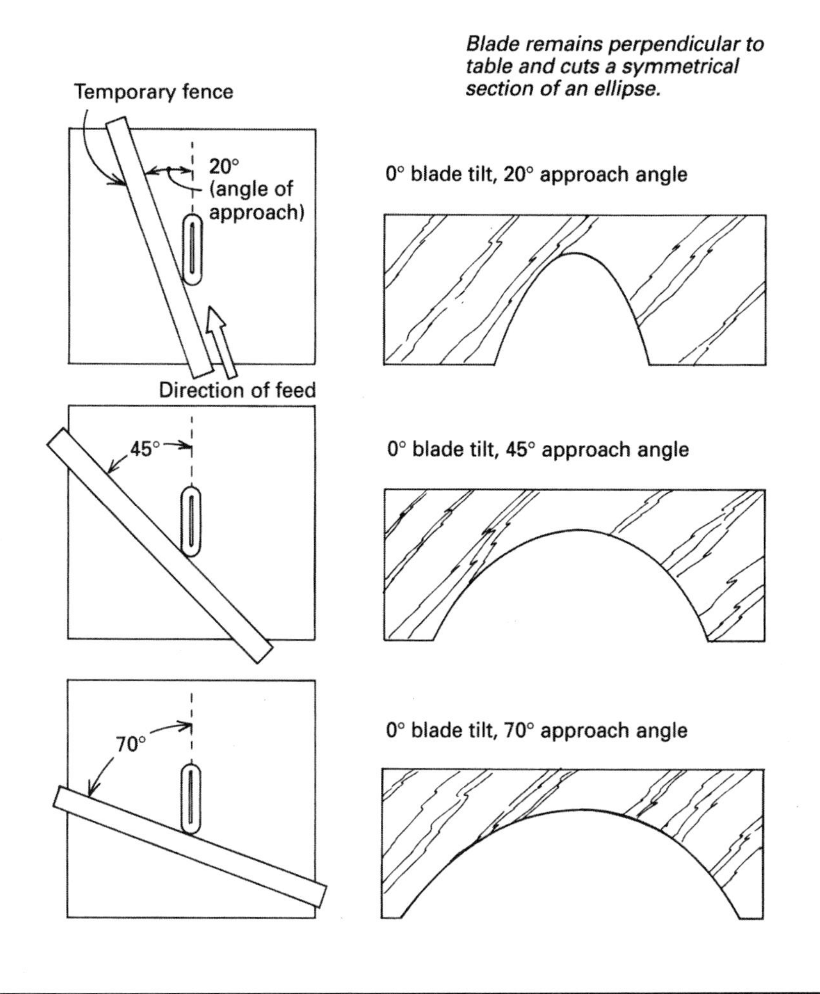

As long as opposite sides are equal lengths, the construction details are unimportant. Adjust the parallelogram, so its width is the same as the widest point of the cove. Then, with the saw unplugged, place the parallelogram on the saw table, so it surrounds the blade. Turn the parallelogram until it just nicks the front and back of the blade. With pencil or tape, make location marks on the saw table inside the leg of the parallelogram that is touching the front of the blade. Measure back from your marks to account for the distance between the start of the cove and the edge of your stock. Clamp a sturdy, freshly edge-jointed piece of wood along your new marks as a fence.

You can cut symmetrical coves with a single fence, though a second fence to create a channel for the stock will make the operation safer. If you do use a single fence, it must be placed to the front (infeed) side of the blade, as shown in the bottom photo on the facing page. Otherwise, the blade will tend to pull the stock away from the fence, making the cut more difficult and more dangerous.

Cutting the cove

After using a tablesaw in the conventional way, it may be natural to assume that a cove could be cut all at once, but it can't. Because the stock approaches the blade from the side, cutting only takes place in an arc as wide as the blade's teeth are high. (And when you are cutting coves with the blade

Safety concerns in tablesaw coving

Even if you are an old hand on the tablesaw, cutting coves on one may raise unfamiliar safety issues.

Setting fences

Whenever you set up for coving, start by pushing your normal rip fence aside or removing it from the saw entirely. Then select planed and edge-jointed hardwood for your coving fences. Clamp them down securely (deep-reach clamps are a good choice), being sure they don't bow off the table at the center. Be sure the pads of your clamps are seated flat on a wide surface under the tabletop.

For symmetrical coves, if you use only one fence, place it to the front of the blade—the infeed side in normal cutting. With the fence to the front, the cutting action of the blade helps keep the stock against the fence, making the cut safer and more accurate. Though one fence is often adequate to cut symmetrical coves, a second fence makes the operation safer and is especially important when cutting deep coves. In all cove-cutting, the stock weakens along the line of the cut; a back fence will provide a margin of safety, acting as a buttress to keep the piece from caving in. The approach to the blade can be from either the left or the right for symmetrical coves.

Use two fences when cutting asymmetrical coves. Always set up the fences for asymmetrical coving so the stock feeds into the blade on the acutely angled side: If the blade tilts to the right, make the approach from the right. If you feed the stock from the other side, it may have a tendency to ride up the blade and off the table, increasing the risk of kickback.

Blade guards

If you want to use a guard over the blade area, you might be best off devising your own and attaching it to one of the temporary fences. Many factory and aftermarket tablesaw blade guards are incompatible with coving. A guard that restricts your view of the workpiece or keeps you from applying constant downward pressure is more of a hindrance than a help.

One guard that works well with coving is the Brett-Guard, a shallow open-bottomed box of clear Plexiglas mounted on horizontal steel bars. It can be adjusted vertically and laterally and can be used to exert some downward pressure on the workpiece. The lowest-priced model retails for $246 and is available from HTC Products, Inc., 120 E. Hudson, P.O. Box 839, Royal Oak, MI 48067; (800) 624-2027.

Feeding the stock

It's essential to keep the stock pressed down on the table while coving. Once it's off the table, the stock can be caught by the teeth at the back of the blade and thrown. To ensure constant contact with the table, raise the blade between passes in increments of ⅛ in. or less. If you try to cut too much, the piece will ride up on the blade.

Unless you have a power feeder, you'll need good jointer-style push blocks to enable you to exert downward pressure over a wide area. If you use the rubber-bottomed kind, clean the dust from the pads before each use to maximize their grip. Keep your push blocks by the fence between cuts, so you're never tempted to use your hand to push the stock from the back.

Because you can't see the blade in cove-cutting, you have to rely even more than usual on listening to it. And listen to the saw's motor. If either one sounds like it's struggling, slow down your feed rate and take smaller cuts.

tilted, the effective cutting height of the teeth is reduced further.) So all cove-cutting must be done in a series of passes.

Start with the blade lowered into the table, and make a pass to see if the clamps are out of the way and you have enough support at the end of the cut. If you are using two fences, the stock should slide easily between them but have no play. Also, be sure your push blocks are handy. Jointer push blocks work well: You can use either the rubber-bottomed kind or the shopmade type with a lip along the underside of the back edge to catch the end of the stock. A regular tablesaw push stick is not appropriate because it concentrates pressure in one spot and doesn't provide the downward pressure required for coving.

Cut the cove in stages, raising the blade 1/8 in. or less with each successive pass. A finish cut of 1/16 in. will give a smoother surface and reduce sanding time.

Asymmetrical coves

Asymmetrical coves are cut with many of the same procedures used for symmetrical coving. The key difference is that asymmetrical coves are produced by tilting the blade as well as angling the fence. This makes asymmetrical coves far more difficult to set up. There are low- and high-tech ways to find the coves you're after. You can proceed by trial and error, eyeballing the shape and building a library of cove profiles, or you can use a computer-aided design (CAD) program.

Finding your cove by eye

To find a cove, squat in front of the saw with your eye at table height, and look across the blade in the path the wood will follow. When making asymmetrical coves, you always feed the stock from the side the blade tilts toward. Because some tablesaw blades tilt right and some tilt left, the angle of approach you take will depend on your tablesaw. As you or someone else changes the tilt of the blade, you will see the potential cove changing. Change your position to see how the approach angle will affect the cut. Closing one eye might help you see the blade as a silhouette.

When you think you have a shape close to the cove you want, set up a pair of fences and make a test cove. As you reset the fence and blade to find the correct shape, remember that you can steepen the acceleration of the cove—making the cove more asymmetrical—either by tilting the blade farther or by bringing the approach angle closer to normal ripping position (see the drawing on p. 96).

A library of coves

If you use the sighting method to find asymmetrical coves, record the angle of blade tilt and the angle of approach on a cutoff from the finished piece. As these templates accumulate, you can easily reproduce old coves, or interpolate between them to get in the ballpark of a new curve. The

A stepped fence raises one edge of the workpiece as Klausz cuts a partial cove in a piece of cherry. For all asymmetrical coves, partial or full, two fences are required, and the stock is fed into the acute side of the blade's tilt.

fuller your collection, the less guesswork. A few hours spent methodically cutting test coves at a series of angles of approach and tilt would be a good way to explore the interrelation of these two variables. And at the same time, you would be building a good foundation for a library of cove profiles.

CAD-generated coves

With access to a CAD program, you can determine the tilt and approach angles for various coves by creating a tablesaw blade in the computer. This will eliminate much of the trial and error involved in the sighting method. Start by drawing two circles 1/8 in. apart. The circles should be the same diameter as your tablesaw blade, most commonly

Asymmetrical coves

Cove becomes more pointed as approach angle is decreased.

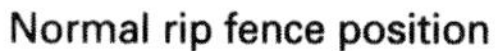

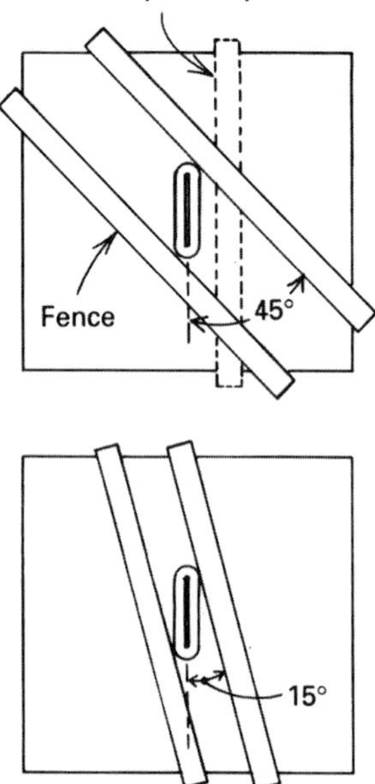

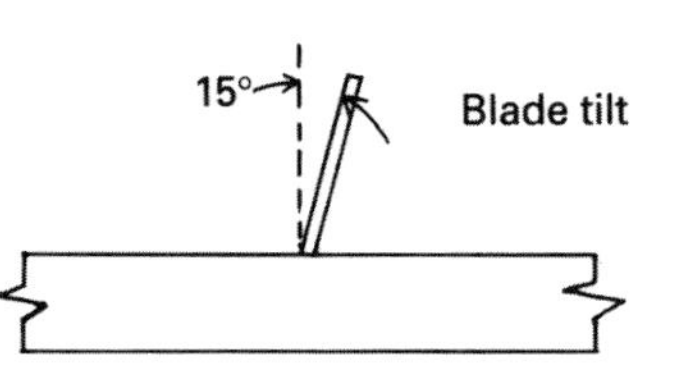

45°

15° blade tilt,
45° approach angle

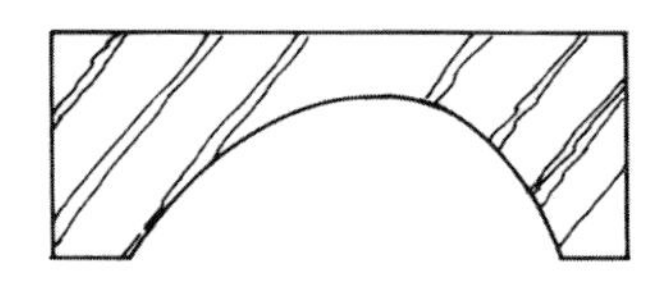

45° blade tilt,
45° approach angle

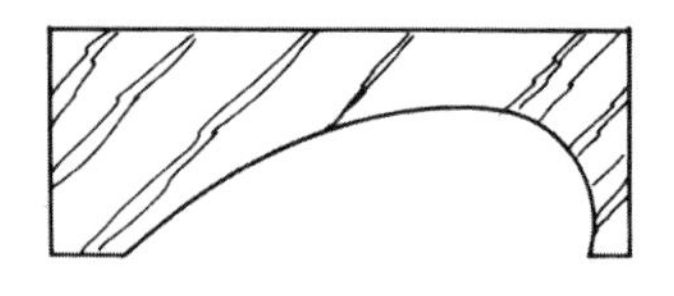

15° blade tilt,
15° approach angle

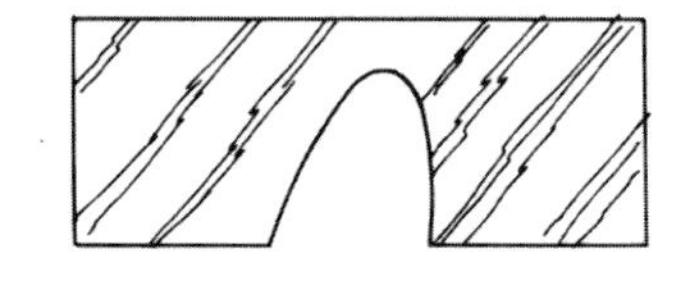

45° blade tilt,
15° approach angle

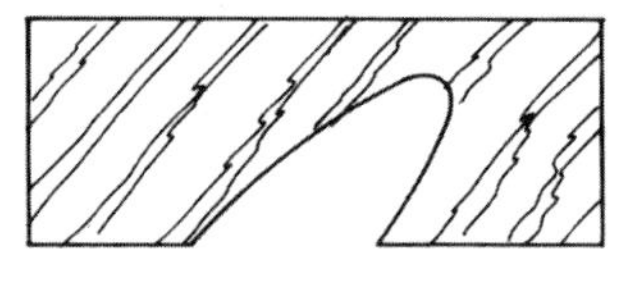

Apex of cove follows tilt of blade.

10 in. Incorporate a baseline 2 in. above the center point to represent the saw table. Then print the image of the blade at various angles of rotation and tilt, being sure to record the angles for each. I have generated a wide range of coves this way and published them in a booklet described at the end of this article.

To set up for asymmetrical cutting using CAD-generated profiles, set the blade tilt using the bevel gauge on the front of your saw. Then raise the blade to the highest point of the cove as drawn on your stock. Set your miter gauge to the approach angle designated on the printout, and slide the front fence into place using the miter gauge. Be certain you set the fence so that the blade will be tilted toward the stock as it approaches. Clamp the front fence in place; then lower the blade into the table, lay a piece of your stock against the front fence and set up a back fence snug to the stock. The cutting can proceed just as it does with symmetrical coving.

Partial coves

This last category of coves is really a variation on the first two. Partial coves are portions of symmetrical or asymmetrical coves. One type of partial cove is cut with a fence that has a gap or cutout in the middle, like the fences on shapers and router tables. The gap allows you to set up the fence right over the blade, and moving the fence exposes more or less of the blade for cutting. Another type is cut with one edge of the stock elevated, riding on a stepped fence, as shown in the photo on p. 95.

Be particularly careful when cutting partial coves to eliminate any play between the stock and the fences, and take a number of test passes to determine if there will be any problems of splintering or compression at the points of contact between the stock and the fences.

HAND TOOLS SHAPE A TRADITIONAL SEAT

by Mario Rodriguez

For the sake of authenticity, when I'm reproducing an 18th-century chair, I use traditional hand tools and techniques. This is especially true when I'm scooping the chair's seat. I conduct workshops on making traditional-style seats, and people are often surprised that I can hand-shape a Windsor, or any other style chair seat, in 40 minutes or less. Here's how I do it.

Most antique chairs have seats carved from a single piece of wood. For my seats, most of which are to be painted (see the photo of the Connecticut comb-back Windsor chair at right), I begin with a 2-in.-thick slab of pine that's sound and relatively clear, except for maybe a few small knots. First, I bandsaw the pine blank roughly to shape (use a bowsaw if you're a pure traditionalist). Then I mark out the pattern to be carved on the blank's top and an edge guide line at the circumference. I also drill holes for the legs and arm posts (stumps) at this time.

Step 1: Rough the seat hollow with an adze.

1) Adze: To begin roughing out a seat, I use a long-handled adze. I straddle the blank, so I can hold it down with my feet (clad in steel-toed boots) while I swing the adze (see the photo at left). Using shallow cuts and fairly short strokes to break up and shorten the grain, I hollow the center of the seat (well within my outline) to about $^{3}/_{4}$ in. deep.

2) Inshave: Next I clamp the seat to my bench and use an inshave to smooth out the seat cavity that's splintered and rough from the adze. Along the edges, I cut to within $^{1}/_{4}$ in. of my pencil line, easing the transition to the $^{3}/_{4}$-in. depth at the middle. To avoid tearing out grain, I shave from the rim down to the hollow (see the left photo below). For clean cuts, I keep my inshave sharp and my strokes light. I also keep tuned to the grain direction and restrict my shaving to the seat's concave area.

3) Drawknife: I use a drawknife to shape the seat's raised curved areas. The drawknife leaves an attractive faceted surface (see the right photo below) that needs little further work. I also use the knife to shape the seat's convex underside and back, working to the perimeter guide line.

Step 2: Sculpt concave area with an inshave.

Step 3: Shape convex surfaces with a drawknife.

4) Spokeshaves: I have two spokeshaves for seat-shaping work: One has a flat bottom and the other is round. I use the round-bottom shave to smooth out the curved surfaces, removing unwanted ridges and tool gouges (see the photo at right); with the flat-bottom shave, I smooth the seat's front and back edges and its underside. Both spokeshaves leave a silky surface with slight tool marks such as those found on original Windsor chairs.

5) Carving gouges: A carving gouge is great for fine detail cutting, carving knotty areas and getting into tight places where other tools won't. I prefer shallow gouges (#2 and #3 sweep) for carving down from the rim outline into the seat. I use 1/2-in. and 1-in.-wide gouges, as shown in the left photo below. If a chair design calls for a rain gutter, I'll go to a 1/4-in. veining gouge.

6) Hand-sanding: Finally, I use sandpaper to give the seat smooth flowing contours. I start with 60-grit to remove any grain tearout and finish up with 100-grit for a paint-ready surface. In keeping with the 18th-century chair look, I sand only the seat's top and front edge while keeping the edge crisp (see the right photo below). On the seat's back edge and underside, I leave the tool marks showing.

Step 4: Remove gouges and ridges with spokeshaves.

Step 5: Carve definition and details with gouges.

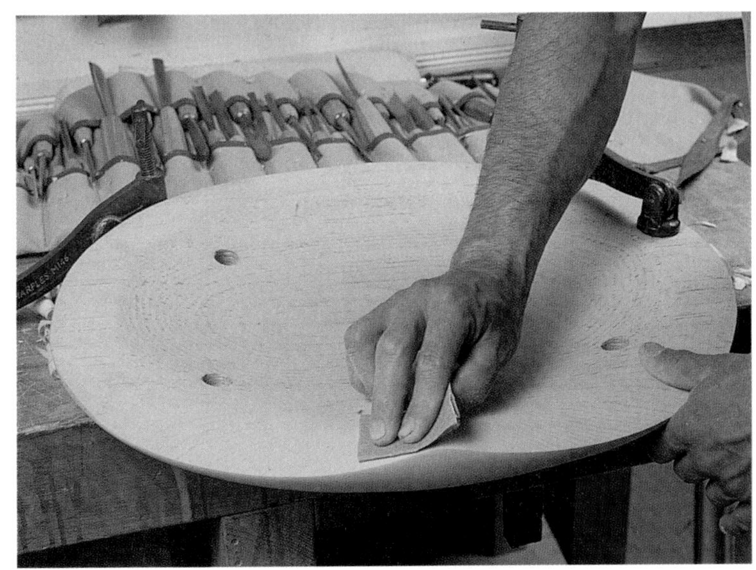

Step 6: Smooth the seat contour with sandpaper.

FOUR

Basic Joints

The first joint most woodworkers practice is the butt joint. It's dead simple: Just two boards butted up against one another and fixed with nails or screws. It has a serious flaw though: it's weak. An open rectangular box put together with butt joints will turn into a parallelogram if you merely pick it up. Drawers built with this joint have a limited lifespan. This is why few woodworkers still have their first projects around.

With experience, a lot of woodworkers move on to more complex joints for greater strength. However, simple joints such as the butt don't have to be weak. You can, as they say, have your cake and eat it too by using joints that are both simple and strong. Among these joints are edge joints, rabbets and dadoes (see *The Basics of Craftsmanship*), splines, and biscuits. Some of these make surprisingly strong joints. A good glue-only edge joint, for example, will be stronger than the wood around it. Biscuits and splines are also tremendously strong: When used in a butt joint, they give it a lot of strength.

Edge joints are often omitted in a discussion of joinery because they seem to be nothing more than a matter of spreading glue on two edges and clamping together. In fact, there are subtleties that can make or literally break this simplest of joints. Anyone with a tabletop that has opened at the ends or has steps between the boards will certainly want to read Jim Tolpin's advice on the edge joint. The same is true of splines and biscuits. Though almost foolproof, these joints have potential pitfalls. The experience of Steven Cook, Ed Speas, and Sandor Nagyszalanczy will steer you clear of the pitfalls and give you a real sense of the breadth and depth of the possibilities these joints offer.

THE EDGE JOINT

by Jim Tolpin

Accessories aid in glue-ups—A laminate-faced gluing stand, hardwood edge protectors and end cauls are all part of the author's clamping routine. The stand provides a flat reference face for the lamination; the edge-protectors keep the edges from being crushed by the clamps; and the end cauls, clamped with C-clamps, flush-up the face of the glue-up at its ends, ensuring that the assembly doesn't become distorted by the pressure of the pipe and/or bar clamps.

Gluing up smaller boards to make a big board—it wasn't always this way. When a 19th-century cabinetmaker needed a wide floating panel for a door or a case side or perhaps a top for a bureau, he went to his stock of wide boards (up to 30 in. was not uncommon) and found what he needed. If he needed 4-in.-thick stock for table legs, the loft of his shop could almost certainly provide it for him. Glue and clamps were used mostly for final assembly.

Today boards of these widths and thicknesses are difficult to come by, and if you can find them, the prices are staggering. Edge-gluing narrower boards to come up with wider ones and face-gluing thinner boards to create thick blanks is now routine for most professional woodworkers. But unless you're careful how you prepare the stock and apply the glue and clamps, the results may be disappointing.

Misoriented boards may cause poorly matched grain patterns; boards with widely varying moisture contents can result in irregular surfaces; and boards with less than perfectly jointed surfaces can produce gaps along the joints or splits in the boards themselves. Too little or too much glue will result in either a starved joint or an engorged glueline, either of which could result in eventual joint failure. Improper clamping techniques cause problems as well: open joints, surfaces that are difficult to flatten, stains and dents. But mastering a few basic principles of stock preparation for glue joinery, glue application and clamp use, for both edge and face laminations, should ensure success.

Sprung joint keeps ends together—The slight concavity of a sprung joint adds an inward stress to the ends of the jointed boards, making the joint less likely to open. The gap between the two boards at center is no more than 1/32 in.; hand pressure should be enough to close it.

Preparing the stock

When joining two or more boards together, you must understand how the boards will move relative to one another. To avoid ridges across the surface of edge-laminations and ledges along the sides of stacked face laminations, I use wood of the same species and moisture content. When possible, I use pieces cut from the same board, a strategy that also helps achieve pleasing grain matches across the joints. I'm also conscious of how I orient the growth rings. Because wood moves significantly more tangentially than it does radially (as much as 3:1 in some species), it's important to keep growth rings roughly parallel to each other (see the drawing on p. 104). As for whether alternating boards should have their growth rings all facing in the same direction or inverted, I generally opt for the former, finding it easier to hold a single arch flat than to try to restrain a wavy surface.

Because it's invariably necessary to resurface glued-up stock to smooth the joined surfaces to one another, I always use oversized stock. For example, to ensure a 3/4-in.-thick panel, I use stock at least 13/16 in. thick, taking 1/32 in. off each face after laminating. If the stock is squirrelly, where the face ripples rather than simply curves, I start with a full 7/8 in. or more. For the same reasons, I make a stacked lamination overwidth, cutting, joining and thicknessing it to final dimension after it's glued up.

Because most commonly used woodworking glues, epoxy excepted, are not strong over a gap, it's critical to get mating surfaces as straight and flat as possible. For edge-gluing, I joint the boards so that the entire length of their edges touch with just hand pressure (see the photo on p. 103). With no pressure on the boards, they should be ever-so-slightly concave. The additional pressure required to close the middle of the joint line adds an inward stress to the ends of the boards that helps inhibit end splits.

However, I've learned that attempting to overcome convexity along an edge with clamps and glue is futile. Though you might get the clamps to close the gaps initially, you're building an outward stress into the board ends that will eventually resolve itself through end splits or by overpowering the glue joint. Better to joint the boards true.

I also check the stock to be face-glued and reject or resurface any board with a warped face. I could subjugate the warp with clamps, but I'd pay sooner or later: The bad board would eventually transmit its distortion to the rest of the assembly.

To ensure a flat surface when joining boards edge to edge, either the edges must be square to the faces or the two boards must join at complementary angles. With my jointer carefully adjusted and using a firm and steady feed technique, I can generally produce a perfectly square edge over the length of a board. But for insurance, I often hold two boards together and joint their edges simultaneously to produce complementary angles, which however negligible, will cancel each other out, resulting in a tight joint and a flat board (see the photo on the facing page and the drawing on p. 106).

Orienting boards properly for lamination

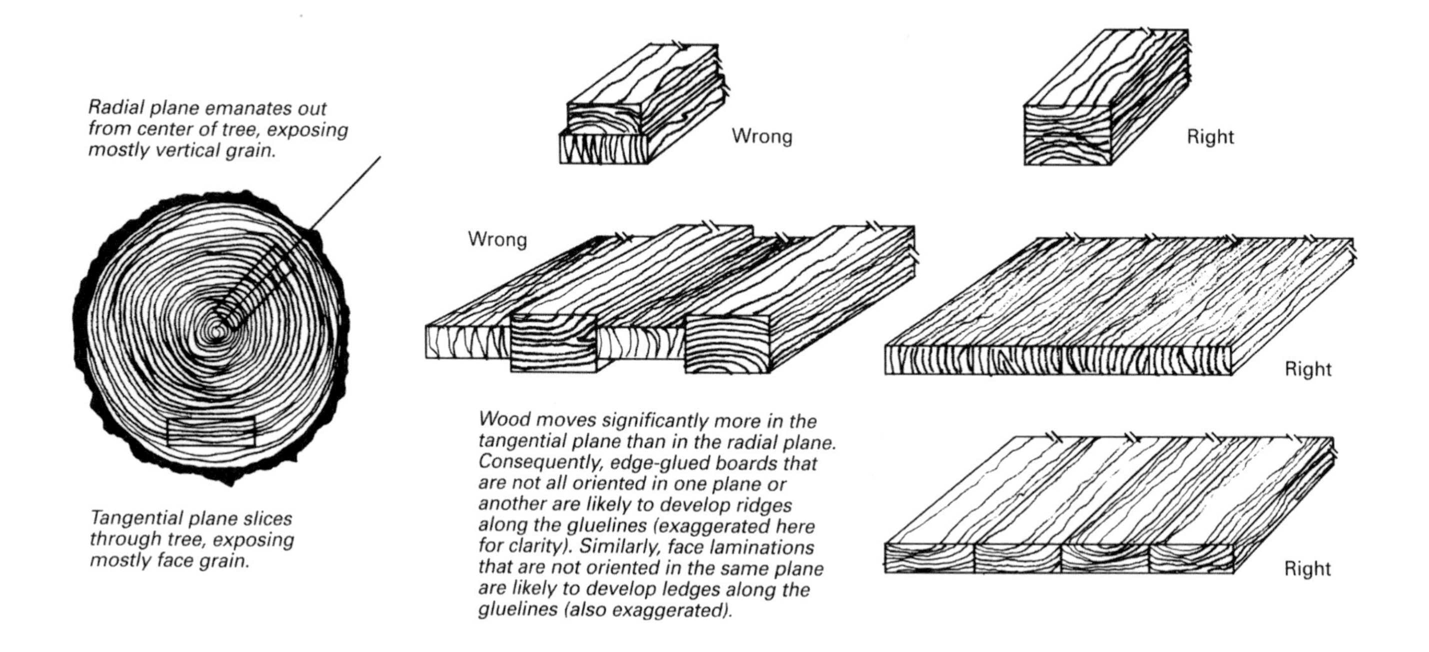

Radial plane emanates out from center of tree, exposing mostly vertical grain.
Tangential plane slices through tree, exposing mostly face grain.
Wrong
Right
Wrong
Right
Right
Wood moves significantly more in the tangential plane than in the radial plane. Consequently, edge-glued boards that are not all oriented in one plane or another are likely to develop ridges along the gluelines (exaggerated here for clarity). Similarly, face laminations that are not oriented in the same plane are likely to develop ledges along the gluelines (also exaggerated).

Maintaining edge alignment

Though it's not necessary for strength, I use dowels, biscuits, a long spline or a routed glue-joint profile along the jointed edges to help keep surfaces aligned. This minimizes the amount of post-glue-up surfacing I'll have to do (see the photo on p. 107). These options are particularly useful when edge-gluing long boards or stubborn, squirrelly stock, especially if you're working alone. With edge alignment taken care of, you can concentrate on closing up the joint or joints before the glue sets up.

Applying glue

Unless I suspect that my joints will require the glue to be strong over a gap (for example, when face-gluing wide boards where clamping near the middle of the faces is awkward), I avoid epoxy. It is expensive and generally runny and messy. Also, because of its toxicity, I have to wear protective gloves and a respirator when using epoxy. For the same reasons, I try to avoid powdered urea-formaldehyde glues, such as Weldwood's plastic resin glue, except when I need to take advantage of its long open time, such as for a project with a lot of parts or one with a complex clamping setup. For most of my woodworking, I rely on the ubiquitous yellow glue (polyvinyl acetate, or PVA). I find that its strength is more than adequate and that its set-up time is ample for most clamping situations.

Using the proper amount of glue is critical for peak performance. If you use too much glue, the joint is only as strong as the internal cohesion of the glue itself, which isn't high for yellow glue or the urea-based glues. Also, a thick glueline looks ugly. If you use too little glue, you've starved the joint, rendering it susceptible to failure under stress.

Unfortunately, knowing how much glue to use is more an art than a hard science. The variables are many and include type of

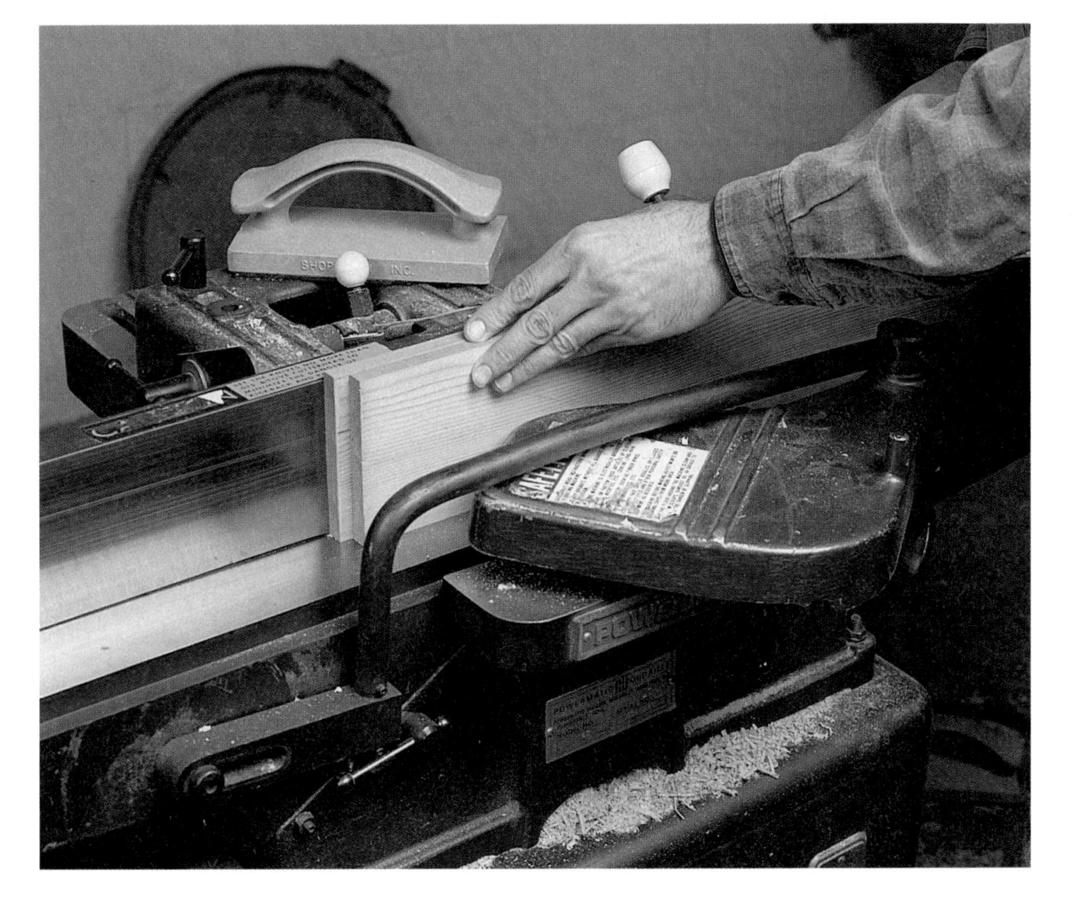

Jointing two boards together can be done safely and easily by pinching the boards together and maintaining steady, even pressure against the jointer fence.

Joining complementary angles for edge-gluing

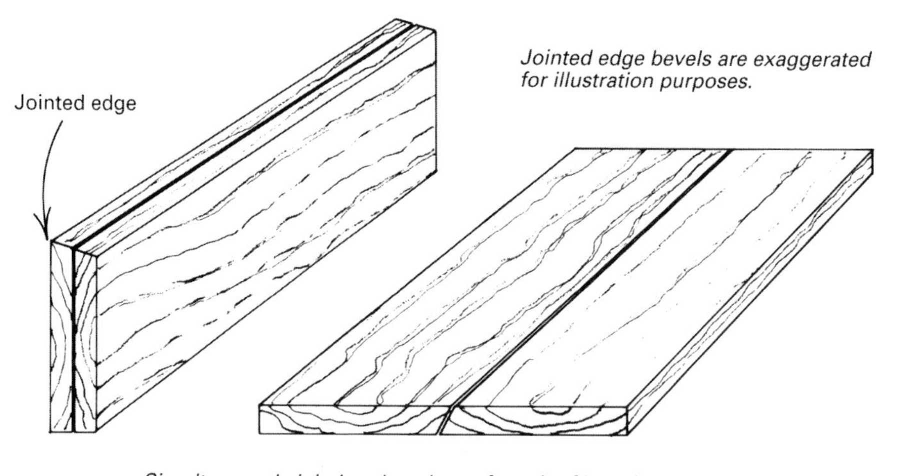

Jointed edge
Jointed edge bevels are exaggerated for illustration purposes.

Simultaneously jointing the edges of a pair of boards that are to be edge-glued ensures a flat glued-up board even if the jointer fence is not perfectly perpendicular to the beds. Any deviation from a 90° edge on one board will be precisely made up in the other.

glue, age, temperature, humidity, type of wood and moisture content of the wood. It's impossible to control all of them. After using a particular type and brand of glue for a while, you become familiar with what that glue looks like at the proper film thickness.

I use a rubber roller or a stiff brush to spread yellow glue evenly across both joint surfaces. If it's opaque, I know I've put on too much, so I wipe a little off. I shoot for a thin, translucent film with no "holidays," or skipped areas, visible in a strong side light.

The glueline tells me if I applied the right amount of adhesive: With yellow glue, if the excess beads up so much it's dripping off the wood, I've put on too much. I look for a bead line of glue, with the boards clamped tight, that stays put. If no bead, or almost no bead, appears, I can tell I've starved the joint, and I need to release the clamps and apply more glue immediately (see the photo on p. 108).

Working with the ureas is trickier yet. This glue is so fluid even a starved joint produces excess that runs out of the joints. As with yellow glue, I look for a thin, even film on both surfaces. To reduce squeeze-out, I don't apply as much clamping pressure. Experience, again, is the best teacher.

Clamping basics

It's important to protect the boards you're gluing up from being damaged by the clamps. Clamps exert tremendous force and can inflict deep dents into most wood surfaces: The softer the species the greater the potential for doing irreparable damage. I protect the laminations by either using pads on the clamp heads themselves or by inserting scraps of wood between the stock and the clamp heads. I'm also careful to protect the stock from being stained by the clamps. Many woods react with the iron of the clamp bars to create stubborn chemical stains. Oak, because of its high tannin content, is especially susceptible. I'm careful either to keep the bars away from the wood or to insert waxed paper, plastic wrap or some other barrier between the wood and clamps.

When deciding where and how many clamps to apply to the glue-up, I shoot for more rather than less in most applications. It's nearly impossible to use too many clamps, though it is easy to overtighten them and starve the joint. If you're stressing your wrist tightening the clamp, chances are you've overtightened it. Back it off a bit, and come back to a comfortable one-hand twist.

Alignment aids make clamping easier—Dowels, splines, biscuits and glue-joint profiles (left to right), are all effective means of guaranteeing alignment when edge-gluing. Though they don't necessarily add a great amount of strength to a joint, any of these will keep your boards flush so that you can concentrate on clamping up.

Being stingy with clamps is just as bad (or worse) than overtightening, though, and more often than not will lead to a failed glue joint. With the exception of epoxy, glues depend on pressure and a tight wood-to-wood bond to reach full strength. Finally, because clamps exert their force over a small area, I use hardwood cauls whenever possible to distribute the pressure more evenly.

Edge-gluing

I use either the common pipe clamp, the bar clamp or the double pipe clamp to join boards edge to edge. Double pipe clamps have a significant advantage over both pipe and bar clamps. Because they apply pressure evenly above and below the boards, your chances of getting a flat, warp-free panel are greater.

Pipe clamps work well for virtually all edge-laminating situations and are both inexpensive and versatile: You can join pipes together to create clamps of whatever length you need, and you can even bend the pipe to go around a curve. The pipe clamp's only major failing is that it doesn't provide a straight, flat support surface for the boards. But it can be dealt with by providing a gluing stand and using cauls on the ends of the boards, as I'll discuss in greater detail below.

Bar clamps lack the versatility of pipe clamps in that their length is fixed, but the bars will generally provide a flat reference surface for the boards you're gluing up. In addition, because of their rectangular profiles, bar clamps are capable of exerting much more force before distorting than pipe clamps, which is useful when gluing up thicker stock.

When I need to do an edge-to-edge glue-up, I begin with a dry run, laying out the boards edge to edge, applying light clamping pressure, and making a final check of the fit of the joints and the match of the grain patterns. When I'm satisfied, I number each board to keep them in order, and I make hatch marks across each joint to aid in alignment later on.

Next I set up the gluing stand, as shown in the photo on p. 102, and reposition the boards on it. I set the hardwood edge protectors in place and then slide bar or pipe clamps under the boards.

Squeeze-out reveals if right amount of glue was used. This photo of a face lamination shows a starved glue joint (top) with no glue beads; a joint with just about the right amount of glue used (center), where the beads are fairly even and stay put on the glueline; and a joint in which too much glue was used and the excess is dripping down the lamination (bottom).

I spread glue on all mating surfaces with a roller or brush and then rub the joints together to even the glue film. I install any splines, biscuits or dowels and then press-fit the boards together. The first clamp I tighten is the one nearest the middle of the assembly. I'm careful not to let the pipe or bar touch the boards, and I apply just enough pressure to bring up a bead of glue. As I'm tightening down on the clamp, I make sure that the faces are flush across the joint. Then I work out from this clamp toward either end. I alternate top and bottom clamps, manipulating the boards as I go by lifting or depressing them near their ends to bring their faces flush. I place the last clamps about 4 in. to 6 in. in from either end.

I use flattening cauls across the ends of the boards, applying pressure either with C-clamps or wooden hand screws, and I check to make sure the joints are flush as I go along. Waxed paper or plastic wrap will keep your cauls from becoming a part of your glue-up. Recalcitrant boards sometimes respond to a firm tap with a hammer; just remember to protect the face of your glue-up with a block of wood.

Once the assembly is clamped up, I usually remove it from the stands and lean it against a wall. To keep the glue-up free of warp, I make sure the assembly stands nearly vertical, with all the clamps parallel to one another.

When the glue beads becomes rubbery, about 20 to 30 minutes in average temperature and humidity conditions, I roll them off with a scraper blade (see the photo on the facing page). If you wait too long, the glue will set up, making it hard to remove, possibly tearing out wood fibers as you chip it away. At the other end of the spectrum, if you hurry and try to wipe up the glue just as it's beading up on the joint line, you risk

Glue can be removed neatly and without any danger of tearout. Wait until the glue has become rubbery, usually a little less than a half-hour with yellow glue in average conditions. Then the glue bead will stick to itself but peel right off the surface of the wood, leaving no trace.

spreading out wet glue in such a thin layer that it's invisible. But when you try to finish the wood, it refuses to take stain or finish wherever glue has sealed the pores.

When the glue has dried, I remove the clamps and scrape off any remaining glue. Recommended clamping times vary; consult the can or bottle, and note that they are temperature-dependent. Then I surface the glued-up panel to final dimension, using either a planer with sharp knives, handplanes and scraper, or sanders.

Face-gluing

When stacking up boards face to face, I usually use the C-clamp and the sliding-bar "speed" or "fast-action" clamp. If I am looking for brute strength, I will use large C-clamps, which are capable of providing over a ton of force. The sliding-bar clamps, though quicker to apply and available with comparatively deep throats, can exert only about a quarter of that amount, so I use them for lighter-duty work.

Wooden hand screws are also useful for face laminations, especially if the top and bottom faces of the assembly are not parallel to one another: The double-screw arrangement allows you to orient the two clamp faces at different angles. While their clamping force is somewhere between that of C-clamps and sliding-bar clamps, hand screws do have the additional advantage of a large, non-marring footprint. For them to be effective, however, they must be adjusted so that the jaws are in full contact with the outer faces of the boards you're clamping.

When I'm face-gluing, I always cut the pieces oversized by at least 1/4 in. in width and length.

Just as when edge-gluing, I set up a gluing stand and dry-assemble, checking to see that the faces fit tightly on all sides. I orient the boards with their hearts out because this tends to keep the edges closed if the boards have any drying left to do. I also make hatch marks across the joints for alignment.

Then I roll or brush the glue onto both faces, stack the pieces on the gluing stand and apply clamps. I generally use cauls top and bottom unless I'm taking off a lot of stock to get down to final thickness. If the stock is 6 in. or wider, I first apply deep-throat clamps to compress the middle of the assembly. Then I apply clamps around the perimeter. I don't worry about putting on too many; it's not a problem having as many as 20 C-clamps in a 1-ft.-sq. area.

Just as with edge-gluing, I wait until the glue has become rubbery to remove it. After the glue has dried, I clean up any residual glue and joint and plane the lamination down to final size.

SPLINE JOINERY

by Steven Cook

In 20 years as a professional woodworker, churning out cabinets, making custom furniture and even some musical instruments, I've always looked for ways to make my two-man shop productive and profitable. One technique I use in virtually all my work is the spline joint.

The spline joint is simply the joining of two boards with a piece of scrap plywood or hardwood that's set into grooves routed in the two boards. Whether you need to align boards to be joined for a large tabletop, make face frames for a set of cabinets or join rail and stile for a frame-and-panel or glazed door, spline joints are useful.

The spline joint is easier than doweling and stronger, too. Locating the splines is easy because the critical dimension is controlled by the depth setting of the router (see the photo below). Just be sure to index from the same face, and whatever you're joining with splines will be in the same

A router and slot cutter substitute for a plate joiner. A steady hand and a keen eye (protected by safety glasses) will yield a strong, quick spline joint.

plane. Since I already have several routers, it's a lot cheaper to use a slotting cutter and splines than to buy a dedicated plate joiner, which makes a similar, though less adaptable, joint. Also, I use mostly scrap plywood for my splines, so there's less chance of swelling or having the spline telegraph through to the surface than with conventional compressed birch biscuits.

The right equipment: a good slotting cutter

Other than a router, the only item you need for spline joinery is a slotting cutter, a generally available router bit. These come in many diameters and slot widths, but choosing the right one needn't be confusing. There are two general rules. First, select the largest shank size that your router will accommodate—usually 1/2 in. And second, go with the smallest diameter cutter you can find because a 1/4-in. shank and a 1 3/4-in. cutter make a weak and dangerous combination. I have a couple of bent shanks in my collection, as well as ruined router bases, due to the mass of the cutter being too great for the shank.

My favorite bit has a 1/2-in. shank, 15/16-in. cutter and a 3/4-in. pilot bearing. That means there's just over 1/4 in. of cutter in the wood, and the 1/2-in. shank can handle that easily. Also, the depth of cut, which is actually 9/32 in., means that your spline is more than 1/2 in. wide (9/32 + 9/32 = 9/16), making for a strong joint.

Cutter widths vary from 1/32 in. up to 1/2 in. or so. Most of my structural joints are made with a 1/4-in. cutter. When joining a frame that is also taking a 1/4-in. plywood panel, it's necessary to use two 3/32-in. cutters with a thin washer between them to make a slot that hugs the undersized plywood.

Making splines

Splines can be made from a variety of materials, including medium-density fiberboard (MDF), plywood and solid wood. My favorite is planed-to-order Baltic birch. I use

Splines can be used as a decorative element in addition to their structural role, as is the case with the ebony splines in the lids of the author's boxes.

You can shape splines in seconds on a variety of common shop machines, including a stationary belt sander.

Slots for frame joinery and panel can be routed simultaneously with a pair of 3/32-in. cutters separated by a thin washer. The result is a strong frame and a snugly fitting panel.

Use solid end pieces with plywood splines to get maximum strength without sacrificing looks or speed.

it all the time for drawers, so there's plenty of scrap. When joining solid boards edge to edge, as for tabletops, I rip thin sections of spline material. When I'm using biscuit-shaped splines to join rail and stile to make frames, I bandsaw the splines to rough size and shape them on either my stationary belt sander or a sanding drum on my drill press (see the bottom photo on p. 111).

If you use solid wood for splines, make sure the grain runs across the joint, rather than parallel to it, for maximum strength and to allow for seasonal wood movement. Frequently, I'll use plywood splines for all but the ends of a long joint, particularly large panel glue-ups, and just use small bits of solid wood at the ends where they'll show. This makes for a strong joint that looks nice and works well for tabletops and box lids (see the top photo on p. 111).

Frame joinery, panel alignment, and decorative edging

I've used slotting cutters for many purposes other than what they were intended for, including rabbeting all around the top edge of a tabletop to inlay a strip of contrasting wood. The most common uses of the slotting cutter in my shop, however, are to join frames and to align and strengthen panels I'm gluing edge to edge.

When I'm joining a frame that takes a flat plywood panel, I make the panel and spline the same thickness and rout both the panel groove and the recess for the spline simultaneously. To do this, I stop just shy of the ends of the stiles and rout right around the ends of the rails, stopping shy of the outside edge (see the top left photo).

For glazed cabinet doors, I want to be able to remove it if it ever breaks, so I use the router and slotting cutter just as I would a plate joiner: I make blind slots in the ends of the rails and the top inside edges of the stiles (see the photos on the facing page). Then I come back later, adjust the router's depth of cut for a rabbet rather than a groove and create a recess for the glass. The corners will be round, but most glass shops will be glad to radius the corners of a sheet of glass for you.

Splines for a glazed door

A slot cutter makes a blind spline recess in the end of the rail. The author makes the cut freehand, using a pencil line to set the limit of the spline groove.

Mating slots are cut in the stiles. With the router and slot cutter at the same setting, the author makes the stile slot. The depth setting of the router keeps everything in line as long as all cuts are from the same side of the frame.

Plywood makes a biscuit-style spline. A piece of plywood sanded to shape fits snugly in the finished slot. The author will reset the depth of cut for a rabbet to create the recess for the glass.

PLATE-JOINERY BASICS

by Ed Speas

Proper grip and stance make it easy to cut accurate, tight-fitting joints. The left hand firmly holds the joiner's fence to the workpiece with the right arm locked to the body. The legs do the pushing. A stop clamped to the workbench holds the piece steady. Cutting the other end of the workpiece or replacing it with another is easy because the workpiece is not clamped to the bench.

Cutting an offset joint using a shim spacer, the author kerfs a table apron that will be set back from the face of its leg by the thickness of the shim. The template in the foreground helps to lay out the kerf in the apron's narrow end.

I could build furniture and cabinets without a plate joiner, but after using one for several years, I wouldn't want to. Plate joinery is a satisfactory and speedy alternative to some traditional joinery.

A plate joiner is a small, hand-held saw with a 4-in.-dia. blade. The blade plunges into a workpiece to cut a radiused kerf. A football-shaped joining plate is then glued into the mating kerfs in the pieces to be joined, like a loose tenon, to create a strong joint. The joining plates (called biscuits by some Yankees who don't know that biscuits are served with gravy for breakfast) are made from solid beech and are slightly compressed. Moisture from the water-based glue causes the plates to swell in the kerfs for a tight fit and strong bond. All you have to do is clamp the members together, and precise joint alignment takes care of itself.

There are many different applications for plate joinery, but I've grouped them into four categories based on the machine setup required to cut the kerf. These categories are flush, small offset, large offset and miter. Before discussing how to set up and cut these joints, lets look at which jobs are best for plate joinery and some basic requirements for cutting accurate joints with a plate joiner.

When to use plate joinery

Plate joinery is one of the best systems I've found for joining man-made sheet materials. But you should use as many plates as possible when joining pre-finished or pre-laminated sheet goods because glue won't adhere well to finished surfaces.

The system also works well with solid-wood joinery, but you need to consider grain direction. When joining face frames, frame and panel, and legs to rails, one of the butt-joined surfaces is end grain. The joint's strength is in the glueline of the plates, without much assistance from the butt joint itself, and it may be inadequate for the application. To strengthen these joints, use two plates side by side. This effectively doubles the strength of the joint. One way to test the strength of any joint is to plate join a sample, and when the glue is dry, try to break the joint apart.

When doubling plates, allow 1/8 in. between kerfs and at least 3/16 in. between the kerf and the face of the board to avoid telegraphing. Telegraphing happens when boards are planed or sanded flat while still swollen from the moisture of the glue and the swelling of the plates. When the wood shrinks later, there will be a slight depression at each joining plate. Leg and rail joints can be further strengthened by adding triangular, corner glue blocks.

Laying out the joints is done by using plates to visualize spacing. The straightedge clamped to the carcase side holds the shelf in place for layout and becomes the reference surface when cutting the joint.

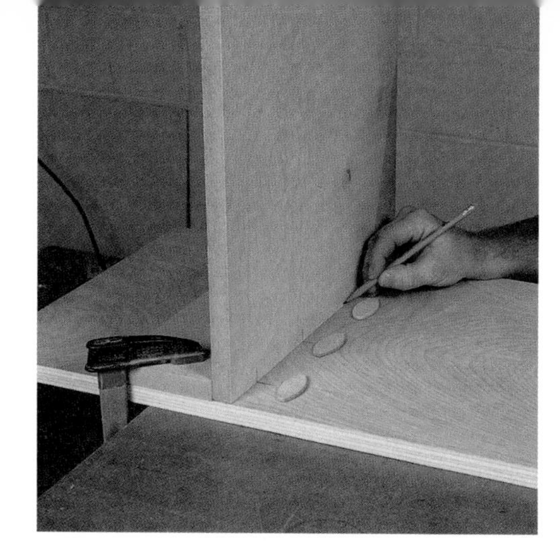

Adjusting a plate joiner

The parts of a plate joiner that position it on the work need to be true and square to cut accurate joints. The base should be absolutely flat, as must the face. The face also must be at 90° to the base. When attached to the joiner, the fence should be flat and perpendicular to the face. If the base, face and fence check out, you have a good machine. But, if even one part doesn't pass the test, you'll have to replace it or exchange the whole machine for a new one.

Most plate joiners have three preset depth-of-cut stops, which correspond to the most popular sized plates: #20 (about 2$^{3}/_{8}$ in. long), #10 (about 2 in. long) and #0 (about 1$^{7}/_{8}$ in. long). Some machines have additional settings to accommodate new plates. For any given joint, you will want to use the largest plate possible—the larger the plate, the greater the gluing area and the stronger the joint.

You can fine-tune the depth of cut (set it slightly deeper than half the width of the plate, so the plate doesn't prevent the parts from butting tightly together during assembly). I check the setting by inserting a #20 plate into a kerf cut at the #20 setting. I draw a line down the middle of the plate along the edge of the board, turn it 180° and put it back in the kerf. If the pencil line still shows, the kerf isn't deep enough. If the line disappears into the kerf, I draw another line as before, pull the plate out and check the distance between the two. It ought to be between $^{1}/_{16}$ in. and $^{1}/_{8}$ in. Once the depth is set for one size plate, it will be correct for the other plate sizes. Because the depth adjusting knobs may vibrate loose, I periodically check them.

Three factors influence the amount of pull to the left exerted by the cutting force of the blade: how fast you plunge the tool, your grip and stance, and the sharpness of the blade. Most joiners have two small pins in their face that penetrate the workpiece to help prevent the machine from pulling to the left. But the pins aren't necessary if you use a strong grip and proper stance (see the photo on p. 114) and make a slow plunge with a sharp blade. In fact, I prefer to take the pins out because they keep the joiner from sliding freely along the workpiece when aligning the cut. When I'm joining miters, the pins are a particular problem because they're pushed into the workpiece at an angle. This can cause the pins to jam and hold the machine's face off the workpiece, which results in a misaligned cut.

The plate joiner is a simple machine and requires little maintenance, but there are a few areas that need attention to keep the tool operating at peak efficiency. To prevent excessive wear (which can render the joiner totally useless), clean and lightly oil the slide mechanism frequently. The blade should be kept free of pitch and residue, and sharpened as needed. A plate joiner has a small motor; taxing it with a dull blade will shorten its life. The blade should be only face ground when sharpened. If the sides of the teeth are ground, the kerf will be too narrow for the joining plate.

Four basic joints

Virtually all joinery situations fall into one of the four following categories depending on how you set up your plate joiner.

Flush joints

The most common joinery situation is when you join two pieces flush on at least one edge. A butt joint is one example. Another would be a right-angle connection flush only on the outside, such as a drawer or cabinet. For all such operations, the fence is set the same for cuts on both pieces. The marks go on the outside of the pieces, and the fence registers on the face, or edge, that has the mark.

Small offset joints

The next situation includes joints where two pieces are at right angles, but not flush, and where the distance of the offset is within the range of the fence. Examples are attaching a rail to a table leg, where the rail is set back from the outside of the leg, or attaching a face frame to a cabinet side where the face frame extends past the side. Marking out is the same as for the flush joints.

Cut small offset joints two ways: The first way is to set the fence so the kerf is centered on the edge of the piece that will be set back, such as a table's rail. Then, before cutting the joint in the table leg, raise the fence the amount of the offset.

The second method uses a shim block the same thickness as the offset. The distance from the fence to the center of the blade is half the thickness of the piece to be set back, plus the thickness of the shim block. For example, for a 1/4-in. offset using 3/4-in.-thick stock, set the fence 5/8 in. (3/8 in. plus 1/4 in.) from the blade's center.

To cut the kerf in the edge of the piece that will be offset, use the shim block between the joiner's fence and the board, as shown in the photo on p. 115. To cut the kerf in the overhanging piece, rest the fence on the stock. You don't have to change the fence, so there is less chance of error.

Large offset joints

These joints are similar to small offset joints except that the offset is beyond the range of the fence. Examples are a shelf or a divider in a cabinet. For simplicity, I'll use a shelf to describe the process.

Draw a line across the upright where the shelf will go, and clamp a straightedge on the line. Hold the shelf in position tight against the straightedge, and mark the locations of the joints. I lay plates on the cabinet side, space them by eye and then mark both the shelf and cabinet side, as shown in the top photo on the facing page.

Because the fence is removed for this operation, the registration point becomes the base of the joiner. To cut the kerfs in the upright, hold the joiner's face on the upright with the base against the straightedge. Line up the joiner's center mark with each pencil mark and cut the joints.

To kerf the edge of the shelf, clamp the shelf to a flat bench with the pencil marks showing. With the joiner's base flat on the bench and its face against the edge of the shelf, align the machine with the pencil marks and cut the joints.

Angled shelf joints, such as for a magazine rack, are cut in the same way. Simply clamp the straightedge at the desired angle.

Mitered joints

The fourth situation is joining mitered pieces, such as in a carcase corner or a drawer. For mitered joints, the joiner's fence must be at 45° to its face. Some machine's fences are preset for 90° and 45° only. Others are adjustable between 45° and 90° for more versatile mitering. There are two different setups for the 45° fences depending on the brand of joiner. Some joiner's fences angle up away from the base, and some angle down toward the base. The direction of the fence's angle determines whether the miter joint aligns along the inside or outside surfaces, as shown in the photo on p. 118.

When the fence goes up, the cuts are referenced from the inside surfaces of the stock, thus aligning the inside corner. If the fence goes down, the kerf is registered from the outside, ensuring that the outside of the miter is flush. If the pieces being joined are the same thickness, both fences yield the same results. But when dealing with unequal thicknesses, you must decide whether to align the inside or the outside of the corner joint.

Laying out plate joints

After you've cut the project parts to width and length, identify and mark the orientation of each piece to avoid confusion at glue-up time. Next mark where each plate will go. Hold or clamp two pieces together as they will be in the final assembly, and draw a line for the center of each plate across the intersection of the two pieces. If the parts are too large to handle, lay out the cuts with a tape measure. A soft-lead, 2B or 4B drawing pencil makes a dark line that won't dent the wood but that can be easily removed after the joints are cut. A white pencil works well for darker woods.

How far apart you put the plates will vary according to the size of the joint and the stress it will take. I lay out the plates by eye, as shown in the top photo. Usually, 6 in. to 8 in. apart is fine. In most cases, you will

Alignment of a miter joint, either along its inside or outside surfaces, is determined by the miter fence when joining boards of unequal thickness. If the fence angles toward the base, the outside of the joint will be aligned. Conversely, an upward angled fence produces a joint aligned on the inside.

want the kerf to be close to the center of the board's thickness. Again, eye-ball accuracy is just fine.

Tips for safety and control

Before cutting the kerf, secure the workpiece. Holding the workpiece and the machine at the same time can be dangerous, and it makes it difficult to control the machine. You can either clamp the work to the bench, or clamp a stop to the bench to keep the piece from sliding, as shown in the photo on p. 114. The stop makes it easy to turn the piece around and replace it with the next one without re-clamping.

Though the joint may be ready to be cut, you first need to understand how to use and handle the tool properly. Stance, grip, and movement are all important. Stand with your feet far apart, one in front of the other, like a runner's starting position. The push comes from your legs, not from your arms. One hand holds the tool and operates the switch while the elbow stays locked to the body and moves with the body. The other hand holds the joiner's fence securely to the workpiece. Different styles of fences require slightly different grips. But whatever the grip, you should be able to hold the machine stable with only the hand on the fence.

Use the handle on the top of the machine only to carry it around the shop, not for operating the machine. Remember, the plate joiner has a small motor, so take it easy while cutting the kerf—in slowly, out slowly. This gives you better control and reduces the chance the tool will wander during the cut. Hold the tool steady. Any movement up or down will result in an enlarged kerf and a loose-fitting plate.

On large pieces, it's best to start on the right side because the dust is ejected out that side of the machine. Starting from the left leaves the dust in the path of your next cut. The dust can keep the fence from lying flat on the face of the board and cause your joint to misalign.

A few practice cuts will help you eliminate sloppy joints on your first project. Remember, it's a hand-held tool and will operate only as effectively as you do.

Gluing and clamping

Because the plates start to swell immediately, you don't have time to run around the shop looking for clamps and trying to figure out what goes where at glue-up. So it's best to dry-clamp your projects before you start gluing. That way you'll have your clamps and clamping blocks ready, and your act rehearsed, when the time comes.

Apply glue in the kerf only—not on the plate. The plate can swell and make assembly difficult. Don't just pour glue into the hole either. Spread the glue on the sides of the kerf where the wood-to-plate contact is. The easiest way to apply glue to the kerf sides is with a glue bottle designed specifically for this purpose. Once you've got glue in the kerfs, apply it to the rest of the joining surfaces.

Some say that clamping time can be reduced because the swollen plates hold the pieces together. But, for best results, leave the clamps on as long as for any other joint.

BEYOND BISCUIT JOINERY BASICS

by Sandor Nagyszalanczy

When biscuit joiners first became popular in America more than a decade ago, it was nothing short of a revolution. Even so, many woodworkers haven't climbed on board—perhaps because they think those little pressed-wood plates are less effective for solid-wood furniture and other framing tasks or perhaps because they can't justify the expense of another dedicated machine.

However, all that a regular biscuit-joining machine does is run a 4-in.-dia. sawblade a little way into the work in a controlled way. The biscuit fits into a pair of 4mm-wide slots, the biscuit's grain runs diagonally across the glueline, and the water-based glue makes the biscuit swell up tight. Slotting for biscuits never seemed complicated enough to require a special machine, and now there is a new group of devices that adapt common workshop power tools, such as the router, angle grinder and drill press, to do biscuit joinery. Given the modest prices ($35 to $120) of these devices, I was anxious to see what awaited buyers who might be considering them.

For those of us who can't remember what we did before biscuit joinery, there's a whole slew of new gadgets to support every aspect of biscuiting, from slot positioning to glue application to carcase clamping. These accessories are discussed beginning on p. 122.

To make biscuiting more versatile, there's a gamut of special biscuits in new sizes, shapes and materials, and there's ingenious and useful cabinet hardware that fits into biscuit slots, as discussed on p. 125 (also see Sources of Supply on p. 127).

A couple of years ago, all you could buy was the expensive original machine, the Lamello, or less-expensive machines from Freud, Porter-Cable and Virutex. Now you've got a number of very affordable alternatives, plus a lot of ingenious ways to get the most from the simple slot. If you've avoided biscuit joinery up to now, you're just about out of reasons not to try it.

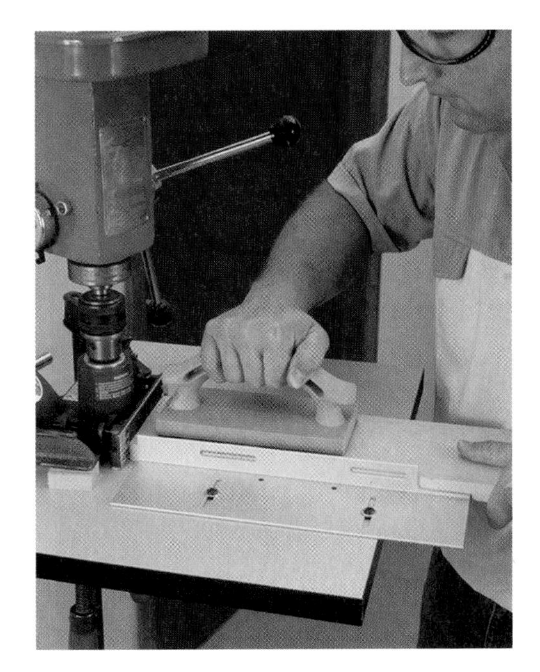

Biscuit joinery with a router, grinder, or drill press

Wolfcraft biscuit joiner attaches to right-angle grinder.

Sears Bis-Kit device replaces the router subbase.

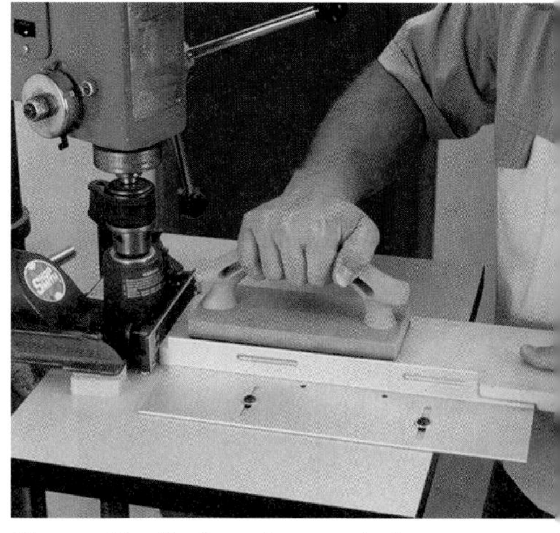

Shopsmith attachment converts the drill press to a biscuit joiner.

You might not be ready to shell out the price of a dedicated biscuit-joining machine ($150 to $400), but with one of the following devices, you can easily convert a portable power tool you already own into a serviceable slot-cutting machine.

Right-angle grinder—You can buy attachments for converting that refugee from the auto-body shop, the right-angle grinder, for woodcarving, corner sanding, random-orbit sanding (see *FWW* #92, p. 51) and now, biscuit joining. The German-made Wolfcraft model 2920 shown at right comes ready to connect to most small (4 in. and 4½ in.) right-angle grinders. Several adapters match arbor sizes. Two metal brackets bolt the mostly plastic device to the grinder's handle-mounting holes. For convenient handling, I mounted my Bosch angle grinder's side handle in lieu of one bracket bolt.

The Wolfcraft has practically all the features of a regular biscuit joiner, including a standard-sized carbide-tooth blade, a quick-set knob for changing slot sizes and an auxiliary front fence that's reversible for square edges or for 45° miters. Wolfcraft also has a dust bag, which didn't work very well, especially when plunging slots vertically.

Unlike conventional biscuit joiners, the Wolfcraft lacks the spring-loaded pins that help keep the stock from creeping sideways. This wasn't a problem on plywood, but when edge-slotting smooth maple, I had to press hard to keep the machine from creeping. This is a small minus for a machine that's lightweight and very nicely designed. If you already own a right-angle grinder, $50 isn't much to pay to add biscuit joinery to your repertoire.

Router—Manufactured for Sears by Vermont American, the plastic Bis-Kit replaces the subbase of a standard or plunge router to provide many—but not all—features of a conventional biscuit joiner. The Bis-Kit's spring-loaded carriage rides on guide rods attached to the base with a depth rod for different-sized slot cuts. The kit's ¼-in. shank, three-winged, carbide-tipped cutter chucks into the router's collet. It's called a kit and so it is—there's about 20 minutes of assembly and adjustment needed.

To use the Bis-Kit, you bring the carriage face against the workpiece and plunge the machine forward. The router's depth of cut locates the slot in the thickness of the work. It's a lot like running a regular biscuit joiner with a couple of important exceptions. First, the cutter is small, so the unit must be plunged and then moved side to side to form each slot. Second, the base overlaps the face of the workpiece by about 2¼ in., so you must mark long centerlines for the slots (see the center photo above). Third, because of the overhanging router, you can't make cuts in the center of a panel. It's very awkward, but you can clamp the work vertically to the side of the workbench to make slots near the edges of a face for joining cabinet sides, tops and bottoms. What you can't do is join a center partition or shelf. At about $40, the Bis-Kit is an inexpensive way for the hobbyist to try basic biscuit joinery. Its

Woodhaven router-table system uses non-standard biscuits.

limitations, however, are liable to dissuade the buyer from getting more deeply into this joinery method.

Router table—If you own a router and a router table with a fence, all you need to start slot cutting is Woodhaven's Biscuits and Bits kit. Developed by router wizard Brad Witt, the system uses a non-standard biscuit and two carbide-tipped cutters.

A two-winged slot cutter (available with either a ½-in. or ¼-in. shank), with a ball-bearing pilot, mounts in the router table for slotting the ends and edges of work. For edge-joints, set the bit's height, mark the center of the slot on adjacent workpieces and slide the stock into the spinning bit until the mark hits the bearing. For endgrain slots, set the router-table fence to guide the cuts (see the photo above).

The second cutter is a straight bit used in a plunge router to make slots in panel faces for joining tops, bottoms and dividers to sides. Set the plunge depth, mark the slot positions, clamp a fence to the stock as a guide and you're ready. The straight bit's diameter of 6mm is slightly more than the thickness of the kit's biscuits to yield a snug fit.

The Woodhaven system excels at something other biscuit systems aren't much good for: face-frame joinery. Woodhaven's 1½-in.-dia. piloted cutter makes a 6mm slot that just fits their oval-shaped 15⁄16-in.-wide (the same as a #20 biscuit) by 1¼-in.-long biscuits, allowing strong end-to-end or right-angle joints in parts as narrow as 1½ in.

The Woodhaven kit also comes with spline strips made from the same compressed composite wood as biscuits, so you can use the kit's router bits to cut continuous slots for spline joints. At $60 for the router bits, 100 biscuits and 10 ft. of spline (plus a metal can), I think the system is a bargain. You can buy just the two-winged slot cutter and 100 biscuits for $35.

Drill press—The Shopsmith Universal Biscuit Joiner is essentially a stationary biscuit machine designed to install on any standard drill press that's capable of spindle speeds between 2,000 and 4,100 rpm. The cast-alloy unit comes preassembled. All you need to do is screw it to the 14-in. by 18-in. baseplate, clamp the baseplate to the drill-press table and connect the ½-in. shaft directly to the drill-press chuck.

Just like a regular portable machine, the Universal Biscuit Joiner's face is spring loaded and retracts to expose the blade when you push the workpiece into it. By design, however, the machine primarily allows slotting on ends and edges. It can only slot the face of a narrow strip, so it can't be used to join up a plywood carcase. Also, because the workpiece must be brought to the tool, I found the unit best for slotting small- and medium-sized parts. To assist end-grain slotting, an auxiliary fence screws to the baseplate (see the right photo on the facing page).

To keep the workpiece from slipping around, the face of the Shopsmith attachment is covered with strips of coarse abrasive paper and also sports spring-loaded pins. I found these worked well, and the overall feeling during plunging was one of control and comfort. The blade was a little grabby when I ran it around 2,200 rpm, but the action smoothed out with the drill press stepped up to around 3,200 rpm. The rear of the head unit has a built-in dust collection port, which worked exceptionally well. Shopsmith also includes a plastic push block for holding down the stock without getting fingers too close to the blade.

My only real peeve with the Shopsmith is the setting for various biscuit sizes. The process requires adjusting two Allen screws while lining up marks on two plunge rods. It's just tedious enough to have made me want to use only one size biscuit during my trials. But beyond this inconvenience, and provided that you accept the limitations of the unit, Shopsmith offers a quality tool for about $120.

Accessories for biscuit joinery

Woodworker's Supply's stand converts portable biscuit joiner to a stationary tool.

Whether you run a professional cabinet shop or have a hobby-woodworking studio in your garage, here's a collection of accessories and devices that can make biscuit joinery less hassle and more productive.

Benchtop stand—Woodworker's Supply sells a $20 pressed-steel device that converts your portable tool into a stationary machine. Mounting is straightforward: Two bolts screw into the machine's handle holes, and a spring stretches over the barrel to secure the rear end of the tool. The catalog says the stand fits Freud, Lamello and Virutex machines, but I had to redrill holes and add a small spacer block to get my older Virutex to work. With the biscuit joiner's front fence as a little table, workpieces can be plunged into the stationary tool for slotting (see the photo above). I used the setup to slot smaller parts for a jewelry box, but with auxiliary side supports, you could probably slot the edge of longer stock.

Positioning jig—If you use biscuits to join lots of cabinet parts and find you're all too often engaged with the tedious task of marking standard biscuit positions, the Lamello Assista positioning jig may be just the ticket. Made in Switzerland, the Assista features a 39-in.-long extruded aluminum track in which rides a carriage that you bolt to your biscuit joiner. Lamello machines attach directly, the baseplates on other machines may need to be drilled and tapped. A spring-loaded bullet catch on the back of the carriage engages notches on wooden sticks held in a groove at the back of the track. The spacing of these notches determines biscuit spacings; you make new sticks to fit your application.

To use the Assista, first fasten the track to any worktable (or workpiece), 40 in. or narrower, with two special clamps that slide in grooves on the underside of the track. Then you butt the workpiece—usually a carcase panel—up against the track and clamp it down. Then you slide the car-

Lamello system includes the Assista slot positioning jig, the Spanbox clamping set and an optional pistol handle for the biscuit joiner.

riage along the track, stopping at each notch to plunge a slot. The apparatus allows horizontal or vertical plunging as well as slotting 45° beveled edges (see the photo above).

Because the jig supports the weight of the biscuit joiner, I found the Assista comfortable to use. It performed flawlessly as I slotted a half dozen cabinet sides in five minutes. The convenience doesn't come cheap—the Assista is about $300—but it still could be a good investment for a small cabinet shop.

Miter jig—Designed for precisely slotting the ends of mitered stock, the Woodhaven miter jig is designed to work with the router table. Set the angle of the jig's white plastic fence, then mount the fence on the right or left side. Place the workpiece against the jig fence with the tip of the miter against a stop, and tighten a keeper post to prevent the work from sliding around. Then push the jig into the router bit. If you join a lot of picture frames, the jig's $44.99 price quickly will be paid in time saved.

Strap clamp—The Lamello Spanbox strap clamping set consists of two buckles, two 25-ft.-long web straps and four 23¾-in.-long extruded aluminum corners. To clamp up a basic cabinet, you put the corners in place, thread the straps into the buckles and then lever over to apply tension. The Spanbox works with odd-shaped carcases and furniture assemblies as well. Two special tension hooks are included, for clamping flat panels, and shorter (5 in.) corners are also available. It's a fast and effective clamping system, but at $175 a set, it's an expensive proposition if you need to clamp lots of boxes at one time.

Pistol grip—Lamello also makes a pistol grip-style handle, which sells for $18.95, and is designed to replace the stock D-handle on most plate joiners (see the photo on the facing page). I found its large size comfortable in my big hand, one-hand controllable and less tiring than the regular handle.

Accessories for biscuit joinery *(continued)*

Glue applicators—One of the more tedious, not to mention messy, aspects of biscuit joinery is squirting glue in all those slots—two for every biscuit. You can use a small, stiff brush, but to make this a quicker and neater operation, there are four special glue applicators on the market, three from Lamello and one from Woodworker's Supply (see the photo below). The flagship of the line, the Dosicol ($57) is designed for more serious production users. Its special tip is shaped like half of a biscuit and works in #6, #10 and #20 slots. After slipping the tip into a slot, a gentle push on the bottle pumps out a precise amount of glue. I found I could easily apply glue to more than a dozen slots in about 15 seconds. The amount the pump expels is adjustable, and when you're done, a locking ring closes the pump. The applicator head sets into a special base equipped with a sponge to prevent drying out between uses. I especially liked the bottle's large removable end cap, which allows refilling while the Dosicol rests in its stand.

Lamello's two other glue bottles, the Servicol and the Minicol, are lower priced ($12.50 and $28.50) and designed for general gluing of all size slots. They'll also get glue to the bottom of dowel holes, small mortises and Woodhaven biscuit slots. While both models have straight applicator tips that distribute glue to the sides of the slot, the metal Minicol tip is more durable and easier to clean. And while the Minicol stand is heavier and more stable, both models offer an air-tight seal to keep the tip from drying out and clogging.

Woodworker's Supply glue applicator set (an identical set called G100 is offered by Freud with their biscuit joiner) comes with a flat-tipped plastic glue bottle that fits into slots for any size biscuit. While this dispenses glue more quickly than the straight-tipped bottle, you must mush the tip around to distribute the glue on the sides of the slot; otherwise, you end up with a gooey mess. The bottle has its own cap, permanently attached with a short plastic cord (a nice touch, no lost cap and dried-out tip). So that you don't have to cap the bottle during a longer gluing session, there's also a special bottle holder that contains a large moist sponge.

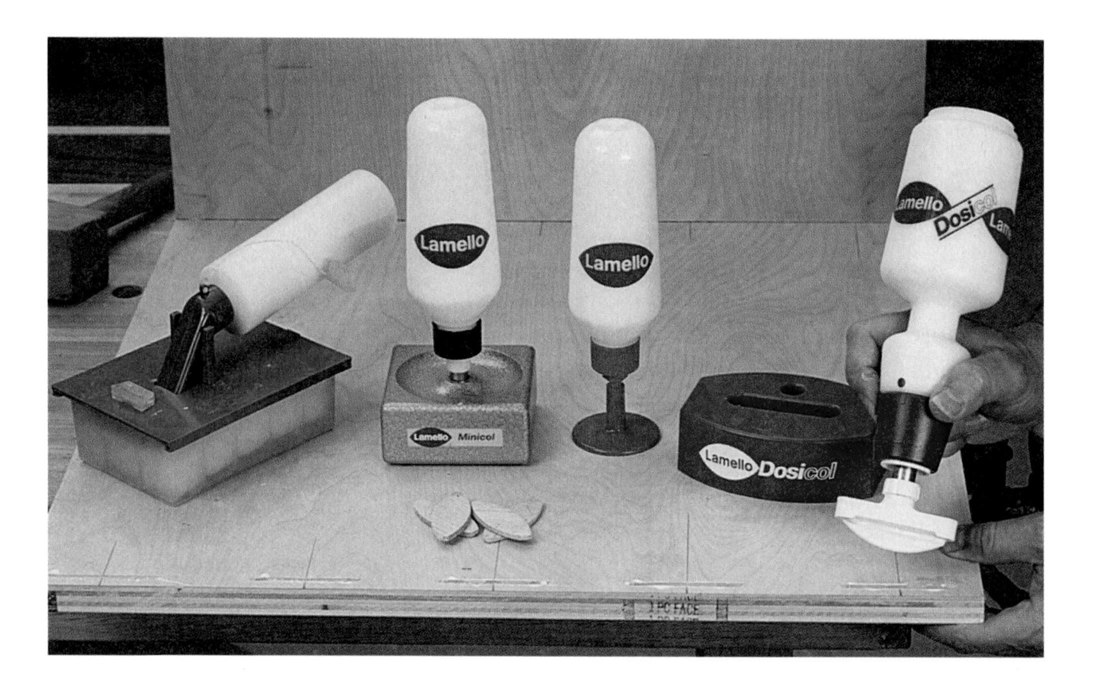

Woodcraft glue bottle and three different Lamello bottles.

New biscuit sizes

Lamello and Woodhaven recently released several new biscuit sizes, as shown in the photo below, designed to fit situations beyond the capacity of standard-sized #0, #10 and #20 biscuits and expand the repertoire of this already versatile joinery method.

Lamello #6—The #6 biscuit is a big football that costs $63 per 1,000 and is designed for heavy-duty joinery in large, thick stock. Measuring 13⁄16 in. wide and almost 3½ in. long, #6 biscuits are standard thickness. With Lamello and DeWalt machines, you simply turn the slot selection dial to MAX, and move the machine about ½ in. side to side to cut the long slot. Other biscuit joiners can also be adjusted to cut the deeper, wider slots, although you may have to remove their anti-slip pins to allow smooth sliding.

Lamello #H9—If you need to make edge-to-face joints in stock that's thinner than about 5⁄16 in. (too thin for #0 biscuits), the diminutive #H9 biscuits are your choice ($41.50 per 1,000). The same setting that's used to cut slots for Lamello's largest (#6) biscuits also is used for the smallest, except that you have to install a special blade. It's both thinner (3mm instead of 4mm) and smaller than the regular blade.

Lamello #11 round biscuits—Unlike the biscuits previously discussed, slots for #11 round biscuits can't be cut with a regular biscuit joiner. Colonial Saw (the U.S. Lamello distributor) sells a special piloted four-winged, carbide-tipped bit ($45 with ½-in. shank) to cut these slots with a router or in the router table. Colonial's manager, Bob Jardinico, told me these round biscuits are popularly used for joining stair railings and banisters, but I think they could be really useful for frame joinery in stock 2 in. and wider. At $64 per 1,000, round biscuits would be an economical alternative to dowels or loose tenons.

Woodhaven mini biscuit—A special router cutter ($25) is also used to make slots for Woodhaven's Itty Bitty biscuits, which are shorter than the Lamello #H9 (13⁄16 in.) but thicker (⅛ in.). Like the #H9, Woodhaven minis ($4.99 per 100) are for joining small parts made from thinner materials and would be a good choice for joining the face frame and dividers on that jewelry box you've been promising your spouse or significant other for Christmas.

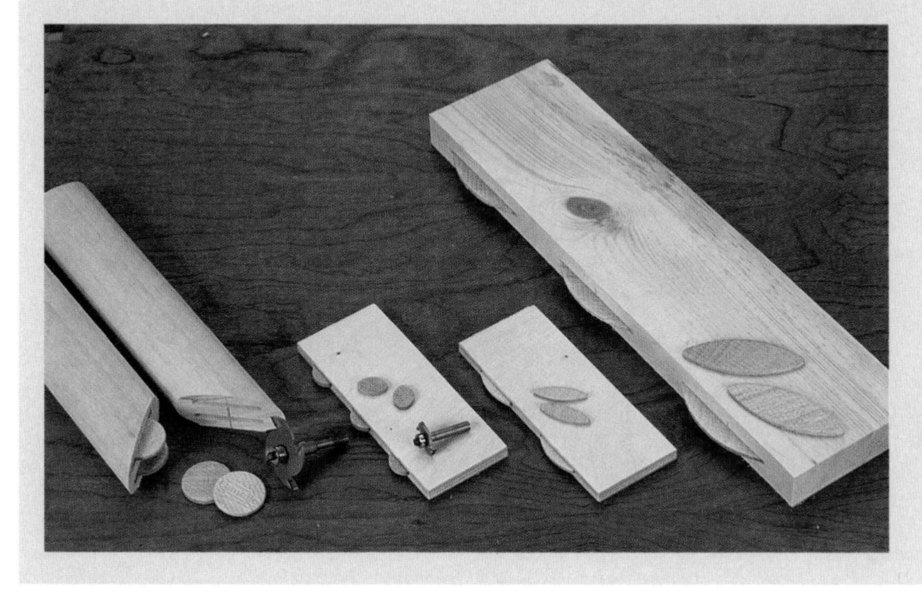

New biscuits (from left): Lamello #11 rounds with four-winged router bit, Woodhaven Itty-Bitty bits with cutter, Lamello's smallest #H9 and jumbo #6 biscuits.

New hardware fits old slots

If you're using only regular compressed-wood biscuits, you're missing half the fun. There's an assorted collection of cabinet hardware and knock-down fittings available from Lamello and Austrian manufacturer Knapp, all designed to work in standard biscuit slots (see the photos below).

Lamello's Paumelle hinges—Paumelle hinges have to be among the easiest to install. Set the biscuit joiner for a #20 cut, and set the fence so the blade makes a 1⁄16-in.-deep mortise on the surface of the work. The hinges hold 10 kilograms (22 lbs.) each and come in packages of 20 hinges (10 right-left pairs) and three finishes: chrome and black ($39) and solid brass ($53). Mounting screws have special heads that must be driven with a #10 Torx bit. Each hinge comes apart (the pin is fixed in one leaf), so the doors are removable. Lamello also has a special spring-loaded awl ($32) for rapidly punching screw-starting holes (see the top photo below).

Self-clamping biscuits—These plastic biscuits fit into regular #20 slots to secure a joint without glue. They're designed to be interspersed with regular glued biscuits along a joint where the parts are hard to clamp. Lamello's K-20 self-clamping biscuits ($14 per 50, shown in the bottom photo below) are made of red plastic with small angled serrations on the sides; one K-20 grips both halves of the joint. In contrast, Knapp's Champ orange nylon clamping

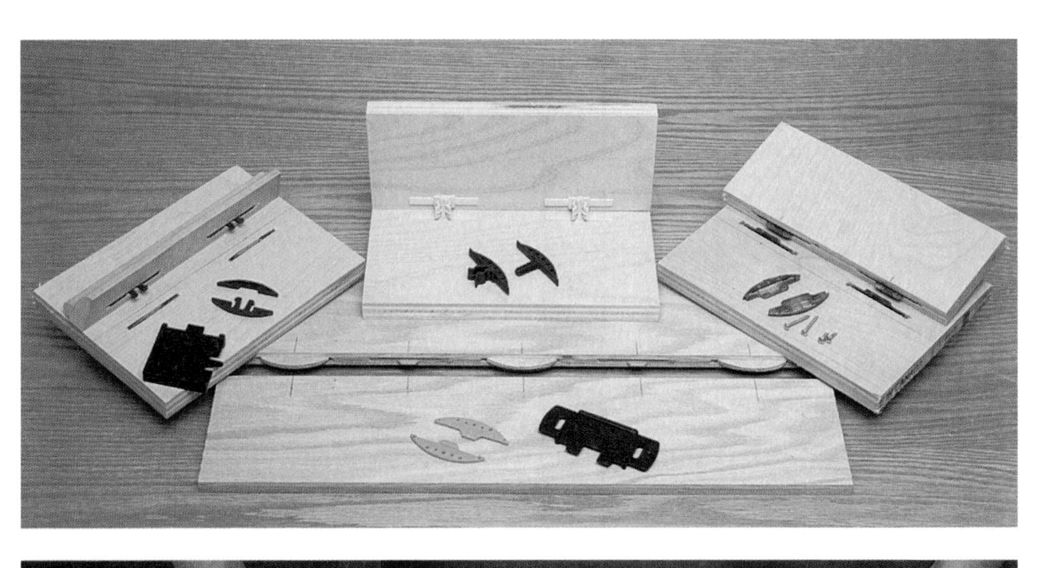

Knapp hardware (from left): Quick detachable fasteners and insertion tool, Mobi-Clips, for creating removable panels, and screw-held Metal knock-down fasteners. Shown in front, Champ self-clamping plates and insertion tool.

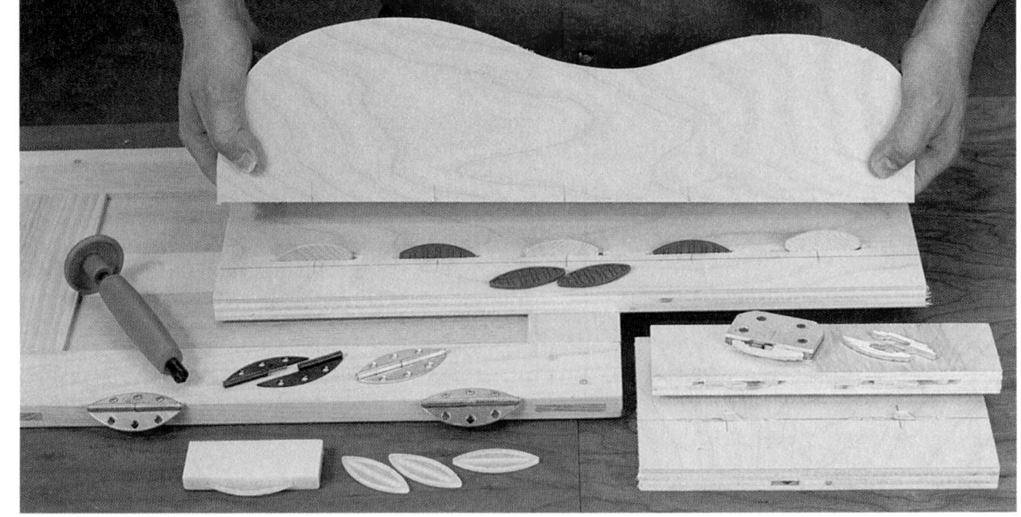

Lamello biscuit-slot hardware (from left): Paumelle hinges with spring-loaded awl for starting screw holes, translucent biscuits for joining solid-surface materials, red K-20 self-clamping biscuits, hook-shaped Simplex knockdown plates with insertion tool.

biscuits must be used in pairs ($49 per 100 pairs). To lock together correctly, each half of a pair must be correctly oriented and epoxied into its slot before the joint is assembled, making Champ biscuits more time-consuming to use than the Lamello K-20s.

Knockdown fittings—A variety of detachable fittings are available that work in standard-sized biscuit slots to create surprisingly strong, tight joints between plywood or solid wood parts. Lamello's pressed-aluminum Simplex knockdown plates (see the bottom photo on the facing page) are driven into slots with a mallet, using a special insertion tool that provides correct alignment and positioning. The surface of each plate is serrated to grip in the slot, so no glue is needed. Knapp's Metal knockdown fasteners (see the top photo on the facing page) are steel plates with small screws that lock the ends of each plate. Either brand of plates is driven into both halves of a joint, but reversed end for end, so their fingers can interlock. Slightly pricey at $47 per 100 for the Simplex, $55 per 100 for the Metal (including screws), these fittings allow clean, sophisticated knockdown casework to be rapidly built.

For less-demanding applications, such as mounting removable moldings on a case or panel, Knapp also offers the Quick disconnectable fastener (shown in the top photo on the facing page). Sold in male-female pairs, these plastic fittings are driven with a plastic insertion tool and epoxied into their slots. They cost $49 for 100 pairs.

Removable panel clips—Knapp makes a set of fittings called Mobi-Clips (see the top photo on the facing page) that allow you to create removable kick plates and access panels (which could function as secret compartments) in your casework. Consisting of a clip half and a stud half, these plastic fittings are epoxied into #20 slots cut into the panel faces. Available in either white or brown plastic ($48 for 50 pairs), Mobi-Clips allow some fine-tuning of the distance between the edge of the removable panel and the carcase.

Plastic biscuits—Compressed-wood biscuits can be used to join countertops made of Corian and Avonite, but they may show through these translucent materials. Lamello C-20 plates (see the bottom photo on the facing page) are milky plastic, specially made for joining these solid surface materials.

SOURCES OF SUPPLY

WOLFCRAFT 2920

Trendlines, 375 Beacham St., Chelsea, MA 02150; (800) 767-9999

SHOPSMITH UNIVERSAL BISCUIT JOINER

Shopsmith Inc., 3931 Image Dr., Dayton, OH 45414; (800) 762-7555

SEARS BIS-KIT

Local Sears stores and catalog sales

WOODHAVEN BISCUITS, BITS AND ACCESSORIES

Woodhaven, 5323 W. Kimberly Rd., Davenport, IA 52806; (800) 344-6657

WOODWORKER'S SUPPLY JOINER STAND AND GLUE BOTTLE

Woodworker's Supply, 5604 Alameda Pl., N.E., Albuquerque, NM 87113; (800) 645-9292

LAMELLO ACCESSORIES, BISCUITS AND HARDWARE

Colonial Saw, 100 Pembroke St., Box A, Kingston, MA 02364; (617) 585-4364

KNAPP HARDWARE

Select Machinery Inc., 64-30 Ellwell Crescent, Rego Park, NY 11374; (718) 897-3937

FIVE

Mortises, Tenons, and Dovetails

It's only natural that this is the largest chapter in the book. These two joints, the mortise and tenon and the dovetail, are classics that every woodworker must know, even if they don't use them every day. Though their technology is ancient, the strongest modern joints can only equal them in long-term holding power. And the cachet of visible dovetails, especially the hand-cut variety, is unmistakable. Their only downside is that, unlike some modern joints, they take some practice to make well.

The mortise and tenon is a joint for all seasons. It can be adapted to a wide range of circumstances, so that few pieces of furniture are improved by using another type of joint. The choice is only complicated by the difficulty in cutting the mortises. Few common shop tools can cut small rectangular holes quickly and easily. Router-cut mortises are relatively easy to make, but there are pitfalls, and the bits leave rounded ends. Specialty tools such as hollow-chisel mortisers do the job well, but require an investment. Mortising chisels are cheap but demand an investment in learning the skills to handle them. The reward, though, is singular. When pegged, mortise-and-tenon joints are completely locked together and stand a better chance than any other joint of surviving intact for many hundreds of years (not that any of us will be around then to check).

Dovetails have a wonderful mystique about them. To a non-woodworker, they can look like a puzzle by Escher. It takes a few heartbeats to figure out what part of what board goes where (if you don't believe this, try drawing two boards joined by dovetails). To a beginning woodworker, dovetails may make perfect sense but are challenging to cut well, which means without gaps, serious tearout, and uneven lines. Watching a master woodworker such as Frank Klausz cut dovetails is an inspiring experience. He saws, chops, and taps them together—perfectly—in about the same time it takes most of us to set a bevel gauge to 12°. Klausz makes cutting dovetails look simple. Once you master cutting dovetails, you can claim a set of excellent woodworking skills, valuable for everything else you do in the workshop.

IN SEARCH OF THE RIGHT MORTISING TECHNIQUE

by Strother Purdy

The first mortise I cut looked as though a miniature dynamite charge had been set off inside the board. Splinters pointed out of the hole in every direction. Inside, my chisel had mashed out nooks, crannies and side passages instead of cutting the straight, flat and square hole I intended. It was plain to see that I had not been born with the skills to chop mortises by hand.

For a while I contemplated buying my way out of learning this skill. Though a good craftsman never blames his tools, I reasoned, a smart one tries to use the best one for the job. My tool wish list, however, was long and underfunded. A jointer and a planer had higher priority than a plunge router or a hollow-chisel mortiser.

In time I learned to cut mortises by hand with reasonable speed and pretty good results. It took a while, but I found I enjoyed the work. The mortises didn't look too hot, but the assembled joint eventually hid them from discerning eyes. I did wonder how strong they were. I knew that yellow glue did not hold across or fill gaps. This told me the uneven fit of my mortise-and-tenon joints couldn't be very strong. Sure, they held together when I tried to pull them apart, but I had no way to test them for the years of use and abuse I wanted them to withstand. It was time to find out how well the mortise had to fit the tenon to stay together and then learn how to cut them that way.

MAN OR MACHINE
Everyone can find a way to cut mortises well, whether through improving skills or finding a better tool. Some prefer the quiet approach of the chisel (right), and others go for the fast and furious router (facing page). Other good options include the drill-press-and-chisel approach, hollow-chisel-mortise machines and dedicated sot mortises.

Good design, fit and glue make strong mortises

I asked Carl Swensson, a woodworker with more than common knowledge about joinery, what made a mortise-and-tenon joint strong. His lengthy reply, which lasted several days, was both enlightening and frustrating.

Boiled down, a strong joint is the product of balanced design (so that one member isn't stronger than the other), an accurate fit and a good glue bond. Everybody knows that glue will make a joint stronger. Swensson was the first who could tell me why. When a joint is under stress, the glue bond spreads it across the cheeks of the mortise and tenon. In a joint without glue, such as one that's only pegged or wedged, the stress will concentrate along edges and at points. This means that the fit must be tight in these places. In a glue joint, the fit is still important, but the accuracy and quality of the glue surfaces are crucial.

To find out more about glue bonds and their requirements, I spoke with Mike Witte, a technical manager at Franklin International. He sent me several manuals about glue, which I read in spite of the great risk of falling asleep. To bond at their full strength, almost all glues need a smooth-but-unburnished surface, free of loose fibers, because glue needs to penetrate a few thousandths of an inch into intact wood. If the surface is burnished—by a dull router bit, for example—the glue can't seep into the pores and has little grip. If the surface is covered with loose fibers, such as a dull chisel might leave, the glue attaches to the loose fibers and not the joint walls. The lesson here is that sharp tools increase joint strength.

Witte confirmed a sobering rule about glue joints: For the glue to do its job, the gap between mortise and tenon should not exceed 0.005 in. This sounded like something I'd need a computer numerically controlled (CNC) router to achieve. However, the way to get these kinds of tolerances really isn't by measuring but by feel. If a mortise and a tenon go together easily, don't need to be hammered home, yet don't come apart without effort, Witte claims they'll be within 0.005 in. apart (see the box on p. 132).

Use chisels for low-cost but high-skill mortising

Chisels are the ubiquitous mortising tool. Everybody has them, but many woodworkers don't use them because they require superlative skill to handle, and they are slow.

What makes a good mortise?

That's simple: a clean surface for a strong glue bond and a tight fit with the tenon.

The fit should be...

Not too tight:

If you have to hammer the joint together, it's too tight. You'll likely split the mortise if you tap aggressivly

Not too loose:

You shouldn't be able to move the tenon in the mortice at all or feel any back-and-forth movement when you try.

But just right:

The tenon should fit into the dry mortise with hand pressure only. It should not come apart easily, and it certainly should be able to withstand gravity. A good fit may even need light mallet taps to drive the joint apart.

For a strong glue bond, the mortise cheeks should be...

- **flat and smooth, so they meet the tenon evenly.**
- **unfinished, so the glue can penetrate the mortise cheeks.**
- **free of loose fibers, which would soak up the glue and not allow it to penetrate solid wood.**

MORTISING CHISEL AND MALLET
Brian Boggs chops a mortise in a chair leg. Though it's the slowest way to cut a mortise, he derives great pleasure from chopping precise joints with good tools.

I found that the first complaint is a half-truth, and the last is, well, true.

I visited Brian Boggs at his chair shop in Kentucky to see whether the humble mortising chisel and mallet were capable of cutting with the precision that glue manufacturers required. When he greeted me, the fact he held a mortising chisel in one hand and a micrometer in the other answered my question. Boggs' recipe is simple: The quality of the mortise depends largely on how the chisel is tuned. Boggs told of the occasion when a student who could not chop a good mortise borrowed his chisel and had no further problems.

Mortising chisels generally have long, stout blades as thick or thicker than they are wide. This allows them to be hammered aggressively and deeply into hard woods without breaking. Unlike most power tools, few chisels arrive from the factory ready to go. To tune one, use an engineer's square to check the surfaces and a benchstone to make them true. The bottom and sides of the blade must be flat and square (the top of the blade is irrelevant). The cutting edge must be both razor sharp, straight and perpendicular to the sides. If not, the chisel will wander no matter how hard you try to keep it going straight down. Never hone a mortising chisel's edge on a buffing wheel because it will round the corners of the blade, right where it should be sharpest to cut the mortise walls.

Boggs begins a mortise by scoring his layout lines with bench chisels to keep splinters from running. He then removes an even 1/16 in. depth across the whole mortise. This creates a shoulder for the chisel to register against. The amazing thing is that a well-tuned mortising chisel is almost self-guiding after the first 1/16 in.

Chopping down as far as the chisel will go in 1/8-in. increments, Boggs travels from one end of the mortise to the other and back again. The chisel's strong bevel breaks out chips as it cuts. Finally, he pares the cheeks lightly with a wide bench chisel.

Carl Swensson also cuts his mortises with chisels, but he begins on the drill press and finishes by paring the cheeks and ends with bench chisels. This method is slightly faster than chopping entirely by hand, but the drill press does take time to set up. Swensson drills a number of non-intersecting holes with a twist drill 1/32 in. thinner than the mortise is wide. The remaining waste between the drill holes is easily tapped out. The ridges left by the drill help him guide

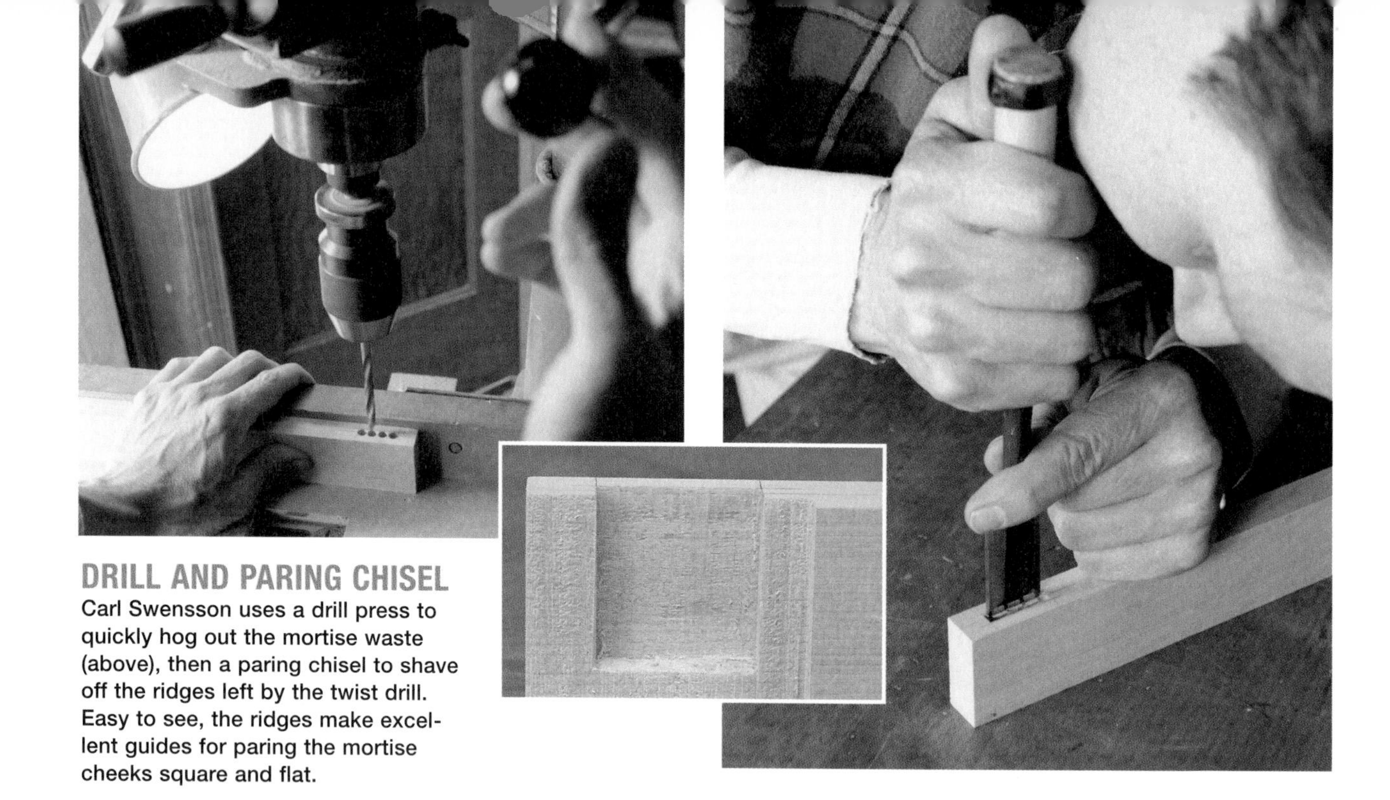

DRILL AND PARING CHISEL
Carl Swensson uses a drill press to quickly hog out the mortise waste (above), then a paring chisel to shave off the ridges left by the twist drill. Easy to see, the ridges make excellent guides for paring the mortise cheeks square and flat.

PLUNGE ROUTER AND JIG
The block-and-clamp jig gives the plunge router a stable base to cut quick and accurate mortises in small pieces.

the chisel when paring the mortise walls flat and square (see the photos above).

It's rewarding work, but cutting mortises by hand is slow and tedious. Chisels do have one important advantage over all other mortising tools, though, and that's their versatility. You can chop or pare a mortise of any size and shape anywhere on any piece of wood, which isn't always true of power tools.

Plunge routers cut fast, simple and precise mortises

The router is to the woodshop what the microwave is to the kitchen. The two are fast, efficient and versatile tools, but I always have a lurking suspicion they're bad for my health. The plunge router, however, is considered by many woodworkers to be one of the most useful tools for mortising.

Jeff Miller, a Chicago furniture maker and instructor, claims to have spent years sorting out the plunge router for mortising. It plunges accurately enough but doesn't move from side to side without help. It's also a top-heavy tool and needs a stable platform to ride on. The key to mortising small parts accurately with a plunge router, Miller found, was a simple, stable and versatile jig to guide it—just a large block with clamps attached (see the photos at left). The clamps hold the workpiece parallel to and even with the top of the block. The router

HOLLOW-CHISEL MORTISER

A drill press that cuts square holes? Faster than a plunge router, hollow-chisel mortisers don't produce much dust or noise, and they leave the mortise ends automatically squared up.

rides on the block, and its fence registers on the opposite edge of the block.

For work that doesn't fit in the jig, the plunge router makes the journey to the workpiece with ease. John McAlevey, a Maine woodworker, uses a plunge router with a fence or a template to cut mortises that would be difficult with any other tool except a chisel and mallet.

Routers are capable of very smooth cuts, but not without some technique. They're light-duty tools, and even the monstrous 3-hp plunge routers need to be handled carefully and used gently. The jig or platform must be rigid to keep the router from wobbling. A bit plunged too fast or without wood on all sides will cut gouges down the mortise cheeks. Probably the best technique is to remove the waste in horizontal increments of 1/32 in., moving the router slowly from end to end. An unstable jig or moving too fast will cause the bit to wander and cut steps in the mortise cheeks. An alternative is to plunge all the way down at either end of the mortise first. Then remove the waste in the middle. Both techniques will cut very clean mortises.

The price for the plunge router's speed is noise and dust

I frankly don't enjoy using routers. They screech loudly and produce volumes of fine dust. Safety goggles, hearing protectors and a good-quality dust mask help, but I dislike working in sensory deprivation gear, unable to hear the phone ring or see my work through the dust and scratches on my goggles. Nonetheless, I have to admit the speed of the router trumps its disadvantages. I watched McAlevey cut 14 mortises with a router in the time Carl Swensson cut three by hand.

Drilling square holes: hollow-chisel mortisers

A dedicated hollow-chisel mortiser is a peculiar and wonderful tool, thereby typically English. In a nutshell, it's a specialized drill press with a hollow and square chisel mounted around an auger bit. A quill feed plunges the spinning bit and hollow chisel into the workpiece, in effect drilling a hole and paring it square simultaneously. A series of these cuts produces a typical rectangular mortise.

Nial Barrett, a woodworker in upstate New York, owns a small one he's found to be a great mortising tool (see the left photo above). It's reasonably quiet, fast, makes chips not dust and cuts square holes. With a price of about $300, it might seem the perfect mortising tool. However, these advantages come with a few problems. The drill-press-style setup limits the size of the workpiece to about 6 in. high. The workpiece must be rectangular in cross section, or

Router milling jigs

A huge number of commercial jigs are available for the router, ranging from the simplest subbase to elaborate computer numerically controlled (CNC) rigs for the most ambitious hobbyist. Among them are a few interesting machines designed to turn the router into an all-purpose production milling tool. I'll call them router milling jigs for lack of a better term. They have names like Matchmaker, Mill-Right and Multirouter. I've had the pleasure to see the Multirouter in action cutting mortises.

The Multirouter isn't hard to describe: It's a router jig gone mad (see the photo at left). There are more levers, knobs, stops, setscrews, tables and fences than any healthy woodworker should be asked to handle. But talking with Peter Turner, a Maine woodworker, made the jig seem devilishly easy to use.

The machine houses a standard fixed-base router in a frame that raises and lowers on linear bearings. The workpiece is clamped on a platform that moves from side to side and in and out. The platform also tilts, making angled work possible. It can cut mortises, tenons, dovetails, box joints and anything in between.

The great advantage of the machine is its speed in cutting more than a few mortises. The initial setup takes a while, but the adjustment for each operation is minimal. Once running, it can cut mortises in 15 seconds and tenons in less than 10. If you blink, you miss the process. Piles of parts for large casework can be milled in minutes. And the quality of the cut is excellent, though no better than any well-jigged router.

The main limitation is the price of the machine. Turner admits that he was not able to afford a new one, which costs about $2,300. But a bit of luck threw an inexpensive used one his way. He bought the machine with a friend, reducing his investment to a fraction of the cost of a new one.

it will be difficult to clamp firmly to the machine. The smaller-sized bits (1/4 in. and 3/8 in.) heat up and burn or crack easily if misused. Finally, even when well-tuned, hollow chisels produce a moderately rough cut (see the inset photo on p. 135).

Barrett does not see the roughness as a problem, and he points out that he's never had a joint fail. I checked with another hollow chisel user, Tom Stangeland, a woodworker in Washington state, who agreed. It's a point well taken: After all, the perfect mortise is simply one that stays mated to its tenon. If the hollow-chisel mortiser cuts well enough, then it cuts perfectly well.

Industrial advantages: dedicated slot mortiser

Dedicated slot mortisers are industrial-grade machines with many advantages over the router and the commercial milling jigs. Slot mortisers have a horizontal drill-style head that slides forward and back, giving the cutter a plunging action. With all other methods, the piece stands still and the cutting tool moves. With slot mortisers, the workpiece is mounted on a sliding table that moves laterally to the head. This table can also be adjusted in height.

Slot mortisers cut very smooth, very accurate mortises even faster than a router (see the inset photo on the facing page). They are surprisingly quiet—quieter than hollow-chisel mortisers—and produce chips not dust. They're made to withstand years of abuse without a whimper. And they're capable of almost any size or type of mortise in a workpiece that will fit on their bed. Maybe this is why I found, without looking very hard, several one-man shop owners who

DEDICATED SLOT MORTISER

Chris Becksvoort cuts a slot for a mortise lock in a finished door. Unlike a router, a dedicated slot mortiser is quiet and a simple pleasure to use.

shelled out several thousand dollars to buy one. In the long term, the machines are simply worth it. Chris Becksvoort doesn't regret a penny he spent on his slot mortiser.

Besides using his slot mortiser for all the common mortises, Becksvoort uses his for end boring bedposts, lock holes in finished doors (see the photos above) and even cutting sliding dovetails in the bases of Shaker candle stands (a long story and a complex jig). Good technique is similar to routing a mortise, with one exception. To get the very best cut, Becksvoort raises the table a hair, recuts one face, then flips the workpiece and cuts the opposite face.

And the right tool is...

With the dedicated slot mortiser, I found a compromise of speed, noise and dust production that I really liked. The stumbling block, of course, is the price. Until I win the lottery, I'll putter along with my chisels, paying more attention to the sharpness of my tools and the fit of my joints. Chisels are hard to beat for their affordability and sheer pleasure of craftsmanship. Although this is my solution to making strong joints, I know much depends on personal preferences, so I don't necessarily recommend this route. I can make sacrifices of speed and ease to avoid noise and dust because I don't run a professional shop. If I did, I might get a plunge router or maybe a hollow-chisel mortiser. Unfortunately, each person I approached might have convinced me his tools and techniques were best, if I hadn't seen all the others.

THROUGH MORTISE-AND-TENON JOINERY

by Jim Richey

It's hard to hide mistakes in through mortise-and-tenon joints. Both the tenon and the mortise are there for anyone to see. I found it tough to get crisp, chip-free mortises that were uniform and had clean, square corners. Then, not too long ago, I came across a drawing of a simple bench made from 1x12 stock, like the one shown in the photo below. I wanted to build several of them, but the joint that held the bench together was a wedged through mortise and tenon. The bench was an incentive. I worked on my technique and experimented with prototypes until I could cut this joint quickly and accurately.

In a through mortise and tenon, the tenon goes all the way through its mating piece and shows on the other side. Wedges are often added to spread the end of the tenon and lock the joint together. It's a strong, attractive joint.

I can cut the mortises by hand, but when I'm faced with making a lot of them, I like to use a machine. In my shop, that means using either the drill press or the router. I prefer using the drill press because it's quiet and setup is fast and accurate. I can easily see the cut in progress.

When I'm boring holes for a through mortise, I try to minimize tearout where the bit exits the stock. If possible, I'll select the side where tearout will be the least noticeable; then I'll lay out and cut the mortise from the opposite side. If tearout is unacceptable on either side, then I'll use a router and a jig. For this bench, though, I decided I could live with some minor tearout on the back side because this area is fairly well-hidden.

Work carefully when joinery is exposed. The author cuts mortises first and then marks the tenons to reduce tearout on the face side.

Cut the mortises first

The usual approach is to build from the "inside out." That is, cut the tenons first,

Cutting through mortises

Step 1: *Back up workpiece with clean scrap; use a Forstner bit to remove most of the waste. Set depth stop so bit just cuts through stock.*

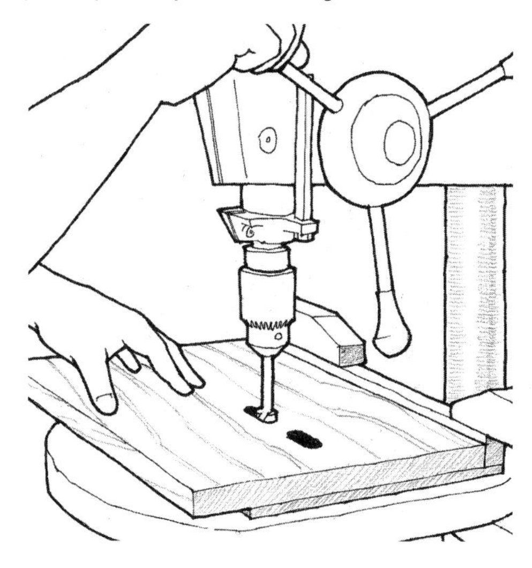

Step 2: *Guide chisel with a straight piece of scrap, and pare remaining waste from walls of the mortise.*

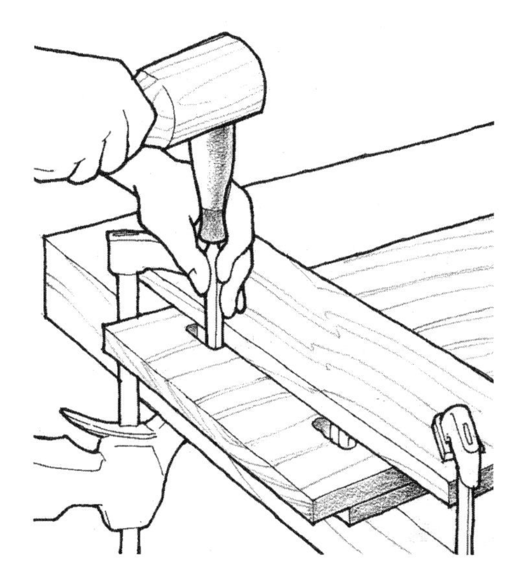

Step 3: *A shopmade saw used like a rough file squares the corners. Carefully work the saw into the corner.*

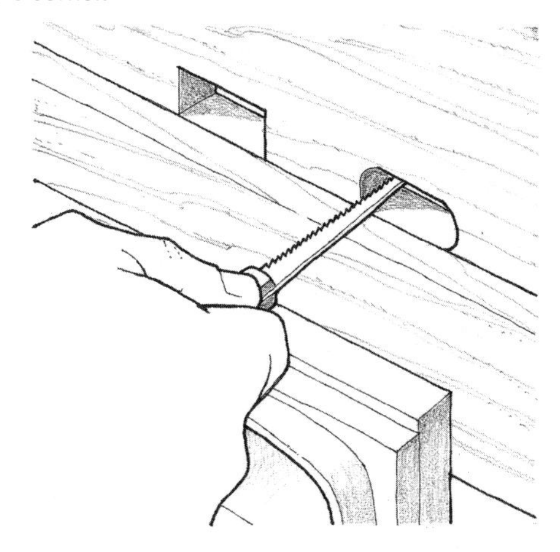

Making the tenons

Step 4: *Transfer mortise location to tenon stock. Use a knife or sharp pencil to mark out the tenon width.*

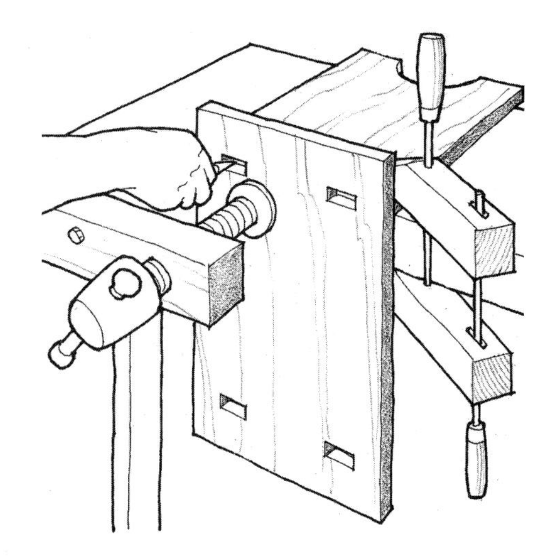

Step 5: *Extend tenon layout lines down the face of the stock with a square.*

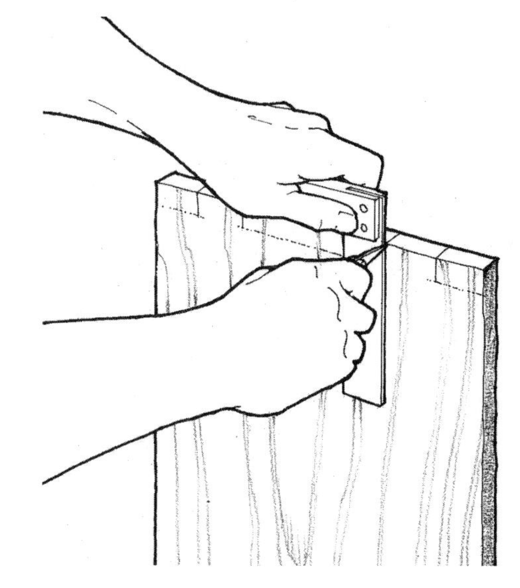

Step 6: *Mark the length of the tenons with a marking gauge or knife, and then cut to the line on a bandsaw.*

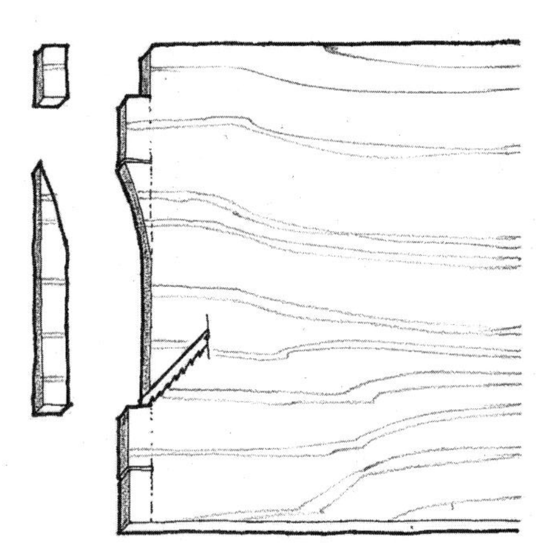

Wedge direction

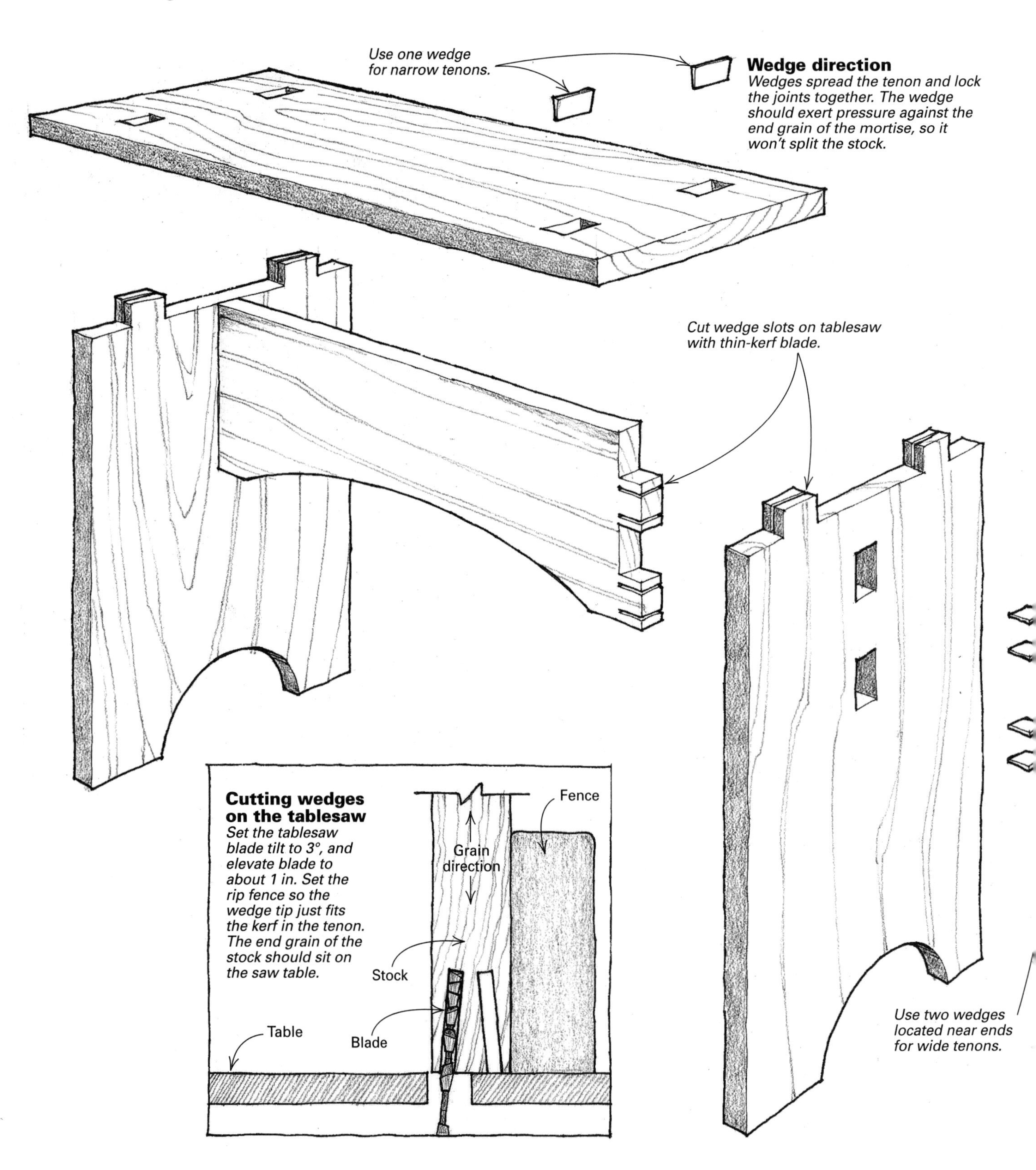
Use one wedge for narrow tenons.
Cut wedge slots on tablesaw with thin-kerf blade.
Grain direction
Fence
Stock
Blade
Table
Use two wedges located near ends for wide tenons.

Wedge direction
Wedges spread the tenon and lock the joints together. The wedge should exert pressure against the end grain of the mortise, so it won't split the stock.

Cutting wedges on the tablesaw
Set the tablesaw blade tilt to 3°, and elevate blade to about 1 in. Set the rip fence so the wedge tip just fits the kerf in the tenon. The end grain of the stock should sit on the saw table.

and then use the tenons as a template to mark the mortise locations. The problem is that you drill the mortises from the back, which virtually guarantees some tearout on the face of the piece, no matter how careful you are. I prefer the "outside-in" approach—cut the mortises first by drilling from the face side, and then mark the tenon locations from the mortises.

To do it this way, I set up my drill press with a Forstner bit and a fence to register the workpiece (see step 1 of the drawings on p. 139). Forstner bits are best for this operation because they make such clean cuts. Just remember that the bit diameter should be equal to or slightly smaller than the tenon thickness. You can always enlarge a mortise that's too narrow.

To minimize tearout, I set the drill-press depth stop so that the bit just goes through the workpiece or leaves a paper-thin layer of material on the bottom of the mortise. It's best to back up the workpiece with a clean piece of scrap.

I drill the first hole at one end of the mortise. Then I nibble away the remaining waste by sliding the work face down on the fence and drilling successive holes every 1/4 in. or so until I reach the other end. Toward the bottom of each hole, I slow down and use light pressure on the drill-press arm.

Shopmade saw cleans out corners

After roughing out the mortise on the drill press, I trim up those little waves on the sides and any remaining waste on the bottom of the mortise with a sharp chisel. This can be done by eye, but you'll get better results if you clamp a straight piece of 3/4-in.-thick scrap across the workpiece to serve as a guide (see step 2 on p. 139). You can use the guide to square up the corners by working toward the corner from one direction and then swinging the guide 90° and working in from the other. If you use a chisel to square up the corners, be sure to work in from both sides of the workpiece, or you'll tear out some really nasty chipping on the back side.

The way I square up the corners is to saw them out with a small, stiff saw (see step 3 on p. 139). I made my saw by filing teeth into the back of a carbon-steel paring knife. But you could also modify a wallboard saw by hammering the teeth flat, filing the sides of the blade to remove all set and then filing the teeth straight across like a rip saw.

I lay the saw against the wooden guide clamped to the workpiece and saw to the corner of the mortise. I use the saw as a rough file to square out the corners (there will be minor tearout on the back side).

Lay out and cut the tenons

I mark the tenon directly from the mortise using a small knife or pencil sharpened to a chisel point. Because the tenon thickness is the full stock thickness, only the width must be marked (see step 4 on p. 139). I use a square to extend this line down the face of the stock (see step 5 on p. 139) and a marking gauge to scribe the tenon length. The tenon should extend completely through the mortised stock with an extra 1/32 in. or so. This will be trimmed flush later, after the wedges have been glued in place.

I bandsaw the tenons using the cutting sequence shown in step 6 on p. 139. If all goes well, the tenons will fit snugly into the mortises on the first try. This never happens for me, though, so some fitting is usually required. Filing either the mortise or the tenon usually will take care of a too-tight fit. If you have some gaps, don't worry. Small shims cut from the same stock will hide them.

Cutting wedges and assembly

After fitting the mortises and tenons, I cut the wedge slots in the tenons. A thin-kerf cutoff blade in a tablesaw will produce a clean slot that's about the right width. Depending on the size of the tenon and its direction in the mating stock, I use one or two wedges to spread the tenon and create a tight joint.

Wedges should always exert pressure against the end grain of the mortise to keep the workpiece from splitting. I locate the slots as shown in the drawing on the facing page.

I saw the wedge material by ripping the stock, on edge, on the tablesaw, as shown in the inset drawing on the facing page. I angle the blade at 3°, and adjust the fence until the point of the wedge will just fit into the kerfs I've sawed into the tenons. I cut the wedge material to length, and now I'm ready to assemble the joint. After clamping everything together, I drive the wedges home with a bit of glue on the leading edge.

LOOSE-TENON JOINERY

by Ken Picou

Loose-tenon joinery is simple and quick. With precut tenon stock, joinery becomes a matter of router-mortising all the parts and then clamping up, with no difficult tenon cutting and no need to square the mortises or round the tenons.

The mortise and tenon is one of the strongest joints in a woodworker's repertoire. Traditionally favored, it remains today the joint of choice for chairs, doors and most other applications where strength is essential. Both the layout and cutting of mortise-and-tenon joints can be time-consuming, requiring much patience and concentration. Switching from the traditional mortise-and-tenon to a loose-tenon (or spline-tenon) system can save you time and effort and ensure consistent results, without sacrificing joint strength.

In loose tenoning, both pieces of stock to be joined are mortised and a section of precut tenon is inserted into the mortises (see the photo above). Once you have a quantity of tenon stock made up, it's a simple matter of cutting the tenons to length and plunge-routing the mortises. A perfect fit is ensured because the width of a router-cut mortise is consistent, and the tenon stock can be planed to the exact thickness desired. Also, because your tenon stock is already rounded, the joint can be entirely machine made with no need to square up mortises or round over tenons.

Tenons vs. dowels: which is stronger?

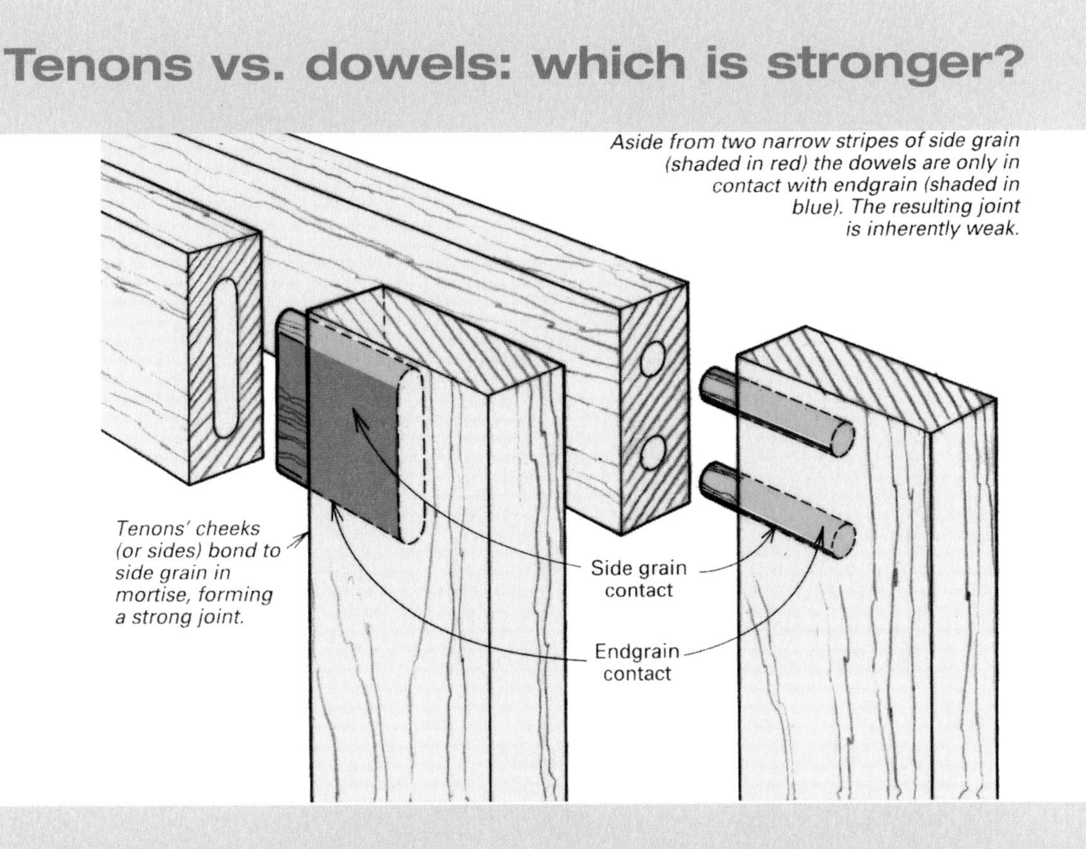

Aside from two narrow stripes of side grain (shaded in red) the dowels are only in contact with endgrain (shaded in blue). The resulting joint is inherently weak.
Tenons' cheeks (or sides) bond to side grain in mortise, forming a strong joint.
Side grain contact
Endgrain contact

Regardless of what the furniture industry would have you believe, a doweled joint isn't nearly as strong as a mortise-and-tenon or loose-tenon joint. There are two reasons for this.

First, endgrain to side-grain glue joints are always weak. The hole drilled to accept the dowel is almost all endgrain, except for two narrow stripes of side grain. There's very little surface that can be successfully glued to the dowel. But the sides of the mortise are all side grain and so are the cheeks of the tenon. These comparatively large surfaces may be glued with success. The resulting joint has the potential for a long life.

Second is the matter of what happens if the wood should shrink. The round dowel (and the hole) distorts into an oval shape. The most likely result is that one of those two narrow stripes of side-grain glue surface will pull loose. If the tenon shrinks a bit, it's less likely to become distorted, and more likely to stay glued.

Another advantage, in terms of layout, is that you cut rails to the exact length needed. There's no need to allow for the tenons and then work back to the length between shoulders. Because the rail is cut to final length in one pass, the shoulders of the joint are always crisp and never accidentally undercut.

Finally, an angled joint—even a compound-angled joint—is easier with a loose tenon. Instead of having to cut an angled tenon, you just rout an angled mortise in one of the pieces to be joined—something you can generally do by shimming the workpiece in your existing mortise fixture.

Mortising

There are many ways to cut a mortise, but I find the plunge router hard to beat for speed and accuracy. On one-of-a-kind items and small production runs, I freehand the mortise using my router with a fence. After chucking the appropriate bit in my plunge router and securing it tightly (especially with

Using standard-sized tenons has many advantages. Picou has accurate gauge blocks already made for 1-in., 1½-in. and 2-in. tenons—which cover most of his tenoning needs.

spiral bits because they have the bad habit of pulling themselves out of collets if not properly tightened), I locate center on a piece of scrap equal in width to the stock I'm mortising. Then I set the fence and depth adjustment on my router and mark the mortise using a shopbuilt gauge (see the photo above).

I like to rout the mortise to full depth with a series of closely spaced plunges, followed by a single cleanup pass. This eliminates the tendency of the bit to wander during a heavy cut and is much easier on the bearings of my router.

If the mortise is located near the end of the stock (which it almost always is), I find it helpful either to rout the mortise before cutting the stock to length or to butt the end of the stock against a piece of scrap of equal thickness to help support the router.

When mortising the end of a rail, I screw a piece of scrap at least 6 in. deep, perpendicular to the fence to ensure that the mortise is true. It's also a good idea to sandwich the end rail between pieces of scrap to help support the router. A simple fixture also can be made for this purpose.

Preparing tenon stock

One of the greatest timesaving features of the loose-tenon system is that you can make a quantity of tenon stock at one time, often from scrap. I maintain an inventory of the most-used widths—1 in., 1½ in. and 2 in.—to cover most of my joinery needs.

Before I start cutting and shaping tenon stock, I first make a long sample mortise with the bit I'll be using for the actual furniture mortises. I then run the scrap stock for the tenons through the planer until I get a perfect fit. I want the tenons to be snug, but not so tight that I can't push the joint together for a test dry-assemble and pull it back apart. I rip the stock to the required widths, then lower my tablesaw blade and cut a couple of channels about ⅛ in. deep on both sides of the tenon stock. These channels give the trapped glue somewhere to go during assembly and go a long way toward eliminating squeeze-out around the base of the joint. Finally, I use a roundover bit in my router table to shape the edges of the tenon stock to the same radius as the ends of the mortises (see the photo on the facing page).

After cutting the tenon stock to size and cutting channels for excess glue to escape, the author routs the edges of the tenon stock to match the shape of the mortises.

Assembly

I glue up loose-tenon joints in the same manner as mortise-and-tenon joints, but there are a few things I do that make the job go smoother. I cut the tenons at least 1/16 in. short to leave space at the bottom of the mortise for excess glue and to allow for any mistake I may have made in measuring the mortise depth.

When applying the glue, I put only enough on the tenon to seal the grain. I apply a much heavier coat to the inside of the mortise by squeezing the glue in and then spreading it with a small plumber's flux brush. This minimizes the amount of glue that gets scraped off of the side of the tenon and deposited on the surface of the project. Finally, if my stock is thick enough, I sometimes run a small (1/16 in. or less) chamfer around the mouth of the mortise to help contain squeeze-out.

I use this system of joinery in my line of side chairs, and I find it to be a great time-saver in both the production and the fitting of the joints.

SOURCES OF SUPPLY

CHUCKS AND END MILLS

MSC Industrial Supply
151 Sunnyside Blvd.
Plainview, NY 11803-1592
(800) 645-7160

MANDRELS

Mooradian Manufacturing Co.
1752 E. 23rd St.
Los Angeles, CA 90058
(213) 747-6348

Note: It's essential that the chuck be centered on the mandrel if the end mill is to run true. For a small charge, Mooradian Manufacturing Co. will thread the shaft end on a chuck you supply and make sure it runs true.

Shop-built mortiser speeds spline-tenon joinery

by Ross Day

Spline-tenon (or loose-tenon) joinery is an easy, fast and strong alternative to the mortise and tenon. The mortises for a spline-tenon joint can be cut many ways, including with a plunge router, but I've found that a dedicated horizontal-mortising machine is a very efficient and enjoyable way of cutting mortises. What's more, the machine is simple and inexpensive to build.

The machine

Horizontal mortisers are available commercially, but they're usually quite expensive. Some tablesaws, European ones in particular, use the saw's arbor as the mortising shaft and have smaller tables that move in two axes mounted just below the shaft. There are also jigs on the market that use a router with a spiral-cutting bit for cutting horizontal mortises. They work quickly but take time to set up because of all the stops, levers and hold-downs, so they are more suited to a production situation than to the custom furnituremaker.

My horizontal mortiser consists primarily of a 1,725 rpm motor; a pulley and V-belt system; a mandrel, shaft, chuck and end mill; and a height-adjustable, flat torsion-box table (a wooden grid with sheets of plywood glued top and bottom). The pulley and V-belt system steps the arbor speed up to 3,450 rpm. The end mill cuts cleanly, spews the chips from the mortise and leaves a flat-bottomed mortise, and the adjustable table allows me to position my mortise.

End mills

It's necessary to use end mills with my mortiser—not router bits. I use a single-end mill made of high-speed steel (HSS) with four flutes designed for bottom-centered cutting. These end mills are fairly cheap, and they last a long time. There are three standard lengths: regular, long and extra-long. I find the regular too short for some work, and the extra-long can flex and throw off your joinery. Long mills are best for most work. They come in increments of 1⁄16 in.; I have a range of them from 1⁄8 in. through 1⁄2 in. I generally make my tenons one-third (or slightly greater) of the stock thickness.

Mortising

I mortise freehand. It takes a little practice, but with end mills it's as safe as any cutting operation can be, and when running only a few pieces, it's as fast as setting stops and so forth. You may be nervous when first trying this method, but if you take it slow, you'll gain confidence. You still need to be conscious of safety, so keep your fingers far away from the end mill, and use a holding jig if you're mortising small parts or if your fingers would have to wander near the mill without one. Remember: This method only can be used with end mills. Never try this with a router bit because it would be extremely dangerous.

To use the horizontal mortiser, first chuck the end mill and set the table height, so the mill is centered in the piece receiving the tenon. (I always glue the spline tenon into one piece first and then treat that piece as though it were normally tenoned.) I begin the mortise, with the workpiece securely in hand or held by a jig, taking light passes, staying just inside the layout lines. Taking light cuts will keep the bit from flexing and creating a mortise that's not square to the stock. Also, it will keep the bit from grabbing. In most cases, the mill will have created a shoulder after a few passes against which the non-fluted portion of the cutter can bump up. Compressed air keeps chips from building up in the mortise, but if you don't want to rig up something similar or don't have compressed air in your shop, you should still clear the chips often.

I sometimes mark my depth of cut on the mortiser table with a pencil line or a piece of tape. I always cut about 1⁄16 in. deeper than my intended mortise depth on each piece to allow room for the glue in the bottom of the mortise. I keep my mortise sides straight—with no taper—and square at the bottom. This is fairly easy to do by watching the workpiece to keep it perpendicular to the bit. After all my mortises are cut, I break the edges of the mortises with a file. This slight shoulder will help ensure that the joint remains clean at the base and not bind when you begin glue-up.

Special applications

One major advantage of spline-tenon joinery over conventional mortise-and-tenon joinery is that it makes angled and curved work much simpler. Instead of

Shopmade horizontal mortiser

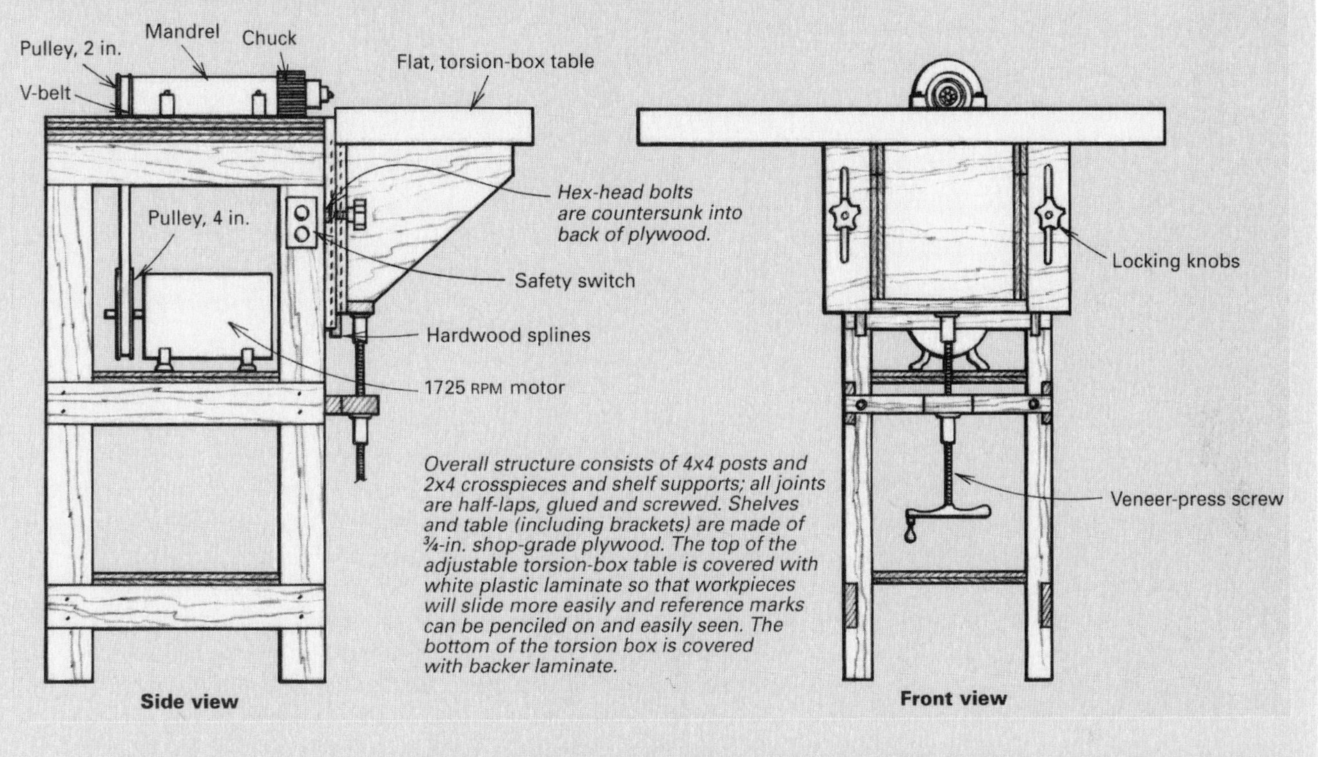
Shopmade horizontal mortiser
A high-quality horizontal mortiser can be built inexpensively and without much difficulty. The critical elements are a precisely adjustable, flat table (hence torsion-box construction and veneer-press screw) and a mandrel and arbor that run true. Torsion box must be parallel to the bit, front to back.
Pulley, 2 in.
Mandrel
Chuck
V-belt
Flat, torsion-box table
Pulley, 4 in.
Hex-head bolts are countersunk into back of plywood.
Safety switch
Hardwood splines
1725 RPM motor
Overall structure consists of 4x4 posts and 2x4 crosspieces and shelf supports; all joints are half-laps, glued and screwed. Shelves and table (including brackets) are made of ¾-in. shop-grade plywood. The top of the adjustable torsion-box table is covered with white plastic laminate so that workpieces will slide more easily and reference marks can be penciled on and easily seen. The bottom of the torsion box is covered with backer laminate.
Side view
Locking knobs
Veneer-press screw
Front view

having to devise torturously complex jigs and fixtures to cut the tenons, I just use a simple jig consisting of an angled block or two (with sandpaper glued on to prevent the workpiece from slipping) and maybe a hold-down clamp (see the photo at right).

You also can use your horizontal mortiser as a lathe to turn small things such as door and drawer pulls. Standard chucks usually have three jaws and won't accept square stock, but a two-jawed chuck will. I just drop the table and clamp a piece of wood to it as a tool rest.

Even curved work is relatively simple to mortise with the author's horizontal mortising machine. A couple of blocks and a toggle clamp hold the workpiece in place, and the mill does the work. This same setup, used with wedges, could be used to cut an angled mortise. By inserting a length of regular precut tenon stock, you'd then have an angled tenon without the hassle of sawing one.

DESIGNING THE WEDGED MORTISE AND TENON

by Carl Swensson

A door can be slammed only so many times before the tenons pull out of their mortises. Even the sturdiest chair will not survive an overweight, hyperactive teen who tilts back on it. These are extremes. Most furniture that falls apart has not been abused. When a chair squeaks or a table wobbles, it's usually just bad joinery design.

Good design buys time against the use and abuse that all furniture will bear. Unless you plan to make all your furniture exclusively for your grandmother, you must choose and design furniture joints to withstand years of stress. Many antique stores offer living proof that well-made furniture can outlive its maker. Look closely at an old chair or door, and you may find the distinctive bands of wedges still holding through tenons in place.

The wedged mortise and tenon is a simply made and very effective woodworking joint (see the photo on the facing page and the photo on p. 150). Two kerfs cut in the tenon accept wedges to make the tenon dovetail-shaped. To accommodate the wedged tenon, most of the mortise wall is relieved (or cut) at the same angle as the tenon wedge. This joint is particularly good at resisting racking, a common stress on table and chair legs. And as a visible and beautiful joint, it will add value beyond its structural contribution.

There are no simple guidelines to cutting a successful wedged mortise and tenon. There are no best angles or right lengths for the wedges nor any proper thicknesses for the tenon strips. Designing the wedged mortise and tenon must take into account not only the many stresses the finished piece must withstand but also the particular characteristics of the wood, even of the particular boards you use. The design process must leave the drawing table and become part of the construction process.

The stresses that break joints

There are two types of forces that work joints loose: internal, from the seasonal expansion and contraction of the wood, and external, from human use. Unless you live in an environment with perfectly controlled humidity, variations in the wood's moisture content are inevitable. Because of the cross-grain construction in joints like a mortise and tenon, these seasonal changes are a long-term threat to the joint's integrity. Quartersawn lumber is more stable than flatsawn and should be used for all joints. This grain orientation ensures that the wood will move the least along its greatest width. It also minimizes the wood's movement against itself.

Normal use will put several forces on a joint: compression and tension, shearing,

The author taps in wedges that won't come out. Careful design will yield a joint that is nearly impossible to pull apart.

The wedged mortise and tenon

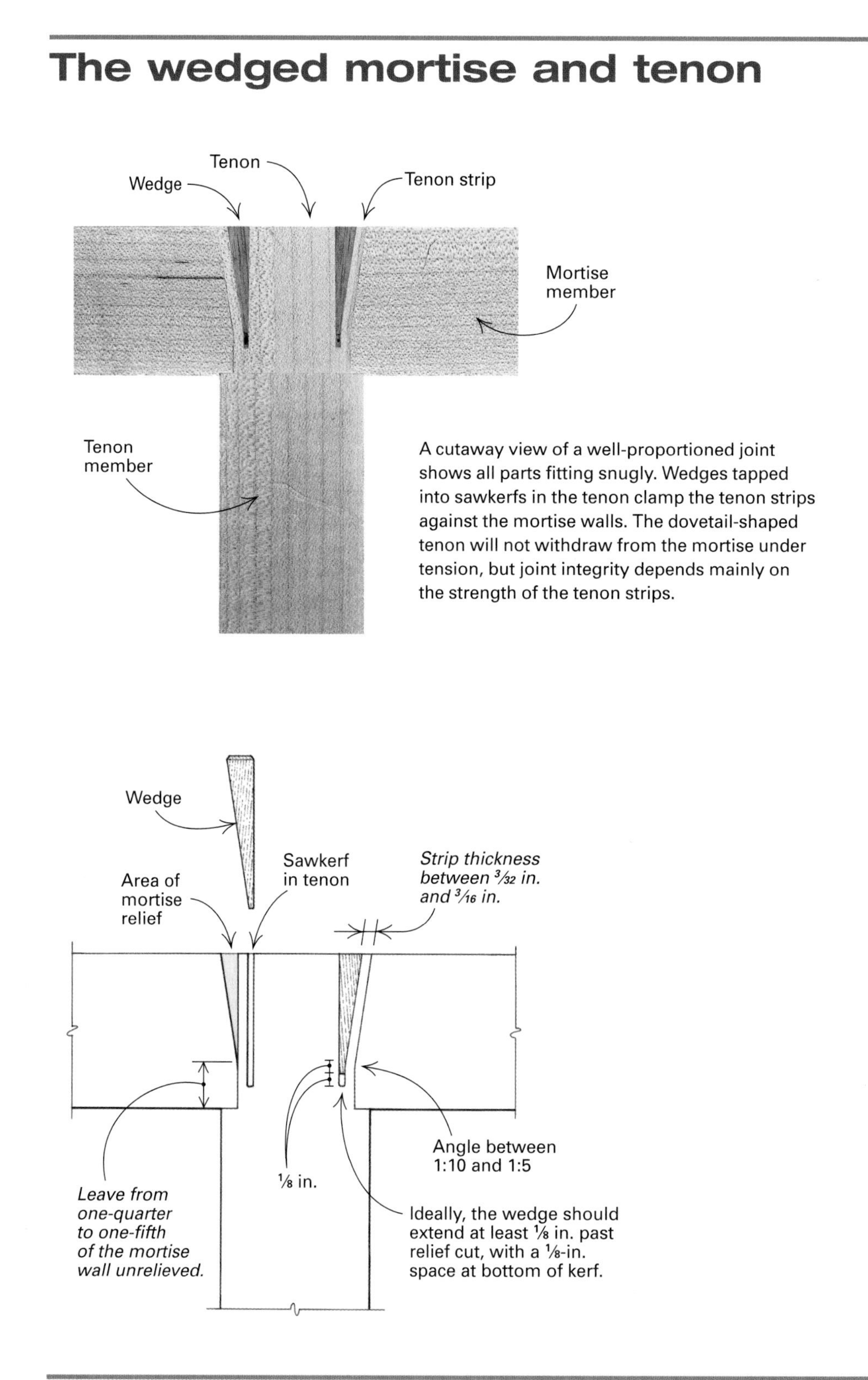

A cutaway view of a well-proportioned joint shows all parts fitting snugly. Wedges tapped into sawkerfs in the tenon clamp the tenon strips against the mortise walls. The dovetail-shaped tenon will not withdraw from the mortise under tension, but joint integrity depends mainly on the strength of the tenon strips.

racking and twisting. The connection between the internal faces of the mortise and tenon does most of the work in keeping the joint together, though the tenon's shoulders help to prevent compression.

Twisting forces are often overlooked in joint design. Kicking a table leg or leaning back on the rear legs of a chair can create very strong twisting forces on a joint. A mortise near the end of a board is particularly vulnerable to this stress because of the short grain. It is better to keep the mortise at least twice the width of the tenon away from the end of the board. These forces will be less likely to cause joint failure.

Wedging the tenon against tension

A simple glued mortise-and-tenon joint with shoulders will resist compression, shearing, racking and twisting forces quite well. But this joint does not respond well to tension. In time, when the glue crumbles away, the tenon will come out almost as easily as it went in.

Wedging the tenon creates an internal dovetail shape that is extremely resistant to tension and does not compromise the joint's strength in any other way (see the drawing on the facing page). Under tension, the mortise walls exert an even clamping pressure along the side of the tenon. This pressure holds the wedges firmly inside the tenon and does not squeeze them out of their kerfs. As long as the tenon keeps its dovetail shape, it will not withdraw under either tension pressure.

The key to the strength of this joint is the integrity of the thin strip of tenon between the wedge and the mortise wall. The joint is nearly impossible to break under tension if the strip remains intact. However, if both strips break, the tenon will not resist withdrawal any more than a plain tenon would. The variables affecting the soundness of the tenon strip are its thickness, the mortise-relief angle, the length of the mortise-relief angle and the length of the kerf in the tenon. Each of these must be determined in turn. As the examples on this and the facing page show, it's easy to misjudge one of these factors.

Templates to test thicknesses and angles

Determining the tenon-strip thickness and mortise-relief angle as a working unit depends largely on the properties of the wood you are using. Hard maple will often work in a wide range of thicknesses and angles. More brittle woods, such as cherry, may require a very low angle ratio and a thin strip to work. Even variations from board to board make it necessary to test the angle and strip for each project.

Make a series of templates with slope ratios from 1:10 to 1:5 to simulate the mortise-relief angles in the actual joint (see the top photo on p. 152). File or chisel a slight round at the angle, both on the test jig and in the actual joint. This slightly reduces the chances that the tenon strip will kink, crack or break when it bends around the angle. Next make five to six strips of various thicknesses from the same wood as the tenon, preferably from the same board. I recommend making them not less than 3/32 in. and not more than 3/16 in.

Clamp the strips to the different templates until you find the combination of greatest thickness and highest angle that will not break the strip. A higher angle gives better withdrawal resistance, but requires a thinner and more vulnerable strip (see the center photo on p. 152). A lower angle can accommodate a thicker strip, which is less likely to break, but will not offer as much resistance to tension. However, really thick strips do not bend as easily and may crack if bent too far (see the bottom photo on p. 152). As a rule, I start testing with a strip 3/32 in. thick and a slope ratio of 1:7 and increase either the ratio or the thickness or both from there to find the best balance.

Strip thickness

Test tenon strip material with a template.
A few outside fibers have failed on this test strip, but it is basically sound.

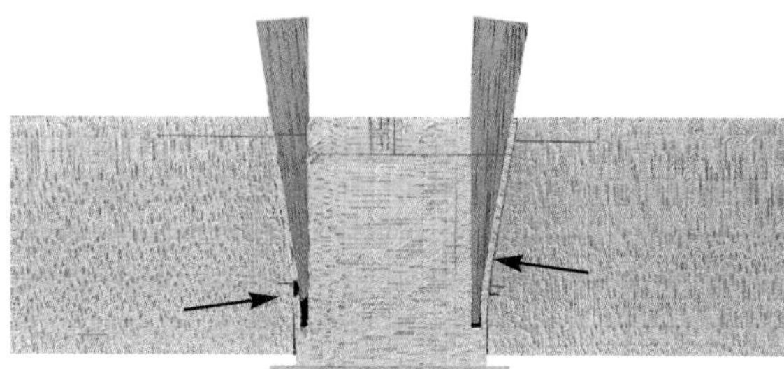

Strips are too thin.
A little tension on the joint has broken one of the strips and allowed the tenon to withdraw. The layout line at the top shows how the parts have moved.

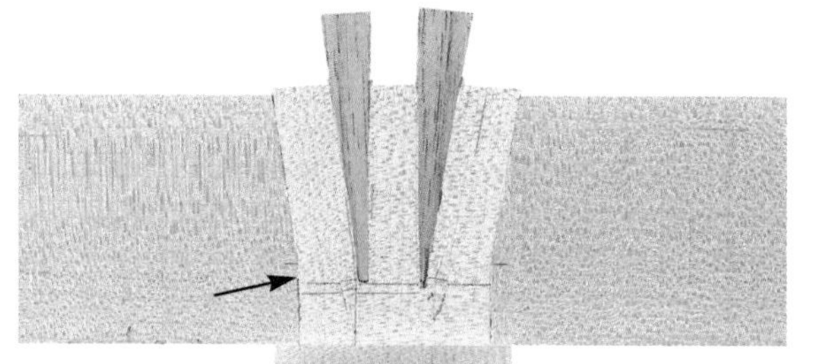

Strips are too thick.
Even though they were tough, the tenon strips were asked to deflect too much and have cracked substantially at the base. Note how the layout lines at the bottom have moved.

Proportions for mortise wall relief and tenon kerf

You now know the angle to relieve the mortise wall and to cut the wedges. The next step is to determine how much of the mortise wall you should relieve. This will, in turn, determine the length of the wedge and the depth of the kerf in the tenon.

The deeper the mortise-relief cut is, the more surface area you create on the mortise wall to resist tension. However, you must leave some room at the base of the tenon so the wedge can be driven past the end of the mortise relief. Leaving from one-quarter to one-fifth of the mortise wall unrelieved works well.

The sawkerf in the tenon should extend beyond the mortise-relief cut, but not by much. This allows the wedge to be driven farther than the end of the mortise relief without bottoming out in the kerf. That ensures the tenon strip will be pressed snugly against the entire relieved mortise wall. Driving the wedge beyond the relief cut also allows the wedge to support the weakest side of the strip where it bends. If the kerf is too shallow, the wedge will bottom out, and the strip cannot be compressed against the mortise wall (see the top photo on the facing page). Trying to insert the wedges farther during assembly may cause a split in the tenon.

If the tenon has grain runout, splits that develop during assembly may follow the grain out of the wood, causing complete joint failure (see the center photo on the facing page). The first defense against such splits is selecting straight-grained wood for the tenon member. Deep sawkerfs and the snug fit of all the parts in the joint also will help prevent this problem.

Another way to keep a strip from splitting is to drill a 1/8-in.-dia. relief hole at the bottom of the kerf. It will distribute the stress at this point. The hole also thins the strip where it bends, helping it to take the bend without cracking. This step should not be necessary if the grain is straight and the relief angle and strip thickness are well balanced.

The wedges for final assembly

Perhaps, without realizing it, you have already designed the wedges. The angle of the wedges is the same as the slope ratio of the mortise relief. The thickness of the wedges at their tip should be a little less than the tenon kerf. The wedges should be at least 3/8 in. longer than the kerf is deep to make it easier to tap in during assembly.

Final assembly, however, is not the time to relax. Much of the joint's integrity depends on how well the parts come together. If you hammer the wedges in unevenly, the joint will rack to one side (see the bottom photo at right). Keep the joint square and the tenon firmly in the mortise as you tap in the wedges.

Yellow wood glue, because it sets fast, can make this joint even trickier to assemble. It sets so fast you won't have much time to make sure all the parts are aligned properly. For this joint, I use a glue with a slower set up time. If you have avoided design mistakes, the result should be a very tight, strong joint and an ornament to your work.

Problem joints

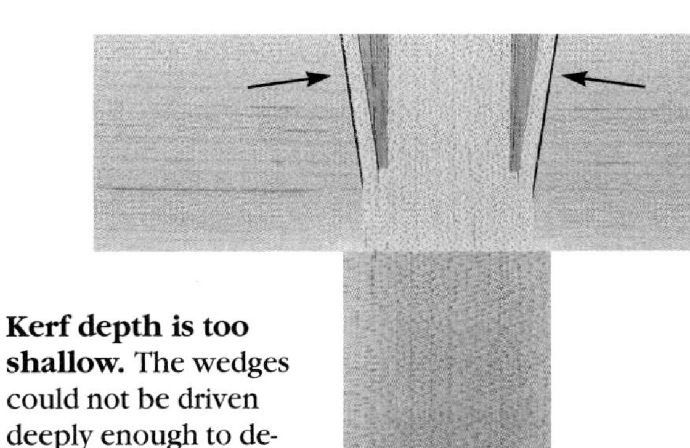

Kerf depth is too shallow. The wedges could not be driven deeply enough to deflect the tenon strips against the mortise wall. Cracks developed at the bottom of the kerf.

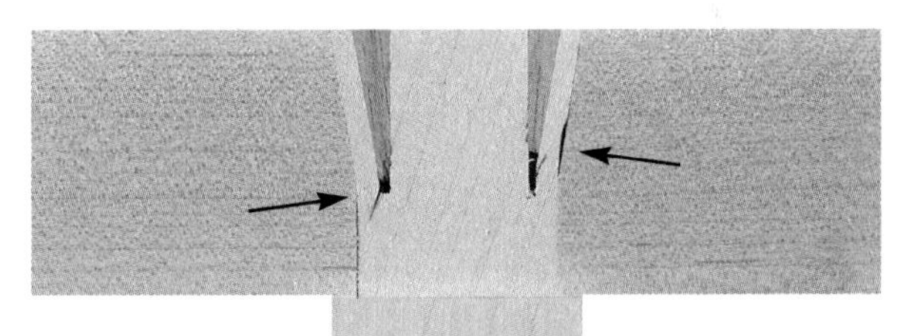

Grain runout causes strip failure. Both tenon strips have cracked along the grain during assembly and will not resist tension.

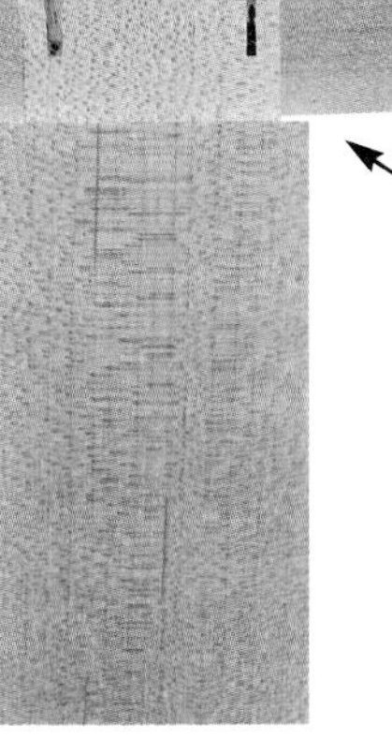

Close, but no cigar. The proportions of this joint are promising, but uneven insertion of the wedges caused permanent racking during assembly.

MACHINE DOVETAILS BY EYE

by Jeff Miller

I like cutting dovetails by hand, but the nature of my business doesn't let me stay in practice. And I admit, I tend to lose a little accuracy when I'm out of shape. I've tried router jigs, but I've never found one I like. I find them fussy to set up, and to my eye, router-cut dovetails never look as good as those cut by hand.

Some years ago, a friend showed me a way to use my tablesaw and bandsaw to make dovetails that look hand-cut. The jig is surprisingly fast to set up, and it lets me cut dovetails of any size and spacing. It's not a production jig, but it's fast enough to use in a professional shop, and it works well in limited production situations.

Disadvantages? The quality of the fit will depend on your ability to cut accurately to a line. But I like that; I find it far more satisfying than using a dovetail jig. In some ways, this is still a hand-cut procedure (I can hear the traditionalists howl). The finished joint certainly looks as if it's been hand-cut (see the bottom photo at left).

A simple jig cuts the pins

The key to this method is a tablesaw jig for cutting the pins. Two fences angled to a narrow V-shape are mounted on a sled that runs in the miter-gauge slots of my tablesaw. I make the pins in two passes over a 1/2-in. dado cutter (see the top photo on p. 156). With the first pass, I cut one side of each pin. Then I rotate the sled and cut the other side. I use the pins to mark the tails before cutting them on the bandsaw.

Tablesaw jig for cutting dovetails

This simple sled is the key to efficient machine dovetails that look hand-cut. Pins are cut in two passes on the jig, one on each side. The author cuts the tails on the bandsaw.

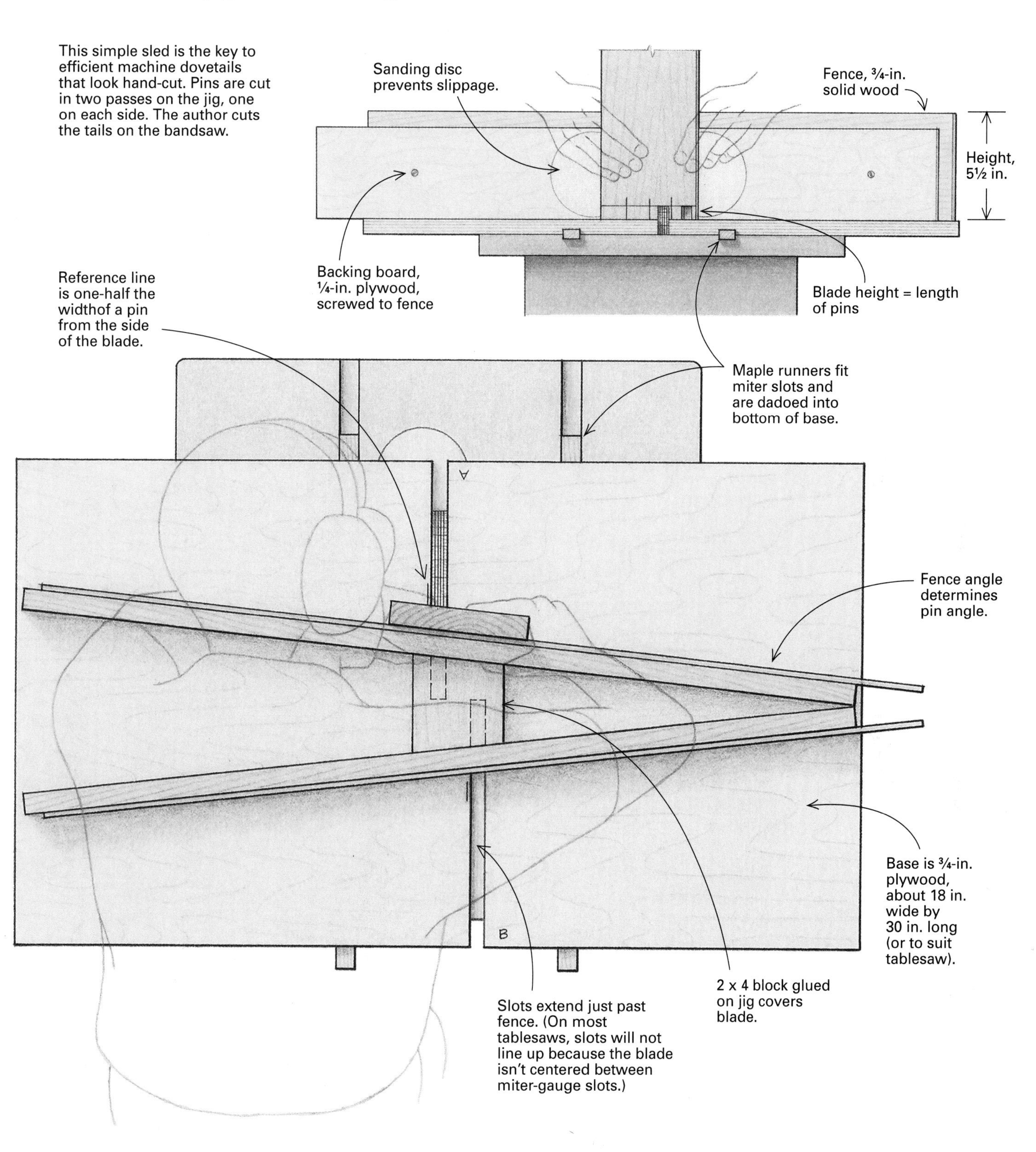
Sanding disc prevents slippage.
Fence, ¾-in. solid wood
Height, 5½ in.
Backing board, ¼-in. plywood, screwed to fence
Blade height = length of pins
Reference line is one-half the widthof a pin from the side of the blade.
Maple runners fit miter slots and are dadoed into bottom of base.
A
Fence angle determines pin angle.
Base is ¾-in. plywood, about 18 in. wide by 30 in. long (or to suit tablesaw).
B
2 x 4 block glued on jig covers blade.
Slots extend just past fence. (On most tablesaws, slots will not line up because the blade isn't centered between miter-gauge slots.)

Cutting wood with the jigs

Make the pins in two passes over a dado cutter. The first pass cuts one side of each pin. The author aligns the centers of the pins with the pencil mark on one side of the sled.

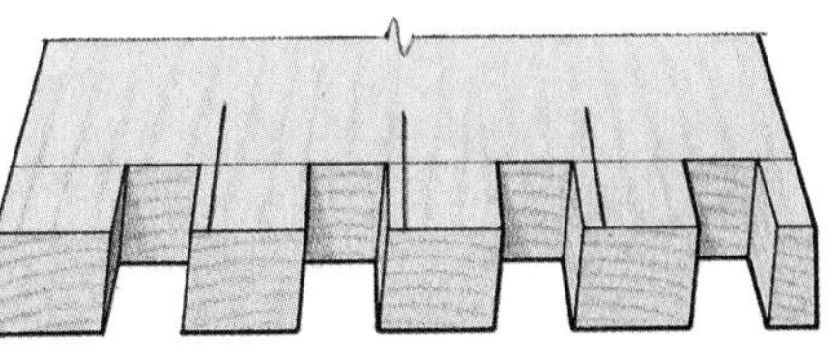

The second set of cuts finishes the pins. After cutting one side of each pin, rotate the jig 180°, and cut the angle on the other side. Align the centers of the pins with the reference mark on the other side of the sled.

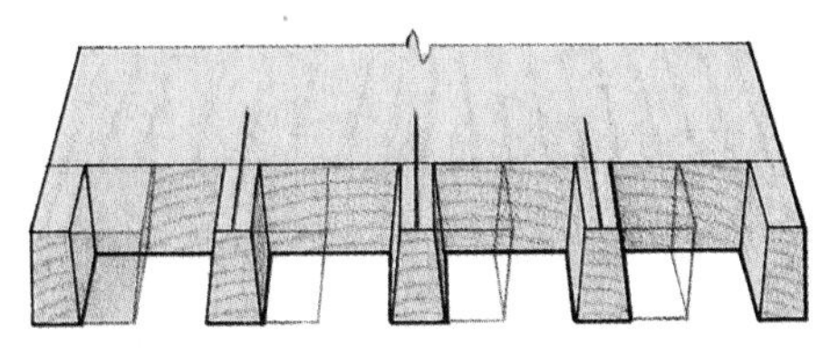

The base of the sled is made of 3/4-in. plywood, 18 in. wide by 30 in. long (see the drawing on p. 155). The runners for the miter slots are glued into shallow dadoes on the bottom of the sled. To ensure the dadoes are parallel to one another, I run the same edge against the fence while cutting each dado.

The fences are set at 6° off a line drawn perpendicular to the blade, which gives a pin angle of 6°. This is a 9:1 ratio. I picked that angle simply because I think it looks best. I recently discovered the jig I had been using for years had one fence set at 6°, the other at 8°. I never noticed until I measured it for drawings. The lesson: Don't worry too much about the angle.

The fences are made of 3/4-in. solid wood, 5 3/4 in. high and fastened from below with screws. Because the blade cuts through the sled between the fences, I glued a block into the space as a guard. After cutting a few dadoes of different widths and heights, the fence was chewed up in the area of the blade. So I mounted 1/4-in. plywood backing boards on the fences to prevent tearout. I move the backing boards each time I change the dovetail profile and replace them when necessary. Sanding discs glued to the backing boards keep the pin board from slipping. Just make sure that the discs are not in the path of the cut or sparks will fly.

Jig setup is based on pin width

Laying out the dovetails is simple. As I do with hand-cut dovetails, I use a marking knife to scribe a line on both faces of the board to locate the bottoms of the pins and to help prevent tearout on the waste portion. I set the dado cutter so the depth of cut just touches the scribed line. On the outside face of the board, I mark the centerlines of the pins. I space them evenly, but you can space them any way you like. The angle of the cut is set by the angle of the fences; the width of the pins is up to you.

I made a pencil line on each side of the jig (see the drawing on p. 155) to determine pin width. The distance from the pencil lines to the cutter is half the width of the pins. When cutting, I align each layout line on the pin board with the pencil line on the jig.

The first round of tablesaw cuts puts the angle on one side of the pins. I line up the reference marks, as shown in the top photo at left, run the sled through the blade and repeat at the next mark. I like the half-pins at each end to be close to full width, so I align the edge of the board with an imaginary line that's twice as far from the blade as the reference mark. When I've cut one side of all the pins, I turn off the saw and rotate the jig 180° to cut the other side of the pins at the opposing angle (see the bottom photo on the facing page). If there's any waste left between the two cuts, I scoot the board over and make another pass.

A bandsaw cuts the tails

The first step in laying out the tails is to scribe a baseline across both sides of the end of the board with a marking knife. Then the tails are scribed with a sharp awl. I do the marking on my jointer because it has a handy right-angle surface (see the top photo on p. 158). The outside face of the tailboard goes down on the jointer table, and the pin board stands on it with the marked face (outside) against the fence. Before I go any further, I label all the mating pieces to avoid confusion.

Cutting the tails is nothing more than cutting to the line on the bandsaw. And this is the crucial task here. In the woodworking classes I teach, many beginners have trouble cutting to a line. There are three things that go into cutting to a line accurately: sharpening the perception of the line, sharpening the perception of the cut and practicing to get the two to meet.

Consider the line first. I like a scribed line because it makes a precise mark, as long as the scribe is made with consistent pressure. A scribed line is actually a little canyon cut into the wood. To make this clearer, I have students trace the scribed lines with a dull pencil (see the top drawing on p. 158). The result is two pencil lines, one on either side of the impression left by the scribe. Cut

Tails on the bandsaw

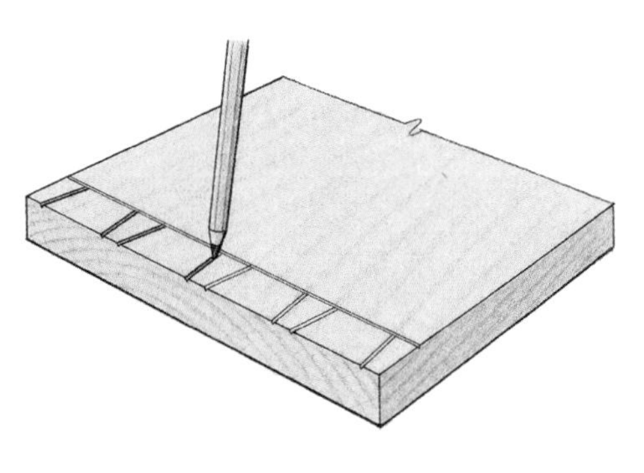

An awl followed by a dull pencil makes lines for the tail cut.

Use an awl to mark the tails from the pins. The author supports the pieces on his jointer as he scribes the marks for the tail cuts.

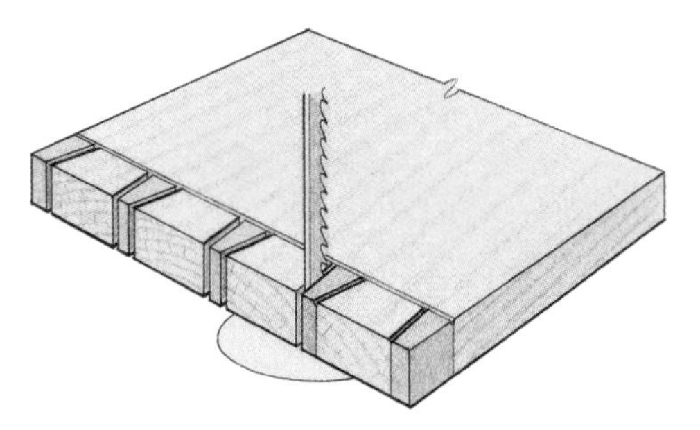

A bandsaw completes the job. Cut to the lines on each side of the tails, and then nibble away the waste. Take care not to cut beyond the scribed baseline.

The author gets an almost perfect mallet-tight fit right off the bandsaw. With a little practice, anyone can have the same results.

away one of the pencil lines, and you've cut to the line.

I cut sides of the tails to the line and use the blade to nibble away the rest of the waste, being careful to stop at the scribed baseline (see the bottom photo on the facing page). I rotate the piece 90° and cut along the scribed line for the bottoms of the half-pins at the ends. Slightly ragged bottoms on the tail can be cleaned up with a chisel. After some practice, you can dispense with this step.

The moment of truth

The first few times I cut dovetails this way, the fit was a little tight, and I had to pare the high spots with a chisel. If one section is loose, a small wedge glued in place can make an almost invisible repair. Sanding dust mixed with finish can make a good joint look almost perfect.

HOUSED SLIDING DOVETAILS

by Tony Konovaloff

Key size is crucial

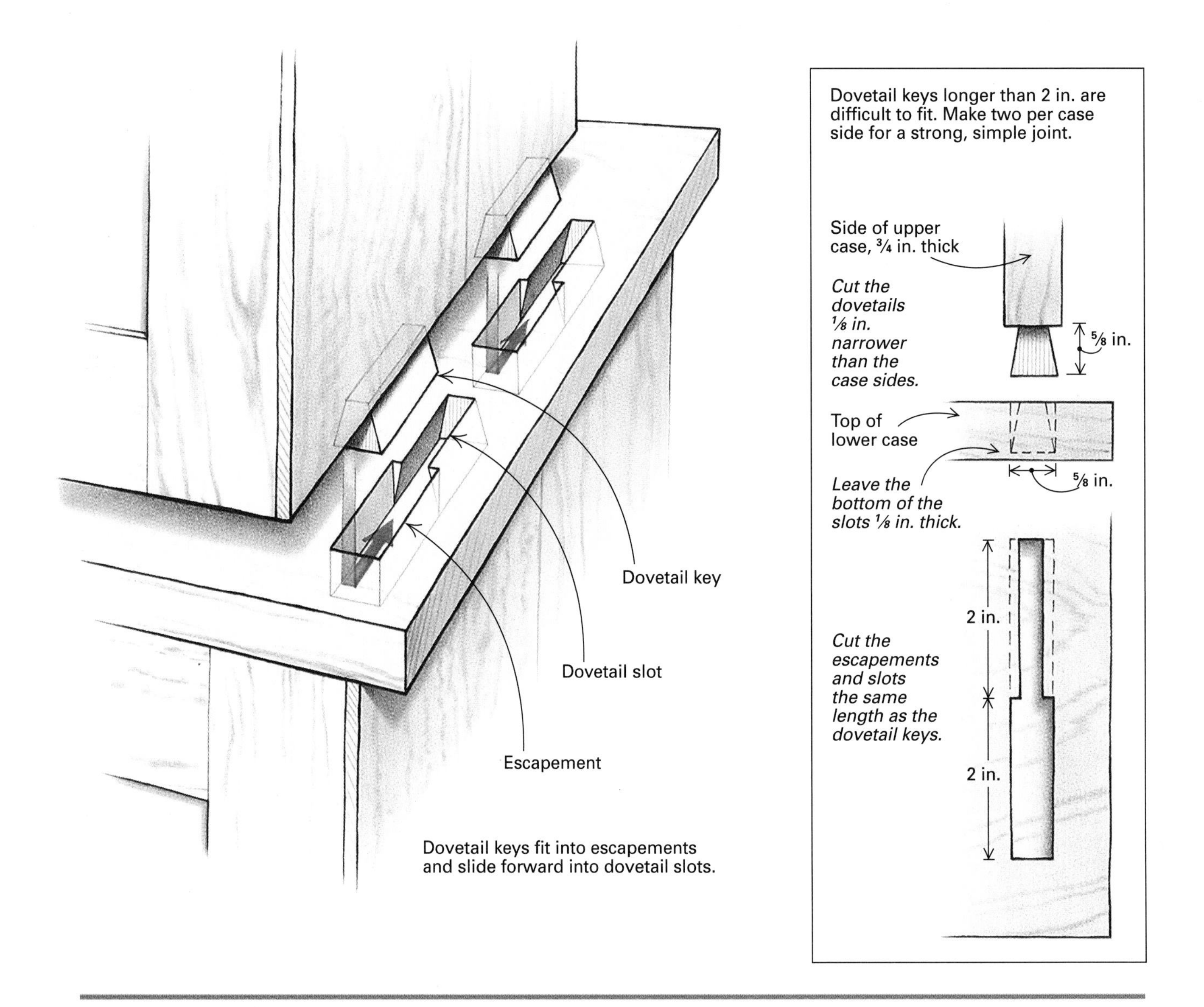

Dovetail key
Dovetail slot
Escapement
Dovetail keys longer than 2 in. are difficult to fit. Make two per case side for a strong, simple joint.
Side of upper case, ¾ in. thick
Cut the dovetails ⅛ in. narrower than the case sides.
⅝ in.
Top of lower case
Leave the bottom of the slots ⅛ in. thick.
⅝ in.
2 in.
2 in.
Cut the escapements and slots the same length as the dovetail keys.

Dovetail keys fit into escapements and slide forward into dovetail slots.

My shop is quite small. There is just enough room for a bench, a tool box and a place to stand and work. I like it that way. My tools are always within easy reach and are hard to misplace. And the shop doesn't require much heat in the winter. But there's one problem: Large cabinets don't leave much room to work. Even desks take up all the available floor space. And to work on large china cabinets, I have to take down the ceiling lights.

Having a small shop doesn't keep me from making large cabinets. However, I do make a lot of knockdown joints to keep big pieces of furniture manageable.

There are endless ways to connect large case pieces, but most knockdown designs I've seen are lacking in one way or another.

After cutting a dovetail the full width of the upper case side, cope out the dovetail keys (above), and then clean up the shoulder with a chisel (below). Pare carefully: The line of the finished joint depends on the flatness of the shoulder.

Large cases joined securely

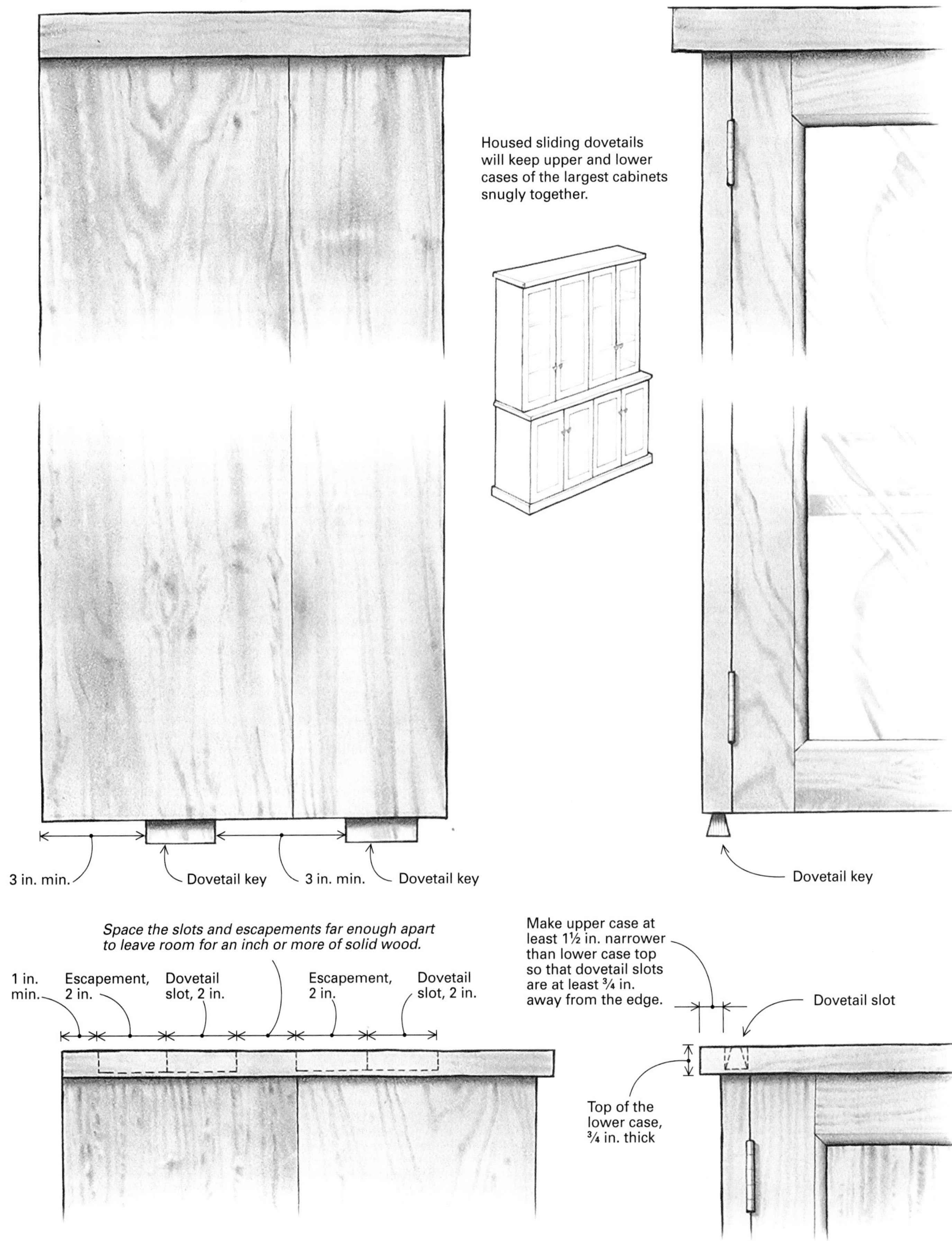

Housed sliding dovetails will keep upper and lower cases of the largest cabinets snugly together.
3 in. min.
Dovetail key
3 in. min.
Dovetail key
Dovetail key
Space the slots and escapements far enough apart to leave room for an inch or more of solid wood.
1 in. min.
Escapement, 2 in.
Dovetail slot, 2 in.
Escapement, 2 in.
Dovetail slot, 2 in.
Make upper case at least 1½ in. narrower than lower case top so that dovetail slots are at least ¾ in. away from the edge.
Dovetail slot
Top of the lower case, ¾ in. thick

Mark the dovetail slots first. The locations for dovetail slots in the top of the lower cabinet are marked directly from the dovetailed keys.

Lay out the escapements using the dovetail slots as a guide. When you cut the joints, remember that the escapements are at the back of the cabinet.

Some are weak; others require clunky or expensive hardware. Sliding dovetails are an option, but they show at the back of the case, and they tend to bind.

To solve some of these problems, I devised a strong connection using housed sliding dovetails (see the drawing on p. 160). I cut small dovetail keys on the bottom of the sides of the upper case and dovetail slots with escapements on the top of the lower case. The keys fit down into the escapements and then slide forward into the slots, locking the cases together and eliminating the need for hardware. And nothing shows in the front or back when the cases are assembled.

The joint holds upper and lower cases tightly together but knocks down smoothly and easily without binding. It doesn't require special tools to make or very much time. But to make sure that you understand what's going on with the joinery, it's a good idea to work up a practice piece.

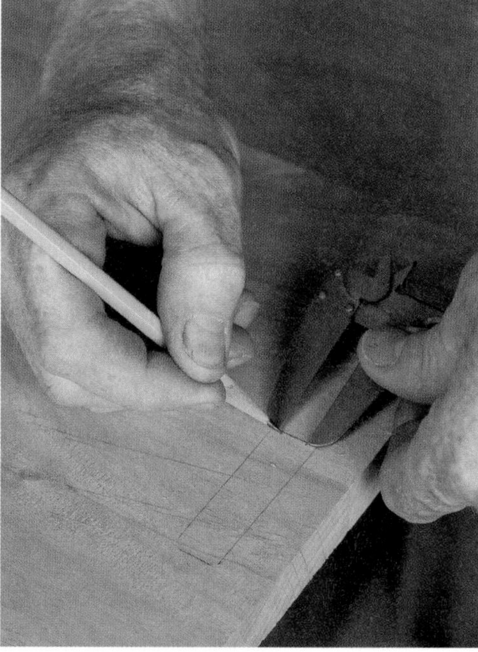

Don't measure, transfer. The tops of the dovetails and slots should be the same width. Find the width with a vernier caliper (left), and then mark it in the middle of the slot (above).

Cut the dovetails first

Before gluing up the top half of the case, I cut the dovetails on the bottoms of the case sides. There are many ways to do this. I use a dovetail plane, but a router and jig would work as well.

Next I cut out sections of the dovetails to leave two keys, each about 2 in. long (see the photos on p. 161). The proportions of the keys depend on the thickness of the stock you use. Generally, I cut them 1/8 in. narrower than the case sides and 1/8 in. shorter than the thickness of the top of the bottom case (see the drawing detail on p. 160). Their placement is important. They must be far enough apart so they don't interfere with each other. If the dovetails are 2 in. long, the escapements and slots must each be 2 in. long. To maintain strength, each slot and escapement pair should be at least an inch apart. This means that 2-in. dovetails must be spaced at least 3 in. apart, and the front of the rear dovetail must be 3 in. from the back of the upper case.

After I cut the keys to length, I complete the upper case. It's important to remember that the shoulders of the dovetail keys rest on the top of the lower case. Only the keys should extend below the line of the shoulders; otherwise, the upper case will not sit evenly on the lower case, and the joint will not function properly.

Lay out the dovetail slots and escapements

Once the upper case has been glued and assembled, I can lay out the escapements and dovetail slots on the top of the lower case. I start by placing the upper case onto the lower case and marking the front, back and sides of each slot and escapement. To determine the width of the top of the dovetail slots, I transfer the measurement from the dovetails themselves with vernier calipers (see the photos above). It is impor-

Carefully pare the slot walls. Cut a little at a time, and test the fit frequently. Pay attention to the angle. It's easy to wander from it.

Just pull back and lift out. The housed sliding dovetail requires no contortions to take apart, even though it is very solid when assembled.

tant that the upper case be assembled: It's the only way to be absolutely sure the slots will be in the right place. However, this isn't necessary when making a practice piece.

Cut the escapements before the dovetail slots

I remove the bulk of the waste from the escapements with a brace and bit and pare to the lines with a chisel. I cut them just slightly deeper than the dovetails are tall. You don't need to leave as much stock in the bottom of the escapements as you would for a sliding dovetail, just enough to keep them solid. I leave about 1/8 in. of material at the bottom of each. I test-fit the dovetails in the escapements before I cut the dovetail slots. The dovetails should just slip into the escapements with no extra room front or back. The shoulders of the dovetails, not the bottoms of the escapements, hold the weight of the upper case.

Fit the slots to the dovetails

I cut the slots slightly undersized and then pare them to fit the dovetails bit by bit. I work slowly, keeping an eye on the angle and the marked lines. The hard part is that you can't really see what you are trying to fit. Don't try to get it all at once (see the left photo above).

Fitting the first 1/4 in. or so of each dovetail makes a good reference for cutting the rest of the slots. The finished joint should feel snug, neither binding nor loose. Putting it together and taking it apart shouldn't take a mallet or Herculean strength.

After you've finished the joint, apply a good coat of paste wax to all parts of the dovetails and slots. The wax helps the joint work smoothly. You now have a hidden, stable and graceful knockdown connection for a two-piece cabinet.

SIX

Modern Joints

If you've been woodworking for even just a couple of years, you've seen the speed at which tool designs change. Woodworking tools are not as fast-changing as computers, but they're still difficult to keep up with. Not too long ago, slotted screws and orbital sanders and were stock items in woodshops. Now, biscuit joiners, hex- or square-drive screws, and random-orbit sanders with dust collection chutes have largely replaced them.

With the changes in tools have come changes in joinery. Though routers have been around for a long time, the tooling has evolved substantially in the last 10 years—especially for joint making. The list of joints the router can cut well is long and includes rabbets, dadoes, mortises, tenons, dovetails, and even biscuit and spline slots. With specialty bit sets, the router can now cut finger joints, lock miters, and cope-and-stick joints quickly and easily. These bits set open up possibilities that only industrial shops had in the not-so-distant past. Jeff Greef offers two extensive articles on router-cut cope-and-stick joints, and the many options are peppered with a lot of how-to.

While evolving tools make cutting joints easier, they also persuade the joint to fit the tool better. An example of this is the mortise and tenon with a mason's miter: It is rarely done because the router can't cut it. You have to stop the router before the end of the cut, risk burning the wood or overcutting, and incise the corner with a chisel. This is too much fussing for most of us, so we opt for a coped or simple mitered joint instead.

Some relatively new joints come from cross-pollination. Threaded inserts have been around for a long time and are an excellent knock-down joint. Their cousins—threads cut directly into the wood—are a little more unusual. They require a metal worker's tap and die tools, which many woodworkers don't have around the shop. Still, these joints offer a viable and interesting alternative worth investigating when the traditional options start to bore.

FRAME-AND-PANEL JOINERY OPTIONS

by Mac Campbell

Decorative moldings running along the inside edges of joined frames interfere with one another at the corners. It's necessary to devise some form of non-structural joint. Here, the author uses a fixture to miter the molding (or sticking) with a paring chisel. There's a plan for the fixture on p. 171.

An easy technique for sticking a frame is to dry-assemble rectangular stock for the stiles and rails, joined with either mortises and tenons or dowels, and to then rout the desired profile and the panel groove with bearing-guided bits.

Frame-and-panel assemblies, whether doors or panels in carcase work, are one of the basic building blocks of furniture. They're rigid, strong and stable. These assemblies also offer interesting design opportunities, particularly in the molding decorating the inside edge of the frame where the frame members trap the panel. This molding, known as sticking, can be as simple as a small chamfer or roundover for contemporary style work to a more elaborate ogee or other multi-curved form.

A separate molding can be added after the frame and panel is assembled, as discussed in the box on p. 170. But, I don't think applied moldings give as clean a look as molding cut directly into the frame members. Integral molding, however, quickly raises a question: How do you join the corners?

There are some alternatives. If the frame members are the same width, you can simply miter them, reinforcing the joint with dowels or a spline. Mitered joints have the advantage of simplicity but are not very strong. And they are useless if the frame members are of different widths (as is often the case with doors). A couple of alternatives that I'll mention in this article are the machine cut cope-and-cove joint and routed sticking on an assembled frame. However, my favorite technique takes advantage of the strength of mortise-and-tenon joinery but still has traditional mitered sticking.

Cope-and-cove joints

Most modern shops use a cope-and-cove joint, in which the ends of the rails are routed or shaped to mate exactly with the stick-

Cope-and-cove joint

Although the cope-and-cove joint is quickly machine cut, its strength is based on the glue bond because the short stub tenon provides no mechanical advantage.

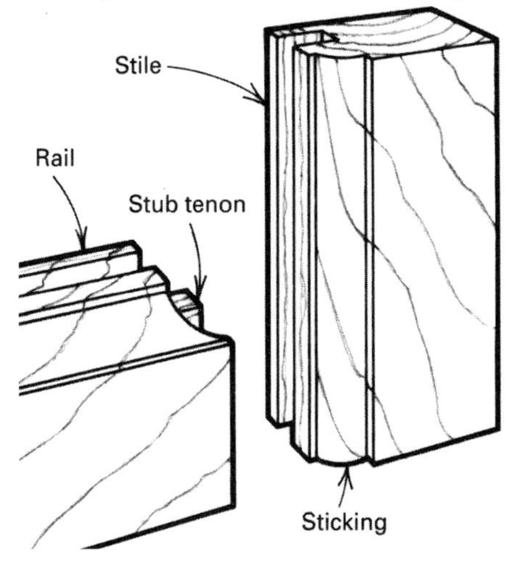

Routed sticking on assembled frames

Sticking can be easily routed on an assembled frame, but the handcut mason's miter can be tricky if the sticking is a complicated pattern.

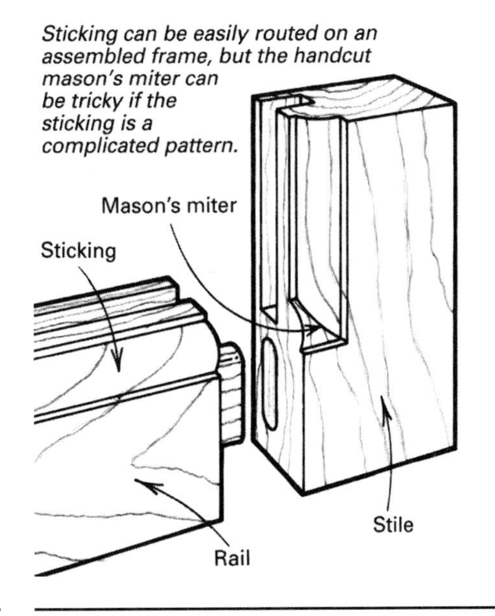

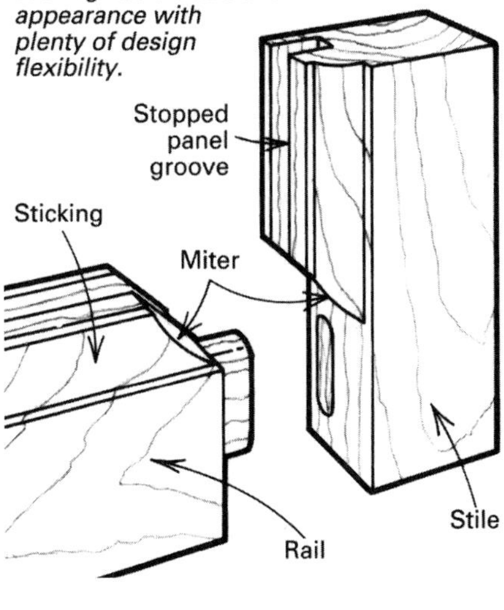

ing on the stiles (see the top left drawing above). The cope-and-cove joint gives a clean look, appears to be mitered at each corner and is fairly strong when the cutters are carefully set up. It is also extremely fast to produce, especially in large quantities. The main drawback of this system is that the rails can fit anywhere on the stiles, so there is no automatic alignment of the assembly. There is little mechanical strength to the joint; it depends entirely on the glue, making assembly procedures much more critical. Another disadvantage is that the location of the panel groove on the inner edge of the frame is predetermined by the cutter you are using. Molding selections are also restricted by the limited variety of cope-and-cove cutter sets available and by the number of these expensive cutters you can afford.

Routed sticking on assembled frames

Another option is to join rectangular frame stock with mortises and tenons or dowels for strength and to align the corners. After cutting the joinery, dry-assemble the frame, and rout the sticking on all four frame pieces at once (see the bottom photo on the facing page). With a wide variety of inexpensive router bits to choose from, almost any sticking profile can be developed. The panel groove is routed separately with a bearing-guided slot cutter. The groove can be inset on the frame's edge to suit the panel thickness or design. The frame is disassembled, glued and reassembled with the panel in place.

Mitered sticking, mortise-and-tenon joint

The mortise and tenon provide a mechanically strong joint, and the mitered sticking has a traditional appearance with plenty of design flexibility.

Stopped panel groove
Sticking
Miter
Rail
Stile

Routing the frame is reasonably efficient for small runs, and the mortises and tenons or dowels provide excellent mechanical joint strength. Routing, however, does leave the interior corners of the sticking rounded. I carve a miter into each corner with a couple of chisel strokes, as shown in the left photo on the facing page. The carved corners are known as mason's miters (see the top right drawing on p. 169) and are not difficult unless the sticking profile is complex.

A mortised-and-tenoned joint with mitered molding

My favorite choice for joining fine work is to combine the strength of a mortise and tenon with the precision of mitered sticking, as shown in the bottom drawing on p. 169. This is the most flexible of all the methods because it will handle any shape of sticking, different widths of frame members, panels set anywhere within the thickness of the frame, and a host of other variables. The sticking and joint are cut separately, so you have many choices for molding cutters or router bits. Also, you can combine cutters for unique sticking profiles. Adding a new profile is not a major investment.

Cutting the joint

I follow a set procedure to make a mortised-and-tenoned frame with stuck molding. After preparing the stock, I cut the joints and then stick the rails and stiles. Next, I bandsaw the sticking from the stiles at the rail-stile juncture, and finally, I miter the sticking for a clean tight joint. Cutting the joint is not particularly difficult, though laying it out requires some care. A little time spent sketching the joint can save time and material in the shop.

Rails for a frame-and-panel door are normally cut to the door width minus the width of the stiles, plus the length of the tenons. For this joint, add in twice the width of the

What's sticking? Here's a glossary

Cope (verb) To shape one part of a joint to conform to the shape of another member. Usually the rail is coped to the stile.

Cope-and-cove joint (noun) As an alternative to a mitered joint, the end of the rail is cut to match the profile of the molded and grooved stile. The rail mates squarely to the stile, yet the sticking appears to be mitered, as shown in figure 1 above.

Cove (noun) A piece of molding with a concave section. (verb) To make a hollow or concave form.

Frame and panel (noun) A door or carcase section composed of a frame that's made up of stiles and rails with a panel. The panel is often made of solid wood trapped within a groove in the edges of the frame pieces, so it can move with changing moisture conditions. The frame provides structural strength with minimum reaction to moisture changes.

Mason's miter (noun) Named for the stone masonry technique from which it is copied, the miter for the sticking is carved into the stile so that the rail can butt squarely to the stile, as shown in figure 2 above.

Molding (noun) A decorative profile worked onto the edge of solid stock (stuck molding) or applied as a separate piece to the edge of a workpiece.

Bolection molding (noun) An applied molding that is rabbeted along one edge, enabling it to fit over a frame work and thus stand proud of the face of the frame.

Rails (noun) The horizontal members of a door or panel frame or horizontal carcase members. Rails are usually tenoned at both ends.

Stick (verb) The process of cutting a molding profile along the edge of solid stock.

Sticking (noun) A molding that is cut along the edge of solid stock as opposed to a separate molding that is applied to the stock.

Stiles (noun) The vertical members of a door or panel frame. Stiles usually run the full length of the frame and are mortised to receive the tenons of the rails that run between the stiles.

sticking. If you are using a dowel joint, do not add in anything for tenon length.

Begin by cutting the mortise and tenon as usual. I leave 1-in.-long ears on the stiles of my frames, but it's easier to cut the stiles to finished length when mitering the sticking. Once the mortises and tenons are cut, stick each piece, using a router, shaper or molding plane. Stiles and rails can be molded from end to end to simplify the process.

Once the sticking is completed, mark the full width of the rail (including the sticking) on the inside face of the stile to mark the point where the miter cut for the molding begins. A marking gauge, used very delicately, will do this job quickly.

A paring fixture for tight-fitting joints

by Tom E. Moore

I use a process similar to Campbell's for assembling stuck frames with mortise-and-tenon joints. I found cutting a smooth, straight shoulder on the stile to mate with the end of the rail to be every bit as difficult as trimming the miters. My solution is the fixture shown in the drawing at right. This fixture not only provides a chisel guide surface for paring the miters but also cleans up the shoulder cut that has been bandsawn shy of my layout line.

For laying out consistently accurate joints, I made a metal template from some scrap duct metal. I cut the layout lines onto the frame stock using a sharp knife with the template, and then I use these lines for both cutting the joints and aligning my paring fixture for final trimming.

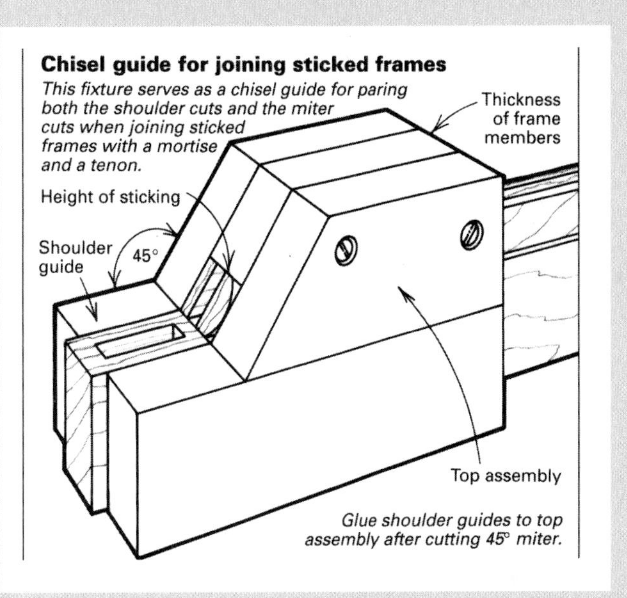
Chisel guide for joining sticked frames
This fixture serves as a chisel guide for paring both the shoulder cuts and the miter cuts when joining sticked frames with a mortise and a tenon.
Thickness of frame members
Height of sticking
Shoulder guide
45°
Top assembly
Glue shoulder guides to top assembly after cutting 45° miter.

A few quick strokes of the chisel will shape the rounded corners left when routing sticking. Although this technique works for all but the most complicated profiles, it can become tedious when making more than a few frames.

Bandsaw the sticking from the stile to provide a clean mating surface for the rail for the mitered molding frame. A fence and a stop block clamped to the bandsaw table help ensure accurate cuts that are later cleaned up with a paring chisel.

Applied moldings can stand proud

MOLDING APPLIED AROUND SOLID PANEL

GLASS RABBET WITH APPLIED MOLDING

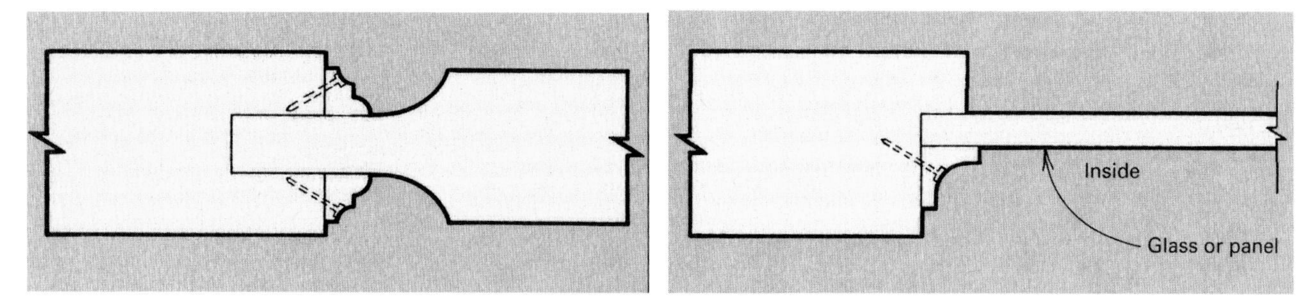

by Jeff Greef

Applied moldings can be added to plain rectangular stiles and rails to achieve the look of cope-and-stick molded frames. And applied molding frames are easier to assemble. If the moldings are properly designed and carefully applied, these frames will be structurally sound with an appearance approaching that of integral moldings. Applied moldings also provide a design alternative that integral sticking does not—bolection molding. This type of molding has a profile that stands proud of the face of the frame, as shown in the right drawing on the facing page.

Applied moldings allow several options for making frames to suit the builder's tools and preferred techniques. The frames can be mortised and tenoned, doweled, mitered, half-lapped or even butted and screwed. The rails and stiles can incorporate a panel groove or rabbet, or the applied moldings can form the panel retaining groove. Whichever method you choose, the following tips will help you get the best results.

Grooved frame—Frames that include a panel groove also should have a stub tenon or haunch on the rail ends that fits into the groove in the stile. Fit the panels in the frame at glue-up, then make moldings and miter them to fit inside the frame against the panel, as shown in the left drawing above. Make moldings by cutting a profile on the edge of a wide board with a router or shaper, then rip the shaped edge off on a tablesaw or bandsaw. Use a molding pattern that can be easily nailed to the frame, like those shown in the drawings. A broad, flat profile, for example, may be difficult to nail. Glue and nail the molding to the frame only, not the panel. Otherwise, the panel can pull the molding away from the frame,

Now cut the slots for the panel. If the sticking is wider (across the face of the stile) than the panel groove is deep, you can plow the panel groove from end to end on both the rails and stiles. The next step of trimming the sticking from the end of the stiles will also cut away the panel groove that runs out the end of the stile. Otherwise, to avoid an exposed groove end on the outer edge of the assembled frame, make sure that the groove stops before emerging from the end of the stile (see the bottom drawing on p. 169).

The next step, trimming the sticking on the stiles, is most easily done on the bandsaw. Set the bandsaw's fence so the cut will just remove the stuck molding, and set a stop block so the cut ends about 1/8 in. shy of the mark made previously at the base of the miter, as shown in the bottom photo. After cutting both ends of all the stiles, make a perpendicular cut with the bandsaw or a handsaw to remove the end of the sticking. I usually just freehand this cut because it is not critical.

Cutting the miters

To cut the actual miters, make up a 45° fixture. This can be made of any dense hardwood, but its accuracy is critical to the fit of the miters. An alternative fixture is described in the box on p. 171. To use the

PARALLEL SETS OF APPLIED MOLDING

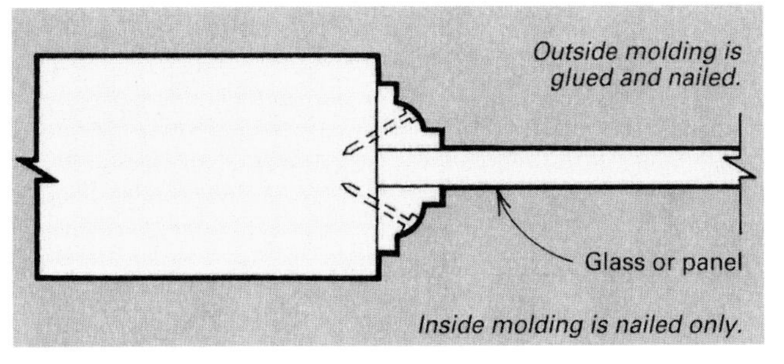

BOLECTION MOLDING

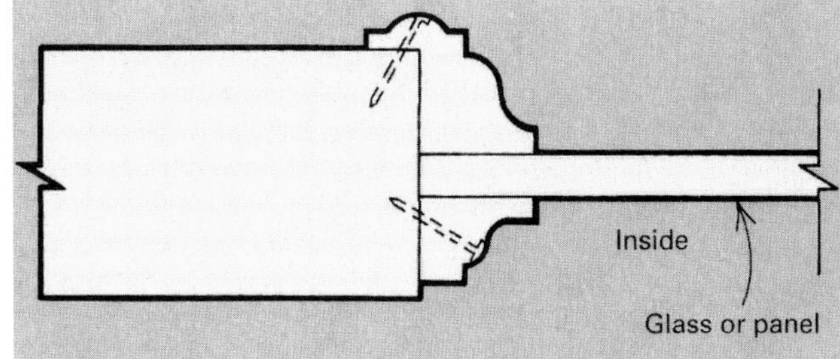

creating an unsightly gap. If the molding is nailed to both panel and frame, it will restrict the panel's movement as humidity levels change and will likely result in a split panel.

Rabbeted frames—If you want to put glass in the frame (as in a cabinet door), you must make the frame with a rabbet rather than a groove, so the glass can be replaced if it breaks. You can cut a rabbet into the frame parts before glue-up, but this requires leaving a stub on the ends of the rails to fill the rabbet at the stile-rail juncture. An alternative technique is to glue up the frame with rectangular stock, rout a rabbet with a bearing-guided rabbeting bit and then square the rabbet corners with a chisel. Moldings are nailed to rabbeted frames (not glued), as shown in the right drawing on the facing page.

Applied moldings—Another possibility for making a glass rabbet or mounting a solid panel, is to apply two parallel sets of molding to the inside of a frame (see the left drawing above). In this case, glue and nail one of the two sets of molding onto the frame, but only nail the other so it can be removed to replace glass. Carefully align the outside set of molding with spacer blocks to position and hold the molding while it is nailed.

Bolection molding solves the problem of locating the first set of molding because this molding has its own rabbet that automatically positions the molding on the frame, as shown in the right drawing above. Because bolection molding protrudes beyond the plane of the frame face, it has a significant visual impact. For some furniture designs, this molding may be too ornate, but it could be just the ticket to dress up an otherwise plain frame.

fixture, place a stile in the vise, and clamp the fixture to the stile so the edge of the fixture lines up with the miter mark. With a very sharp chisel, gradually pare the stile down, using the 45° angled face of the fixture to guide your chisel for the last cut. The rails are mitered in the same fashion by lining up the angled surface of the fixture with the base of the sticking at the end of the rail. Because this process miters the stiles and rails across the inside edge of the frame on both sides of the panel groove, you can stick both front and back of the frame without altering the process.

Dry-assemble the stile and rail to check the fit of the miter. Square the two pieces accurately, and make sure that the outside of the rail lines up with the end of the stile. Make any needed adjustments, and then cut the rest of the miters.

Final assembly

I like to prefinish the panels to prevent unfinished areas from showing along the sides if the panels shrink slightly due to humidity changes. Prefinishing also helps prevent squeeze-out from gluing the panels to the frame during assembly. A panel that is glued in this way will surely split as it tries to move with changes in humidity.

ROUTER BITS TACKLE COPE AND STICK

by Jeff Greef

You don't need a shaper for cope-and-stick joinery anymore. Now the market is teeming with router bits in a variety of styles competing for your cope-and-stick business.

Making frames with molded edges for glazed or raised-panel doors like the one in the photo above is a lot easier now that there are specialized stile-and-rail router bits on the market. But there are over 50 bit sets to choose from. To sort through this wide array of offerings, I obtained bits from 16 suppliers and manufacturers and put them through their paces. My objective was to find the real differences between bits and to provide guidelines for choosing a set. I inspected each set closely, scrutinizing for quality by eye. Then I tried out each set on pine, poplar and oak to check the cut and the fit of the joints they produced.

Stile-and-rail bits cut two profiles: a stick profile and a corresponding cope cut. The stick is the contour on the inside edges of a door or window frame on both the vertical members (stiles) and the horizontal ones (rails). The cope is a negative version of the stick and is cut into the ends of the rails, so

Solid bit sets like these come in pairs and have cutters that cannot be removed from the shank.

they fit over the stick on the stiles, as shown in the drawing below.

All the stile-and-rail bit sets I examined cut a tenon and open mortise joint in addition to the cope and stick. The open mortise is the last few inches of the groove that also holds the panel. This joinery is adequate for small- and medium-sized cabinet doors. You can beef up the joint with dowels or loose tenons in open mortises. Also, with some bits, you can make a rabbet for glass instead of a groove for a panel. If you make the glass rabbet, use a reinforcing joint because the tenon-and-open mortise joint is eliminated.

Solid bit sets

Cope-and-stick bit sets come with solid bits or stacking bits. The cutters on solid sets cannot be removed from the shank for shimming or reconfiguration. As a result, the quality of the fit of cope to stick is entirely a function of how the bits are ground. Solid bit sets have two bits, one for sticking and one for coping, as shown in the bottom photo on the facing page. The main advantage of solid sets is ease of use. You just chuck 'em up and go. The main drawback is lack of adjustability. If you get a set that gives a good fit, you'll be fine, but if not, you're stuck.

Sharpening is another consideration with solid sets. Carbide router bits are sharpened by grinding the flat face of the carbide. When the face is ground, the profile changes slightly as the cutting edge recedes along the bevel of the edge grind. Consequently, the fit of cope to stick changes a little, too. Because there is no adjustment with solid sets, you can't compensate for these changes.

A solid set would be a possible choice for someone who is willing to sacrifice precision for ease of use and doesn't intend to use the bits enough to require resharpening.

Stacking two-part

Like the solid types, these bits come in pairs, one bit each for coping and sticking (see the photo on p. 176). But with these bits, the slot cutters and profile cutters are separate and can be removed from the bit shank. This allows you to place shims between them to adjust the fit of the joint.

Cope-and-stick joint

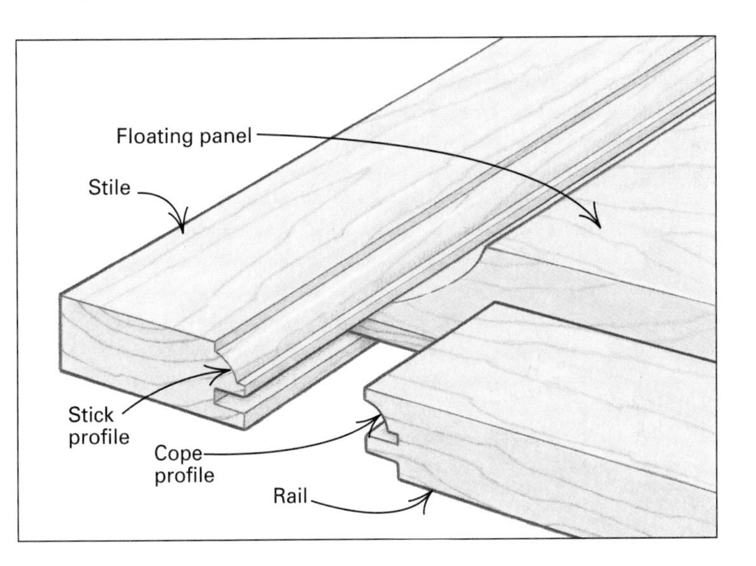

Reversible sets use one bit to cut both sides of the joint. The cutters can be shimmed to fine-tune the fit of cope to stick.

The shims, provided by all manufacturers, are thin washers that fit over the shank. Shims won't cure all mismatches but should take care of 90% of them.

Two-part stacking bit sets are among the most costly of all stile-and-rail sets. And there is more set-up time because you must adjust the fit with shims when making test-cuts. But once the bits are properly shimmed and set up in two router tables, you never have to change setups. For any production situation where the bits would be used a lot, a stacking two-part set is the logical choice.

Stacking reversible

Unlike all the other bit sets, which come with mating pairs of cutters, these use a single bit to cut both the cope and the stick. After cutting the copes, you remove the cutters from the bit arbor, and rearrange them to cut the stick. Just like the stacking two-part sets, reversible sets are adjustable with shims, as shown in the photo below. These sets cost less because you buy only one cutter assembly instead of two. But they won't last as long between sharpenings as a two-part set because the cutters in a reversible do twice as much work.

If you want adjustability and you plan to make only a few doors, I would consider the reversibles because they cost less than two-part sets and their results are just as good. If you make a lot of doors, though, the constant need to switch a reversible set between cope and stick would become irritating.

The reversibility of these bits, while making them inexpensive and convenient, limits the range of possible profiles because a single cutter must shape both the cope and the stick.

Hybrid

With hybrid bit sets, you use a separate cutter for each part of the joint (see the top photo on the facing page). You make separate setups for each of the sticking, coping, grooving and tenoning passes. This can be tedious, but there are no shims to fuss with, and there is wide adjustability. And hybrids let you vary stock thickness. All the previously mentioned cutters are designed for specific stock thicknesses, usually 3/4 in. Hybrid sets are the logical choice for special applications where you need to use odd stock thicknesses or for panel grooves that are wider than the standard 1/4 in.

Architectural

These sets are designed specifically for making architectural windows and doors. The cutters are stackable and come in both reversible and two-bit sets, as shown in the bottom photo on the facing page. Cutting standard architectural stock at thicknesses of 1 3/8 in. or 1 3/4 in. with such bits will require either a 3-hp router or multiple passes with a less powerful machine.

Which bits are best?

Once you've narrowed your search to a particular type of bit set, there are a number of factors to consider in choosing between bits.

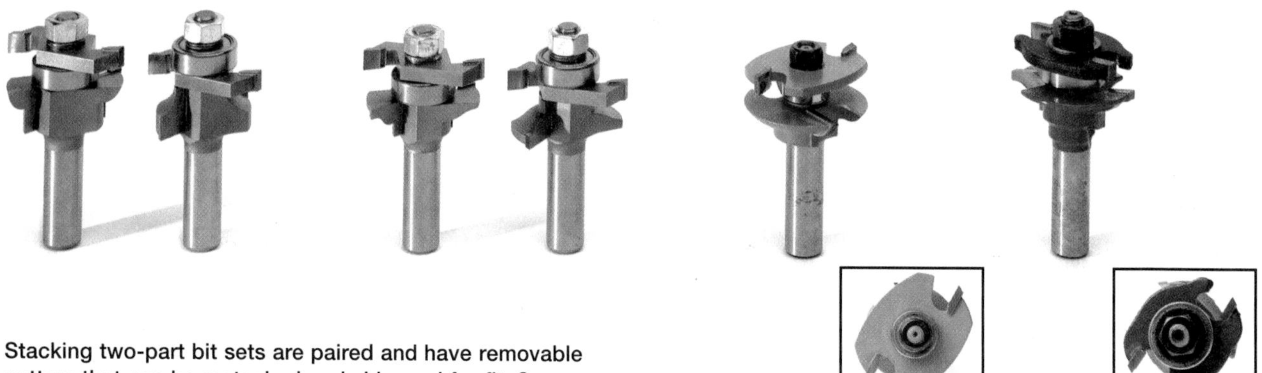

Stacking two-part bit sets are paired and have removable cutters that can be restacked and shimmed for fit. Some have the anti-kickback design shown in the inset photos.

They run from the purely objective—price and specifications—to more subjective considerations. I've compiled data from my review of the bits in the chart on pp. 180-181, and I'll explain what I looked for and why. When you buy bits, keep in mind that quality varies from bit to bit even from the same manufacturer. Examine bits closely, and return any that aren't up to snuff.

Grinding quality

You need a sharp edge on the carbide to get a smooth surface on the wood. Both the face and edge of the carbide must be ground smoothly. I found all bits had smooth face grinds. The major variable was the quality of the edge grind. I evaluated edge grinds by running a pencil tip along the carbide to see whether it slid smoothly or scraped along. Then I examined the stick each cutter produced, looking for nicks in the cut. Generally, I found bits with the best edge grinding left the best finish cuts.

Back grind

Another critical aspect of grinding is the angle of back grind. In back-grinding, the edge is ground at a sharp enough angle that only the very point touches the wood; the portion behind the edge should not. Without that clearance, burning will result. The heat can ruin the carbide, not to mention the workpiece.

Cutter balance

If bits are not balanced, they will vibrate while in use. I checked for mismatched cutters with the bits in the router. With the router unplugged, I held a steel rule on the router table and spun the bit. When the end of the rule just scraped one cutter, I spun the bit around to see how the other side compared. This technique will only show gross deviations from proper grinding indexing but is worth using whenever you chuck up a new bit or if an old bit is cutting poorly or with excessive vibration.

The fit of cope to stick depends upon two factors. The first and most important is how well the manufacturer ground the cutters so that the cope is an exact match for the stick. The second is how well you set up the adjustments (where possible) to make the matching parts align. You can produce ill-fitting joints with well-ground cutters if you don't shim properly. But no amount of shimming will fill gaps in joints made with poorly ground cutters.

Solid cutters are not adjustable, so how well the joint fits is up to the manufacturer. Of those I tested, all had good matches of cope to stick, but several had poor fits of the

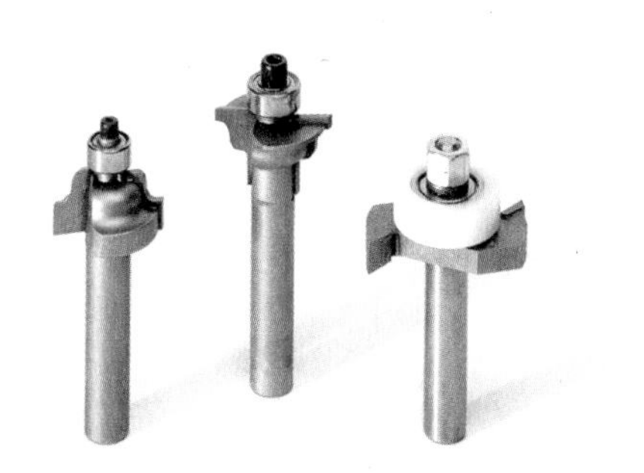

Hybrid bit sets separate the slot cutter from the profile cutters. This set has mated profile cutters; two-bit sets, which have reversible profile cutters, are also available.

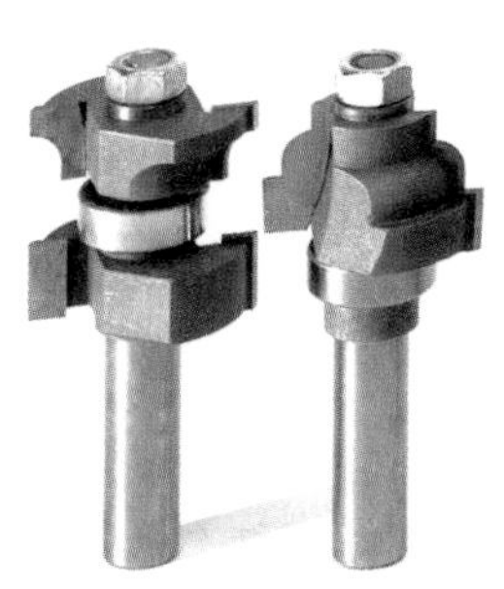

Architectural bit sets will tackle full-sized windows and doors and come in both paired and reversible sets.

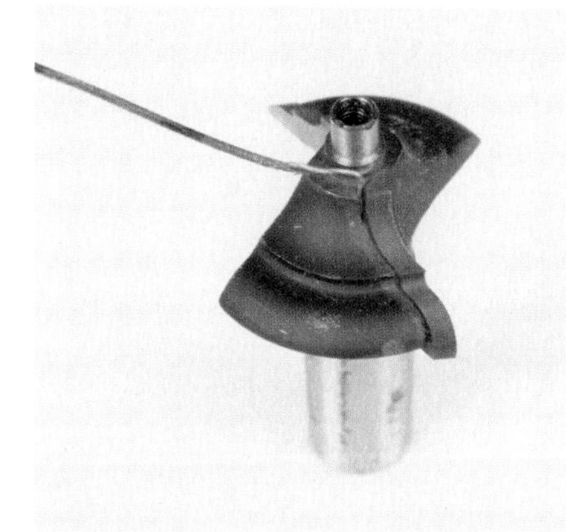

Voids in the brazing behind the carbide cutter can compromise the safety of a bit. The wire in the photo points to a void that is larger than the pinhole most manufacturers permit. But because it's within the diameter of the guide bearing, it's not likely to cause a problem.

A defective shank like this one, left rough on one side, can cause serious vibration. Remove the cutters to inspect a new bit before running it.

tenon in the groove. The fits varied with different types of wood, which is common because router bits are ground at an angle that is a compromise between the optimum rakes for cutting hardwoods and softwoods.

Anti-kickback design

The Italian bits (Freud and CMT) are well-made and impressive-looking with their anti-kickback design that limits the depth of cut, reducing the danger of kickback and severe injury (see the inset photos on p. 176). Most technical representatives I spoke with thought this feature was a good idea on larger diameter cutters, such as panel raisers where kickback is a serious threat, but overkill on smaller bits like these. I tend to agree.

Price and value

Why are there such wide price variations between bits of the same type? There are a number of factors that affect the quality and price of bits: different grades of carbide, types of brazing and brazing material, various edge-grinding and shank-grinding techniques. But it's difficult for the consumer to ascertain by observation or inquiry which materials and techniques were used to make a particular bit. I talked to Steve Cash, who runs a sharpening service here in Santa Cruz and sees thousands of bits a year. He said that, roughly speaking, higher price reflects the use of more expensive materials or processes in manufacturing.

In selecting for price, look for the lowest cost per cut. If you do a lot of cope-and-stick work, it makes sense to spend the money for a higher priced bit that will cut cleanly for a long time. If you have just a few doors, buy a less expensive bit. You may have to do some touch up sanding behind the bit, but you'll still come out ahead.

Personally, I think the best values among cope-and-stick bits are the reversibles. Because you're only paying for one shank, the prices are considerably lower than for two-part bits of comparable quality. Unless I knew I'd be in a production situation, I'd accept the extra toil involved in changing setups and get reversibles. The solid bits, though they seem like a bargain, didn't impress me with their performance. They were the only bits I tried that burned, and I also dislike their lack of adjustability.

Defective bits

When you have your new bits, take a close look at them before putting them to use. Defective bits are not unheard of, and some potential problems will be evident on visual inspection.

Brazing voids

The brazing between a router bit's carbide cutter and steel body attaches the cutter to the body, and it acts as a cushion that protects the brittle carbide from fracturing under impact. Wherever there are gaps in the braze line, the possibility of fracture

SOURCES OF SUPPLY

Amana Tool Corp.*
120 Carolyn Blvd.
Farmingdale, NY 11735
(800) 445-0077

Bosch—SB Power Tool Co.*
PO Box 12217
New Bern, NC 28562
(800) 334-5730

Carb Tech—Trendlines
375 Beacham St.
Chelsea, MA 02150
(800) 767-9999

CMT
5425 Beaumont Center Blvd., Suite 900
Tampa, FL 33634
(800) 531-5559

DML—Primark Tool*
1350 S. 15th St.
Louisville, KY 40210
(800) 242-7003

Eagle America
PO Box 1099
Chardon, OH 44024
(800) 872-2511

Freud
218 Feld Ave.
High Point, NC 27264
(800) 334-4107

FS Tool*
PO Box 510
Lewiston, NY 14092
(800) 387-9723

Grizzly
PO Box 2069
Bellingham, WA 98227
(800) 541-5537

Hartville Tool and Supply
940 W. Maple St.
Hartville, OH 44623
(800) 345-2396

MLCS
Box 4053 C13
Rydal, PA 19046
(800) 533-9298

Porter-Cable *
4825 Highway 45 N.
Jackson, TN 38305
(800) 321-9443

SY—Cascade Tool Co.
Box 3110
Bellingham, WA 98227
(800) 235-0272

Velepec*
71-72 70th St.
Glendale, NY 11385
(800) 365-6636

Whiteside Machine Co.*
4506 Shook Rd.
Claremont, NC 28610
(800) 225-3982

Woodtek—Woodworker's Supply
1108 N. Glenn Rd.
Caspar, WY 82601
(800) 645-9292

* These companies do not sell directly to the public but will tell you who their local distributor is.

increases. If the carbide breaks while the bit is spinning, the result can be like shrapnel. The consensus among the manufacturers I spoke with was that nothing larger than a pinhole void in the brazing was acceptable. But the location of the void is important, too. The bit in the top photo had a void larger than a pinhole, so I sent it to Jim Effner for expert evaluation. (Effner is a former technical services engineer with Leitz, the German manufacturer of cutting tools, and is the author of *Chisels on a Wheel,* a book about motor-driven cutters.) He said that because the void was at the small diameter of the cutter and within the span of the guide bearing, it wouldn't get much stress and wouldn't pose a problem.

Misground shank

I learned my lesson about carefully inspecting bits from experience. One bit that looked fine at first vibrated so much when I started it up that I immediately shut off the router. When I removed the cutters from the shank and looked closer, I found that half the upper shank was rough and unground, as shown in the bottom photo. In addition to checking for this type of defect, look at the lower section of a bit's shank. For the collet to grip it properly, the shank should be polished smooth and be free of blemishes.

It's not the bit, it's the collet

While you're paying all this attention to your bits, don't forget that they're in a partnership with your router's collet. Collets take a lot of abuse, and if they start to become egg-shaped, through wear or metal fatigue, they'll cause problems with your bits. According to Jim Effner, collets have a fairly predictable life span of 1,000 hours of use. So keep track of their birthdays, and replace them before they get too ancient.

Cope-and-stick router bit sets

Manufacturer/ supplier	Country of manufacture	Manufacturer's stock number	Price	Stock thickness ✷	Profile type	Profile depth ✷
Solid bits						
Carb Tech	Taiwan	AY12	69.95	¾	Ogee	⅜
Hartville	Taiwan	83641	65.00	¾	Bead	⅜
MLCS	Taiwan	849	74.95	1 (min.)	Step ogee	½
SY	Taiwan	C1393	99.95	¾	Round	¼
Woodtek	Taiwan	821026	74.95	1 (min.)	Step ogee	9/16
Stacking two-part sets						
Bosch	U.S.	85625M	133.40	¾	Ogee	⅜
CMT	Italy	891-502	129.00	¾	Round	9/16
DML	U.S.	02024	150.00	¾	Round	⅜
Eagle	U.S.	185-0900	99.99	¾	Bead	⅜
Freud	Italy	99-261	153.00	¾	Ogee	10mm
MLCS	Taiwan	843	74.95	¾	Round	⅜
Porter-Cable	U.S.	43550 & 51	144.00	¾	Bead	¼
Whiteside	U.S.	6002 A & B	126.00	¾	Ogee	⅜
Stacking reversible bits						
Amana	Israel	55350	117.60	¾	Ogee	⅜
Eagle	U.S.	184-0105	59.99	¾	Ogee	⅜
F.S. Tool	Canada	FRB27	109.00	¾	Ogee	12mm
Grizzly	Taiwan	G2926	49.95	¾	Step ogee	½
Hartville	Taiwan	82141	39.00	¾	Ogee	⅜
MLCS	Taiwan	894	69.95	¾	Ogee	⅜
SY	Taiwan	C1654	49.95	¾	Step ogee	⅜
Velepec	U.S./Israel	ROSRA-90-8	110.00	¾	Ogee	⅜
Whiteside	U.S.	6151	69.95	¾	Ogee	⅜
Woodtek	Taiwan	820739	37.50	¾	Step ogee	⅜
Hybrid bits						
Freud	Italy	99-060 & 062✚	60.00	unlimited	Step ogee	½
Velepec	U.S./Israel	3-piece set	140.00	unlimited	Ogee	⅜
Architectural bits						
Amana	Israel	55340	156.45	to 1¾	Ogee	¼
Freud	Italy	99-050 & 051	96.00	to 1¾	Ogee	6mm
MLCS	Taiwan	893	54.95	to 1¾	Ogee	¼
SY	Taiwan	C1552	89.00	to 1¾	Bead	5/16

Shank diameter ✷	Fit of cope and stick	Quality of edge grind	Smoothness of cut	Comments
½	Cope good; tenon loose	Below avg.	Below average	
½	Excellent	Average	Average	Burning—insufficient back grind
½◆	Very good	Below avg.	Average	Burning—insufficient back grind
½	Cope good; tenon loose	Below avg.	Below average	
½◆	Cope good; tenon loose	Below avg.	Average	Burning—insufficient back grind
½	Fair	Best	Best	Without shims, bearing sparks against cutter
½	Excellent	Best	Best	Anti-kickback design
½	Excellent	Best	Best	
½◆	Excellent	Average	Average	
½	Good	Best	Best	Anti-kickback design
½◆	Excellent	Below avg.	Best	
½◆	Good	Average	Average	
½	Excellent	Average	Average	
½	Very good	Best	Average	
½◆	Excellent	Below avg.	Below average	
½	Excellent	Best	Best	
½◆	Excellent	Below avg.	Below avg.—small nicks	
½	Excellent	Average	Average—small nicks	
½◆	Very good	Below avg.	Best	
½	Fair	Below avg.	Below average—small nicks	Out of balance—cutters not ground at equal radii
½	Very good	Below avg.	Best	
½	Excellent	Below avg.	Below average	
½◆	Fair	Below avg.	Below avg.—small nicks	
½	Good	Best	Best	
½	Good—very small gap	Below avg.	Best	
½	Excellent	Below avg.	Average	Vibration
½	Excellent	Best	Average	Anti-kickback design
½◆	Very good	Below avg.	Average	
½	Good	Below avg.	Below avg.—small nicks	

CURVED COPE AND STICK

by Jeff Greef

Cope blocks and templates help cut a curving profile in end grain. Cope blocks pinch the delicate workpiece, providing stability, tearout prevention and a nailing surface for the curved template. After flush-trimming, the same template guides the contoured cope bit.

I learned cope-and-stick joinery for doors and windows while an apprentice at Davenport Mill, a custom architectural millwork shop in Santa Cruz, Calif. Although most of the cope-and-stick work we did there was on rectilinear doors and windows, clients also had us do various curved forms ranging from simple arcs to circles, ellipses and free-form lines. After I left the mill, it occurred to me that I could easily take the curved cope-and-stick techniques I had learned on the shaper and apply them to cabinet work by using some of the rail-and-stile router bits commonly used for kitchen cabinet doors. I think the system I use takes the head scratching out of making sash with curved cope and stick.

The *stick* of cope and stick refers to the molded edge along the inside of a door or window frame and on both sides of a window's crossbars, or muntins. When you want another piece to butt against the sticking to make a joint, the solution is to cut a cope (which is a negative profile of the sticking) on the end of any part that will join the sticking. A good cope produces a tightly fitting, gapless joint that on small pieces can often be glued up without further reinforcement.

With rectilinear work, cope-and-stick cuts are fairly straightforward, as shown in the drawing on p. 185. The edges that get sticking are all straight, and the ends that get coped are all cut at 90°. (For an explanation of conventional cope and stick, see *The Best of FWW: Traditional Woodworking Techniques,* The Taunton Press, 1991.) But a few challenges arise when you attempt to cope and stick curved pieces.

I solve these problems with a system of curved templates like the one in the photo on the facing page, which can be quickly and accurately produced with a router screwed to a shopmade radiusing jig. Three types of templates are required: one for shaping curved glazing bars, another to make cope blocks (disposable pieces that stabilize and back up the cope cuts), and a third to guide the router bearing while coping the ends of pieces that join curved members. I screw handles to the templates to make controlling the cuts easier and to keep my hands well away from the cutters. I'll explain how I make the templates and then how I use them to do curved cope-and-stick work like that shown in the top photo on p. 184.

First, though, a word of caution: These router techniques require that you cut very small parts on the router table, as well as climb cut against the grain. There are safe ways to do both of these, but if you are new to routers, I suggest you use a design that incorporates larger parts with larger radii.

Full-scale sash

The first step in any curved cope-and-stick project is to make a full-scale drawing. I find this essential and constantly refer to it as I'm working to establish the length, location and curvature of different parts and templates. First experiment with various designs on the drafting table using a compass; then draw your favorite design full scale on a sheet of plywood. I use shopmade trammel points to draw the full-scale arcs and record the radius of each arc on the drawing. This is the easiest time to get the radii—all you have to do is measure between the pencil and the pivot point on the trammel bar. This will give you the radii for cutting bar templates; add or subtract the depth of the rabbet from these radii to make templates for cope blocks and end coping.

Turning out templates

Now make a template for every curved part in your door or window. To cut the curved edges of the templates, you can use a simple router jig like the one shown in the top photo on the facing page. The jig consists of a teardrop-shaped plywood substitute base for your router with a long arm of solid wood attached to it. A small block of wood that's clamped to the arm and drilled to accept a 10d nail provides an adjustable pivot point from which to swing the arcs.

I cut the templates from 1/4-in. Baltic-birch plywood, which is strong and stable, routs to a clean edge and is free of voids,

Proceed piece by piece for best fit. For curved cope-and-stick work, the author dry-assembles the frame and then copes and fits the interior components one at a time.

Full-scale layout orients curved parts. Use trammel points to strike the arcs and record their radii for making templates.

providing a smooth surface for the router's guide bearing. Don't forget: Measure from the outside of the router bit to the pivot point on the radiusing jig to cut the internal radius of a template. For an external radius, measure to the inside of the bit. You can use a plunge router to make the arcing cuts. Or do as I do, and simply tilt the router up to turn it on, and then lower it into the ply; make the templates over long, and cut off the plunge point where the cut is not true. I usually cut all the templates at once, making all the radius cuts with the router and cutting the templates free with a sabersaw. To make small-radius templates, I use a circle-cutting setup on the router table, as shown in the photo on p. 189.

Templates for end coping and for the cope blocks are sized differently from templates for the bars. As you can see in the drawing on this page, when you make a curved edge with sticking on it, the outer edge of the sticking has one radius, and the rabbet shoulder has another. When making templates and joining parts, it's important to remember which is which. I call the outer radius the sticking radius, and the other one the rabbet radius. When you cope something, either the end of a part or the edge of a cope block, you'll need a template sized to the rabbet radius of the sticking it will mate with.

Shape the bars

Once you've made all the bar templates, cut the sticking and coping on the rails and stiles. Then cut the joints in the door or window's outer rails and stiles, and glue up the frame. A simple, strong solution is to mortise both rails and stiles and insert floating tenons. By cutting the joints after you cut the cope and stick, you can be sure the joint is in the rabbet and doesn't interfere with the profile. With the frame together, you can begin to fill it in, dry-fitting one bar at a time. For an explanation of the cope-and-stick bits you'll need and the sequence of cuts, see the box on p. 189.

I attach handles to the sticking templates with flat-head screws, countersunk and driven from below. Then I fix the template to the workpiece with nails hammered into the back of the part or into ends that will be cut off, making sure I locate them out of the path of the router bits. Holding the handles firmly, I flush-trim the piece to the template.

Using the template and handles in the same way, as shown in the bottom photo on p. 186, cut the sticking and the rabbet next. Take small passes to come to the profile gradually. On curved parts, you will invariably have to cut against the grain. To avoid tearout, climb the cut—move the part into the cutter with the direction of the spinning bit, rather than against it as is customary. To do so safely, bear down on the safety handles, move the part slowly but steadily and take light cuts.

Rectilinear cope and stick

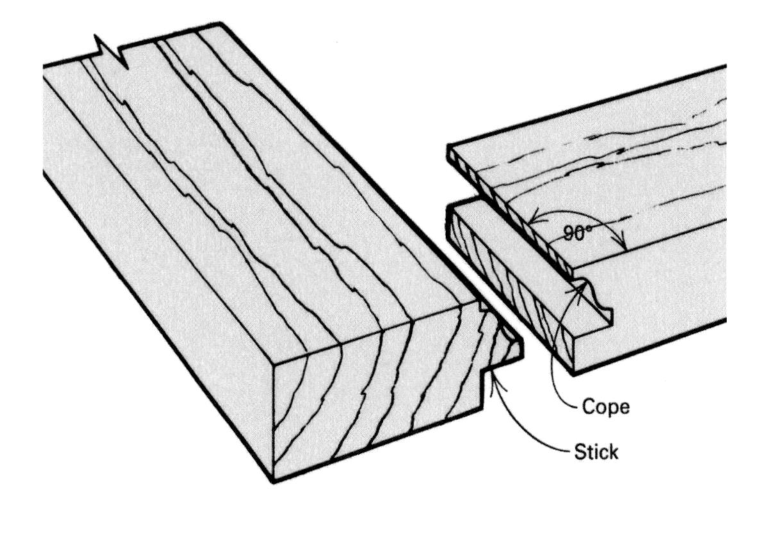

Steps to good coping

With the sticking and rabbets cut in all the bars, begin coping by making cope blocks to fit onto the sticking on either side of the parts to be coped, as shown in the photos on p. 188. The cope blocks serve several purposes. They help eliminate tearout by backing up the cope cut, which is made across the end grain of the small-section bars, while also providing infeed and outfeed surfaces for the router bearing. The blocks also help stabilize the narrow workpiece and give you something to grab as you make the cut.

Rout the arcs for templates all at once, then separate them. The author uses a shopmade jig to rout pairs of concentric arcs in a sheet of stable, void-free Baltic-birch plywood. He'll make end cuts with a sabersaw to free the templates. Template-arc radii are computed from the full-scale drawing.

Start in the middle when sticking curved bars. Half the cut will be with the grain and half against. Climb cut against the grain, holding the handles firmly, making the cut in a series of passes.

And last, they provide a larger surface for mounting the coping templates for more accurate placement. To make the cope blocks, you'll need templates that match the curves of the rabbets on each side of the bar. Use them to flush-trim and cope the blocks.

Press the cope blocks onto the bar, and put them in place on the full-scale drawing. Next place the door or window on top of them with its corners resting on spacer blocks. Make sure it is directly over its corresponding lines on the drawing. Then run a pencil along the curve of the rabbet, scribing a line across the top of the cope blocks and the bar itself, as shown in the top photo on p. 188.

Coping the bars

I set up two router tables to cope the ends of the bars: one with a flush-trimming bit and one with a coping bit. This is important because it is often necessary to go back and forth between the two setups during the fitting procedure. If you don't have two full-fledged router tables, screwing your router to a piece of plywood clamped to sawhorses will work fine.

Lift the door or window off its blocks, and choose a coping template that matches the scribed line. Then nail the template to the coping blocks, as shown in the bottom right photo on the facing page. Use a quick-release clamp to keep the cope blocks tight against the bar. Bandsaw away most of the waste, and flush-trim to the template. From there, go directly to the cope setup, as shown in the bottom left photo on p. 188.

Now duplicate the process to fit the other end of the bar. To establish its length, first lay the bar on the full-scale drawing. Next rest the door on top, and butt the already coped end against the rabbet of the piece it will join. Then scribe along the curve of the rabbet of the intersecting piece at the opposite end. It's prudent to cut the part a bit long at first to see how it fits. Shorten it if necessary by repeating the flush-trim step with the part protruding just a hair and then coping again. And now, voilà, you have a properly oriented and coped curved bar. When all the parts are fitted, glue them in one by one. Use glue with a long open time, like brown glue (urea formaldehyde), so you'll be able to make minor adjustments as you work. Use masking tape to hold the pieces in place as the glue sets. Be sure to apply the tape away from the joint, so you have access to clean the glue squeeze-out.

Curved cope and stick

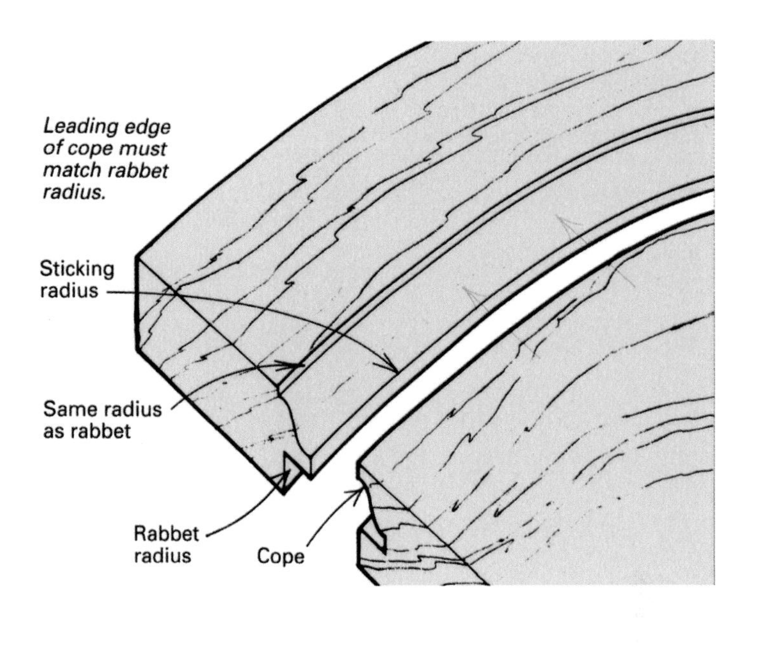

To cut window glass, trace the rabbets from the glued-up frame, and make templates from the tracings. Cutting glass along outside curves is not terribly difficult, but inside curves present more of a challenge. You should at least be prepared for some failures, and perhaps consider letting a professional cut glass to your templates. Once the panes are cut, you can use either putty or wooden stops to hold them in the frame. I use putty because there's a danger of splitting the narrow bars when nailing in stops.

All of the procedures I've described in this article involve curves that are true arcs of circles and, hence, easily made by arcing with a router in a radius jig. But you can use the same system to make cope-and-stick pieces of any curve you choose. This will be more challenging, though, as you will have to make the templates by hand, and coping templates will also have to be sanded to fit adjoining parts.

Marking and coping a curved bar

To mark coping lines, set the part in its place on the layout board, and use spacer blocks to support the frame-in-progress directly above the drawing as you scribe to the rabbet.

Affixing a template—Clamp the cope blocks to the workpiece, and nail a template to the scribe line. Then bandsaw close to the template before flush-trimming on the router table.

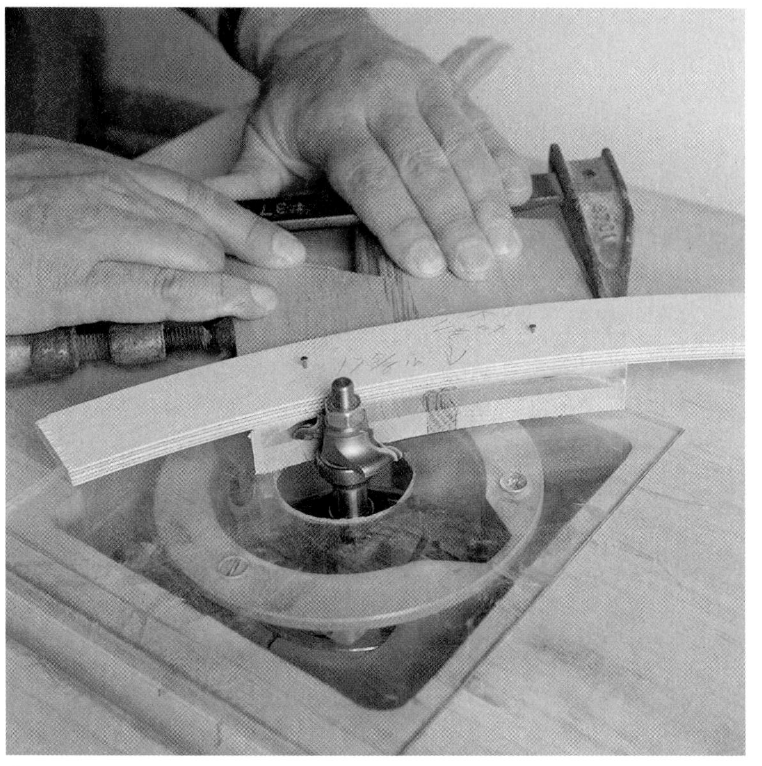

Cutting the cope—After flush-trimming to the template, cut the cope with a guide bearing riding on the workpiece.

It's hard to swing a tiny arc with a handheld router. Small-radius curves are most safely made with a circle-cutting setup. The jig consists of a crossbar clamped to the router table and a pivot pin that goes through the crossbar into the workpiece.

Choosing bits for curved sash

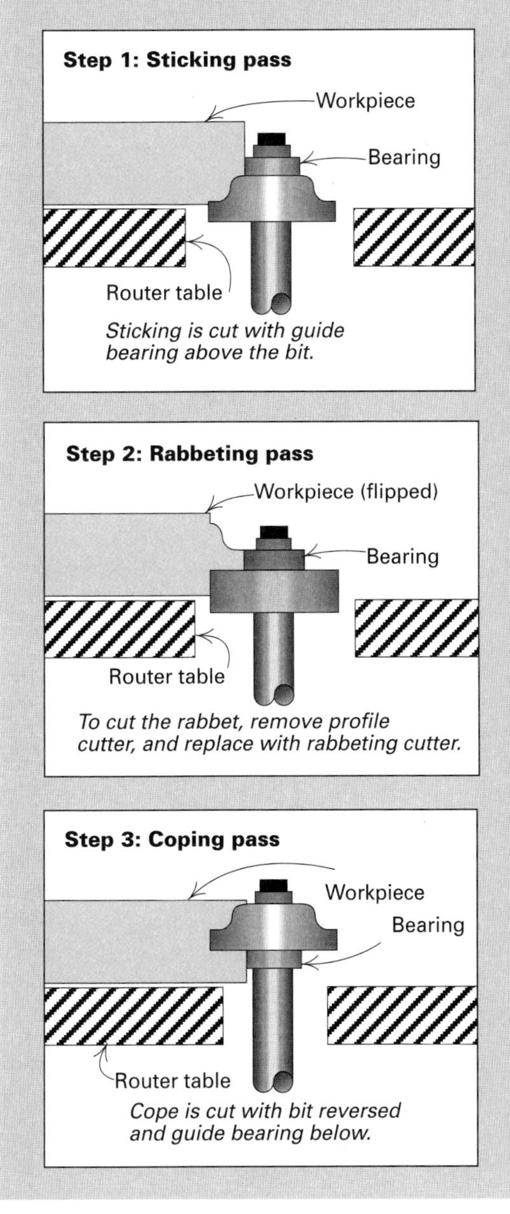

Curved cope and stick can be used with both glass panes and solid panels. Most of the router bits sold for cope and stick these days are designed primarily for making paneled kitchen cabinet doors, for which a groove (rather than a rabbet) is required below the sticking. Many of these bit sets are adaptable for making a glass rabbet, often by simply adding a cutter to the shank, so that the area below the sticking becomes a rabbet instead of a groove.

Solid bit sets that cut the whole bar profile in one pass are available, but it's best to buy stacking bits. With stacking bits, you can switch the guide bearing from top to bottom and change from rabbeting to grooving configuration. As long as the bits you use are capable of the three major steps shown in the drawings below, you'll be able to make cope and stick with either a glass rabbet or a panel groove. I used bits from Eagle America (800-872-2511), part #184-0305, along with their optional accessory kit #100-8420, which allows the set to cut glass rabbets.

THREADED INSERTS

by William Tandy Young

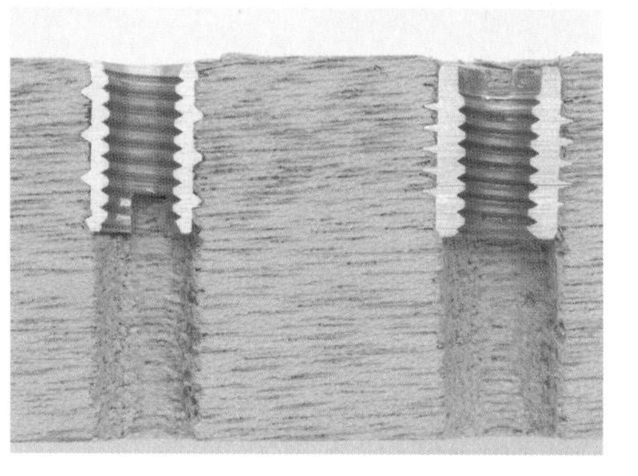

Stronger than screws—Boston furnituremaker Bill Howard uses threaded inserts to attach decorative end pieces to a credenza (above). A ¼-in. Insert (right) has about 50% more surface area in the wood than a #14 screw.

My friend Andy called one day to ask if I wanted to take part in a bulk order of threaded inserts. I'd seen threaded inserts in catalogs but had no experience with them. I asked Andy how he used them, and after a moment of stunned silence he replied, "Where do you want me to start?" He told me he used them on everything from tools and jigs to high-end furniture. Threaded inserts are so valuable around his shop that craftsmen working there guard their private stocks. Andy's never steered me wrong, so I joined the bulk order and got some of my own.

Once I started working with threaded inserts, I quickly saw how handy they are. They look like round nuts with machine-screw threads on the inside and wood-screw threads on the outside (see the bottom photo at left). Threaded into a hole, inserts make it possible to use machine screws to fasten wooden parts. Inserts have a large outside diameter and coarse threads, and their surface area is more than 50% greater than comparable wood screws. The surrounding wood fails long before inserts pull out. Inserts hold so well they can be difficult to remove. Some designs are impossible to remove, short of splitting them out.

Since that first order, I've used threaded inserts to replace wood screws where strength was important and on knockdown furniture. I've fixed wobbly chairs by replacing stripped wood screws with threaded inserts, and I've made all kinds of jigs and fixtures with inserts. I might toss the jig when the job is done, but not before I've salvaged the inserts.

Three types of inserts for woodworking

There are dozens of types of inserts made for use in almost every material. Only three are suitable for wood: inserts that cut threads in the wood, inserts that form threads and barbed inserts, which have no threads. Whatever type you choose, they're generally available in brass, zinc alloy and steel. Zinc-alloy inserts are the least expensive but also the softest. The internal threads will strip after repeated use. Brass is harder, and steel inserts are the toughest of all.

Thread-cutting inserts

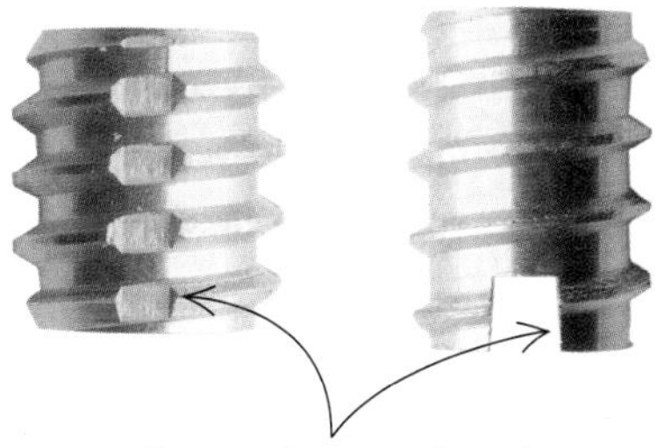

The external thread on a thread-cutting insert isn't continuous (see the photo above). The threads are broad and flat-topped with a notch, slot or groove that breaks the threads in one or more places. As the insert is driven, the sharp edges of the break cut threads into the wood. Thread-cutting inserts are easier to drive. I use them when I'm installing large inserts and when I'm working in hardwoods.

Thread-forming inserts

Thread-forming inserts have continuous thin, sharp threads (see the photo above). These inserts work like wood screws, displacing the wood around the threads rather than removing it. Thread-forming inserts install easily in everything but the hardest woods. I don't use them in thin stock or in the edges of boards because they can bulge the wood around the insert or cause a split.

Barbed inserts

Barbed inserts don't have threads; they have angled fins that let the insert go in but not come out (see the photo above). These inserts are installed with a hammer.

Though barbed inserts are sold for use in solid wood, they aren't as secure as externally threaded inserts. Barbed inserts are designed for engineered wood like medium-density fiberboard where threading an insert is likely to crumble the material.

Choosing the right driver

Driving inserts with a screwdriver is a torturous, experience. You're far better off using a driver made for the job. Stud-type drivers, which screw into an insert's internal threads, are one option. These devices range from the simple nut-and-bolt driver shown in the photo below to more elaborate production drivers, like the ones shown in the photos at right. Although these drivers are able to break a jam between driver and insert, they can't back an insert out of its pilot hole once it's been installed.

Specialty drivers engage inserts either with a hex-shaped stud or with a pair of tabs that fit into the top of the insert. These drivers also are capable of removing an insert.

Nut-and-bolt driver

This non-power driver is simple, but it's slow and fussy to use. You can make one from a nut and a bolt; you will need two wrenches to use it. Here's how it works: Thread the bolt into the insert with the nut between the insert and the bolt head. Tighten the nut to contact the insert, and with a wrench on the bolt head, drive the insert into the pilot hole. If the insert wants

to back out while unthreading the bolt, just hold the nut against the insert with the other wrench and back out the bolt.

Production drivers

At the other extreme are expensive, hardened-steel industrial production drivers for use in a drill press, variable-speed drill or screw gun. There are two types, and they aren't cheap. But if you drive inserts into hardwoods all day long, they may be worth the investment.

Specialty drivers

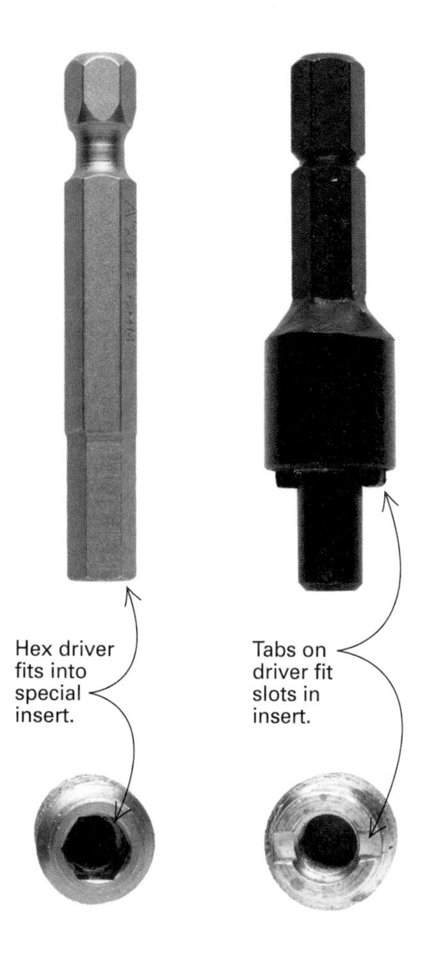
Hex driver fits into special insert.
Tabs on driver fit slots in insert.

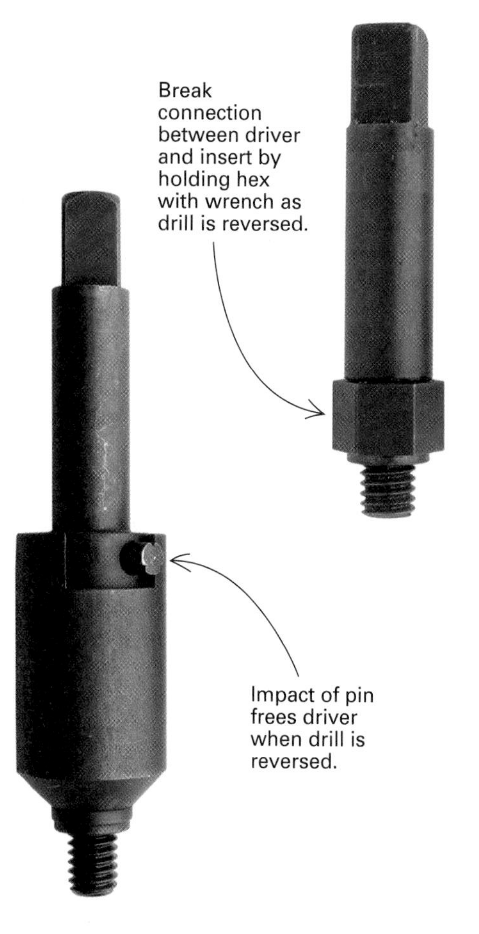
Break connection between driver and insert by holding hex with wrench as drill is reversed.
Impact of pin frees driver when drill is reversed.

The less expensive version is basically a nut-and-bolt driver with a shank that chucks into a drill. A wrench is used to break a jam (see the photo at right above). Prices start around $50.

A more expensive version can break a jam without a wrench (see photo at left above). These drivers look complicated, but they are nothing more than fancy nut-and-bolt drivers that produce an impact to break a jam. They cost upward of $150 each.

Internal-thread drivers can install any insert, but some inserts also can be installed with a specialty driver. Two kinds of specialty drivers are readily available at a cost of around $11 each. One has a smooth shaft to pilot the driver in the bore, with small tabs that engage a slot in the top of the insert, and the other uses a hex socket (see the photos above right).

Specialty drivers have two clear advantages over stud-type drivers. For one thing, jamming isn't an issue. Drive the insert, and then pull out the driver. More important, inserts made for specialty drivers can be removed. If you don't want the insert where you drove it, just reverse the drill and back it out. Inserts without a slot or socket have to be drilled or split out.

Shopmade power driver

Made from commonly available parts, this driver will install inserts efficiently.

Machine screw sized to fit insert. Head is ground to diameter less than coupling.

Hex coupling provides good grip for drill chuck.

Nylon insert nut, small end tightened against coupling

Face of nut is rounded to minimize contact with insert.

Length protruding from nut is less than depth of insert.

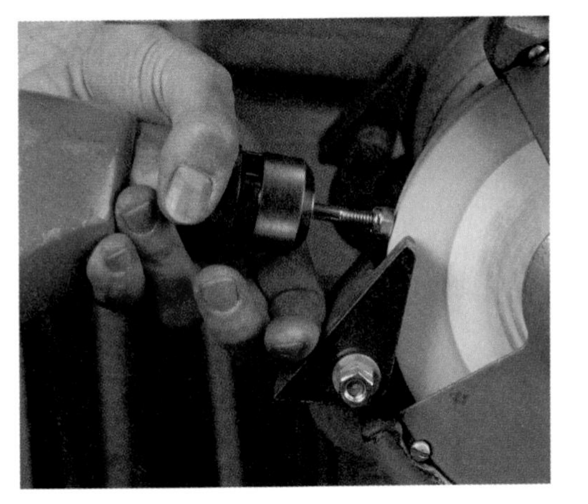

Avoiding jams— To reduce contact between driver and insert, the author rounds over the nut at the bottom of the driver. The nut has been threaded on a machine screw that is chucked in a drill to make grinding easier.

For my work, a shopmade driver (see the photo above) is just as effective as a top-of-the-line production driver. I can make a set to fit every size insert for lunch money or less. I make smaller-size drivers from a machine screw threaded through a hexagonal coupling. To make a good bearing surface against the insert, I snug a nylon-lined stop nut against the coupling. I put the small end of the nut facing the drill.

Before assembling a driver made with a coupling, I grind the head of the machine screw to make it slightly smaller than the diameter of the coupling. This helps the drill chuck grip the coupling, not the screw. Then I grind a radius on the large end of the stop nut, as shown in the right photo above, so the nut touches the insert but not the surrounding wood.

This works well in the smaller machine screws, but the outside diameter of a 5/16-in. coupling won't fit in a 3/8-in. chuck. For larger inserts, I use a bolt that isn't threaded full length and cut the head off.

Drill the right size pilot hole

No matter what driver you use, the right size pilot hole is essential. I determine the right size the same way I do when driving wood screws. For hardwood, I make the pilot hole for an insert slightly larger than the root diameter of the insert. For softwood, I make the hole slightly smaller. I always run a test in a scrap piece of the same wood to make sure the insert drives easily.

Whenever I can, I drill the pilot holes in a drill press to ensure they're square to the surface. I drill the holes a little deeper than the insert by about one diameter, and I keep them one insert diameter from an edge.

SOURCES OF SUPPLY

The following are sources for threaded inserts and drivers:

Groov-Pin Corp. (201) 945-6780. Minimum order $200. For smaller orders, call for name of local distributor.

McFeely's: (800) 443-7937

Paxton Hardware: (800) 241-9741

Professional Discount Hardware: (800) 248-1919

Spirol International: (860) 774-8571

Sta-fast: (800) 782-3278

The Tool Club: (800) 486-6525

Yardley Products Corp.: (800) 457-0154

THREADING WOOD FOR MACHINE SCREWS

by Pat Warner

Tooling to cut threads for 5/16-18 machine screws

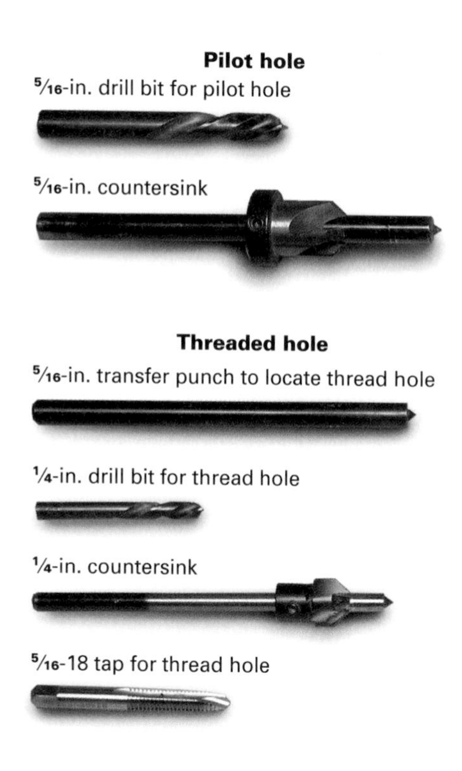

Machine screws make excellent joints in wood. They are hard to break, and some of the head configurations are quite decorative. I use them for knockdown furniture joints and for adjustable jigs that need to be strong. But machine screws are not as simple to use as wood screws because they don't cut their own threads the way wood screws do.

The most common solution is a threaded insert. But I've found you really don't need inserts to make strong joints with machine screws. Metal taps will cut crisp, strong and durable threads in any hardwood. It takes about the same amount of force to strip wood threads as it does to pull a threaded insert out of its hole. And if you tap the wood deeper than a threaded insert requires, the wood joint will be stronger. Machine screws in an inch of wood threads will make a really tough knockdown joint.

Wood threads require careful drilling and tapping. The wrong size drill bit or a misaligned hole will lead to a weak connection. But by following the drilling schedule at right and using the proper tools, you can produce deep, crisp and strong threads without too much trouble.

The only specialized tools that you will need are taps. I have taps in four screw sizes: 3/8-16, 5/16-18, 1/4-20 and #10-24 (the first number is the diameter of the screw; the second is the number of threads per inch). You will also need drill bits, transfer punches and countersinks.

The pilot holes need to be drilled first to locate the thread holes properly. The machine screw should slide easily through the pilot hole, just as a wood screw should. If the head configuration calls for it, I would countersink the pilot holes for the screw heads at this point.

Clamp the piece with the pilot holes to the piece that receives the threads, and transfer the hole locations. I use a transfer punch the same size as the pilot hole, drilling the thread holes on the punch marks. Chamfer the mouth of the thread holes about 1/32 in. greater than the tap diameter. If you don't, the tap may tear out the surface grain when you cut the threads.

I have tried tapping by hand with a wrench, but I just can't tap straight. A drill press will give you excellent results safely every time. Just don't turn on the drill press. In fact, unplug the machine before starting this procedure.

Clamp the work firmly, and put the tap in the chuck. Turn the drive pulley by hand while guiding the tap into the thread hole with the quill feed. Once you've started the threads, you can tap the rest by hand if you like.

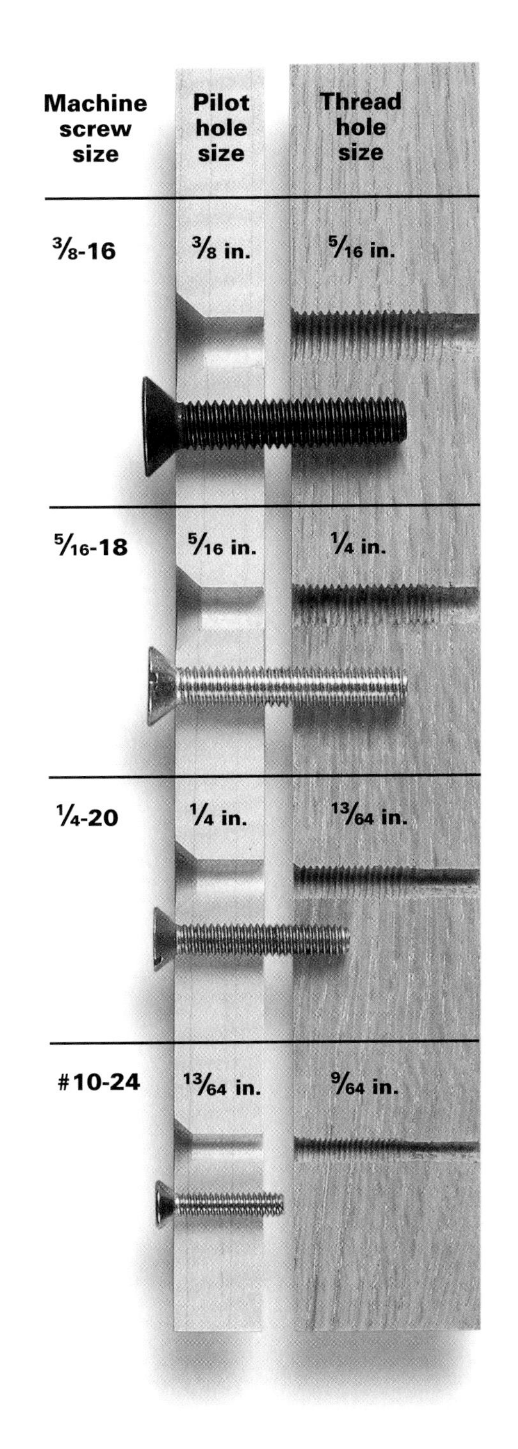

Machine screw size
Pilot hole size
Thread hole size
3/8-16
3/8 in.
5/16 in.
5/16-18
5/16 in.
1/4 in.
1/4-20
1/4 in.
13/64 in.
#10-24
13/64 in.
9/64 in.

ABOUT THE AUTHORS

Anatole Burkin was a daily journalist before joining the staff of *Fine Woodworking* magazine. He's a self-taught woodworker who has built furniture, kitchen cabinets, and a wooden kayak. He lives in Southbury, Conn., with his wife, Robin, and Weimaraner, Trixi.

Mac Campbell is studying theology in Halifax, Nova Scotia, Canada. Previously, he ran a custom furnituremaking shop in Harvey Station, New Brunswick.

Steven Cook has worked on and built pipe organs for most of his life. Since 1992, he has built six handmade organs in his shop, and a seventh is under construction. A lifelong resident of the Pacific Northwest, he lives in Edmonds, Wash., with his wife and children, where he says those rainy days make it easy to stay in his shop and work.

Ross Day is a custom furnituremaker in Seattle. He also teaches fine furnituremaking at Seattle Community College.

Bruce Gray builds custom furniture in Grand Bay, New Brunswick, Canada.

Jeff Greef is a woodworker and journalist living in Santa Cruz, Calif. He is the author of three books, *Woodshop Jigs and Fixtures, Display Cabinets,* and *Wooden Boxes.* In his spare time, he gardens.

Garrett Hack opened his own shop in 1973 and later studied furnituremaking at Boston University's Program in Artisanry. He designs and builds furniture in Vermont and is a regular contributor to *Fin*e Woodworking magazine. He is the author of *The Handplane Book* and *Classic Hand Tools,* published by The Taunton Press.

Kirt Kirkpatrick lives in Albuquerque, N.M. Formerly a journeyman patternmaker and boat builder, he now carves and builds furniture and doors.

Frank Klausz III studied cove cutting for his senior thesis at Harvard University. He works for C.U.C. International in Stamford, Conn. His father, Frank Klausz, and Will Neptune of North Bennet Street School, also contributed their expertise to the article on pp. 91-96.

Tony Konovaloff has been making furniture by hand since 1986. He has written a book, *Chisel, Mallet, Plane and Saw,* which is about the way he works and how he makes his furniture. He hopes to publish it soon. He lives with his wife and three sons in Oak Harbor, Washi.

Jeff Miller is a furniture designer, craftsman, teacher, and author of woodworking books and articles. Jeff's furniture has been shown in galleries nationwide and has won numerous awards. He is the author of *Chairmaking & Design,* which won the 1998 Stanley Award, and *Beds: Step-by-Step,* both published by The Taunton Press.

Tom Moore is a woodworker in Clarksville, Va.

Sandor Nagyszalanczy, of Santa Cruz, Calif., is a professional furniture designer and craftsman with more than 20 years of experience. A former senior editor of *Fine Woodworking* magazine, he has written five books, including *The Art of Fine Tools,* published by The Taunton Press.

Ken Picou is a woodworker and a designer of woodworking tools who holds patents on the Robo-Sander and Mr. Mortise tools. He currently builds giant fishing lures (up to 30 in. long) for hopeful fishermen in Austin, Tex.

John Michael Pierson, a professional designer/craftsman and professor of applied design, lives in Lemon Grove, Calif.

Strother Purdy is a former editor at *Fine Woodworking* magazine. Now he edits books for The Taunton Press.

Mason Rapaport designs and builds furniture in Easthampton, Mass. He mainly works with curves, bending and veneering plywood in a vacuum press, which he says allows for a vast expression of ideas in design.

Jim Richey splits his year between his hometown of Alva, Okla., and a rustic cabin in South Fork, Colo. A serious woodworker since 1972, he likes to build furniture and boxes. Jim is also a photographer, illustrator, and novice blacksmith. He has edited and illustrated *Fine Woodworking* magazine's "Methods of Work" column for nearly 20 years.

Mario Rodriguez is a contributing editor to *Fine Woodworking* magazine and woodworker living in Haddonfield, N.J. He teaches toolmaking, furnituremaking, and antique restoration at the Fashion Institute of Technology in New York City. He is the author of *Traditional Woodwork,* published by The Taunton Press.

Gary Rogowski has designed and built fine furniture in Portland, Oreg., since 1974. He has a school called Northwest Woodworking Studio in Portland. He is a contributing editor to *Fine Woodworking* magazine and the author of *Router Joinery,* published by The Taunton Press. He is currently working on another book about joinery techniques.

Lon Schleining has designed and built stairs in Long Beach, Calif., for 20 years. He is currently working on a book about curves and bending, to be published in 1999. He also teaches woodworking at Cerritos College in Norwalk, Calif.

Ed Speas works for Formica Corp., in Henryville, Penn., as a technical specialist. He enjoys woodworking as a hobby.

Carl Swensson is a professional woodworker and furniture designer and teacher. He has built tracker organs, doors for a Buddhist temple in Japan, and countless Appalachian-style chairs. He lives in Baltimore, Md.

Jim Tolpin is a writer and woodworker in Port Townsend, Wash. He is the author of many books, including *Working at Woodworking, Traditional Kitchen Cabinets, The Toolbox Book, and The New Cottage Home,* all published by The Taunton Press.

Ronald Volbrecht builds and repairs guitars. He has built instruments for John Mellencamp, Richie Sambora, Hoyt Axton, and other artists. He lives and works in Nashville, Ind.

Alec Waters is a former associate editor at *Fine Woodworking* magazine. He lives in Oakville, Conn.

Pat Warner is a woodworker deep into routing, an instructor at Palomar College in San Marcos, Calif., and an occasional consultant for the router and bit manufacturing industry. He has two books published, *Getting the Very Best from Your Router* and *The Router Joinery Handbook.* He lives in Escondido, Calif. He also has a webpage at www.patwarner.com.

Andrew Kimball Weegar is the owner of Kimball Canoe Co. and builds wood and canvas boats in North Bridgton, Maine.

William Tandy Young is a furnituremaker, conservator, and adhesive consultant in Stow, Mass. He is the author of *The Glue Book,* published by The Taunton Press.

CREDITS

David Arky (photographer): 97

Vince Babak (illustrator): 76, 87, 155, 156, 158

Jonathan Binzen (photographer): 91, 92, 95

Jim Boesel (photographer): 147

Anatole Burkin (photographer): 6, 7, 8, 9, 10, 11, 12

Chris Clapp (illustrator): 6, 7, 8, 9, 10, 12

Aimé Fraser (photographer): 154, 158, 159, 166, 190 (top)

Michael Gellatly (illustrator): 160, 162

Jeff Greef (photographer): 174 (top), 178, 182, 184, 186, 188, 189

Sloan Howard (photographer): 174 (bottom), 175, 176, 177

Lee Hov (illustrator): 50

Heather Lambert (illustrator): 175

Vincent Laurence (photographer): 4, 14, 15, 16, 18, 20, 22, 23, 24, 25, 26, 42, 70, 71, 72, 73, 75, 76, 77, 78, 80, 102, 103, 105, 107, 108, 109, 110, 111, 112, 113, 161, 163, 164, 165

Robert Marsala (photographer): 69

John McKeith (photographer): 51

Maria Meleschnig (illustrator): 93, 96, 143, 147, 185, 187

Sandor Nagyszalancy (photographer): 119, 120, 121, 122, 123, 124, 125, 126, 142, 144, 145

Scott Phillips (photographer): 35, 150, 190 (bottom), 191, 192, 193

Dennis Preston (photographer): 27, 28, 29, 30, 31, 32, 33, 34, 52, 53, 54, 55, 56, 57, 58, 59

Strother Purdy (photographer): 36, 37, 38, 39, 40, 130, 131, 132, 133, 134, 135, 136, 137, 149, 152, 153, 194, 195

Jim Richey (photographer): 138

Jim Richey (illustrator): 17, 21, 139, 140

Joe Romero (photographer): 41

Charley Robinson (photographer): 44, 45, 46, 47, 48, 100, 114, 115, 116, 118

Kathleen Rushton (illustrator): 56, 64

Mark Sant'Angelo (illustrator); 169, 171, 172, 173

Alec Waters (photographer): 61, 62, 63, 66, 67, 98, 99, 168, 171

Matthew Wells (illustrator): 59, 104, 106, 189

EQUIVALENCE CHART

Inches	Centimeters	Millimeters
1/8	0.3	3
1/4	0.6	6
3/8	1.0	10
1/2	1.3	13
5/8	1.6	16
3/4	1.9	19
7/8	2.2	22
1	2.5	25
1 1/4	3.2	32
1 1/2	3.8	38
1 3/4	4.4	44
2	5.1	51
2 1/2	6.4	64
3	7.6	76
3 1/2	8.9	89
4	10.2	102
4 1/2	11.4	114
5	12.7	127
6	15.2	152
7	17.8	178
8	20.3	203
9	22.9	229
10	25.4	254
11	27.9	279

Inches	Centimeters	Millimeters
12	30.5	305
13	33.0	330
14	35.6	356
15	38.1	381
16	40.6	406
17	43.2	432
18	45.7	457
19	48.3	483
20	50.8	508
21	53.3	533
22	55.9	559
23	58.4	584
24	61.0	610
25	63.5	635
26	66.0	660
27	68.6	686
28	71.1	711
29	73.7	737
30	76.2	762
31	78.7	787
32	81.3	813
33	83.8	838
34	86.4	864
35	88.9	889
36	91.4	914

INDEX

P

R

S

T

V

W

Publisher: Jim Childs
Associate Publisher: Helen Albert
Associate Editor: Strother Purdy
Indexer: Harriet Hodges
Designer: Amy Russo
Layout Artist: Susan Fazekas

Fine Woodworking **magazine**
Editor: Tim D. Schreiner
Art Director: Bob Goodfellow
Managing Editor: Jefferson Kolle
Senior Editors: Jonathan Binzen, Anatole Burkin
Associate Editor: William Duckworth
Assistant Editor: Matthew Teague
Associate Art Director: Michael Pekovich